W9-CFI-587

SLAVERY AND FREEDOM

The position of the slave per Aristotle

ALSO BY JAMES OAKES

The Ruling Race:
A History of American Slaveholders

JAMES OAKES

Slavery and Freedom

AN INTERPRETATION OF
THE OLD SOUTH

VINTAGE BOOKS

A DIVISION OF RANDOM HOUSE, INC.

NEW YORK

FIRST VINTAGE BOOKS EDITION, DECEMBER 1991

Copyright © 1990 by James Oakes
Maps copyright © 1990 by Alfred A. Knopf, Inc.

All rights reserved under International and Pan-American
Copyright Conventions. Published in the United States by
Vintage Books, a division of Random House, Inc.,
New York, and simultaneously in Canada
by Random House of Canada Limited, Toronto.
Originally published in hardcover
by Alfred A. Knopf, Inc., New York, in 1990.

Library of Congress Cataloging-in-Publication Data
Oakes, James.
Slavery and freedom : an interpretation of the Old South /
James Oakes.—1st Vintage Books ed.
p. cm.
Reprint. Originally published: New York : Knopf, 1990.
Includes bibliographical references and index.
ISBN 0-679-73035-4 (pbk.)
1. Slavery—Southern States—History.
2. Capitalism—Southern States—History.
3. Southern States—History—1775-1865.
I. Title.
[E441.015 1991]
975'.00496—dc20   91-50027
CIP

Manufactured in the United States of America
10 9 8 7 6 5 4 3 2 1

FOR MOM AND DAD,

AND FOR MY BROTHERS AND SISTERS,

JOHN

MARY

JOAN

FRANCES

JOSEPH

THOMAS

AND MICHAEL

That Liberalism may be a tendency towards something very different from itself, is a possibility in its nature.

T. S. ELIOT
The Idea of a Christian Society

Contents

Introduction

BY TRADITION, historians are expected to introduce their books with succinct statements of what they are about. This one is about the relationship between slavery and liberal capitalism in the southern United States during the nineteenth century. As vast and unwieldy as this theme sounds, it is actually an old one in slavery studies. Slavery and capitalism have been the object of scholarly scrutiny at least since Eric Williams published his classic monograph on the subject in 1944. Slavery and liberal politics have received far less attention, but the relationship has been examined with considerable sophistication in essays and monographs by Charles Sellers, Edmund Morgan, and J. Mills Thornton, to name only a few. If I can justify any claims to novelty on this well-trodden turf, it is in the effort to integrate two otherwise distinct bodies of literature—the one focusing on economics and the other on politics—into a single interpretation of slavery in the Old South.

As I worked toward this synthesis I was drawn, finally, to the deceptively simple problem with which this book begins: What was slavery? The question would scarcely have seemed serious a generation ago, when most historians more or less "knew slavery when they saw it," even if they disagreed vehemently about how to interpret it. But as the study of New World slavery has pushed beyond traditional boundaries of time and place, its very definition has become obscured. At the same time, however, students of slavery in the Old World—classical antiquity, medieval Europe, early modern Russia, and Africa—have been moving in the opposite direction, toward a complex understanding of the specific character of human slavery. Within this literature M. I. Finley's studies of the ancient world have been critical.[1] Over the course of his long and fruitful career, Finley carefully developed a precise definition of "slavery" that distinguished it from other forms of subordination, and of "slave society" as distinct from a society with slaves. With Finley's categories as their starting point, students of Old World slavery have gone on to produce monographs of considerable analytical sophistication.[2] Also drawing inspiration from Finley, but operating from explicitly sociological premises, Keith Hopkins has worked out more carefully than anyone else the historical character of the slave society of Ancient Rome, while Orlando Patterson has provided an important definition of slavery based on a comparative analysis of dozens of societies in which slaves were present.[3]

Finley also intervened in a second field of inquiry—the so-called "other transition," from ancient slavery to medieval feudalism. The starting point in this discussion was Marc Bloch's brilliant, posthumously published essay "How and Why Ancient Slavery Came to an End." More recently, significant contributions have been offered by Perry Anderson, Chris Wickham, Pierre Bonnassie, and others. Their sustained investigation into the causes of this epochal transformation has helped distinguish slavery and slave society from serfdom, feudalism, and feudal society. This is a distinction of no mean significance.[4] If the shift from slavery to serfdom involved profound changes that took several centuries to complete, the emergence of modern slavery must therefore have required an equally momentous turn away from feudalism. By studying the transition from Ancient Rome to Medieval Europe I was able to disentangle the "totality" of the master-slave relationship from the "organicism" of feudal social relations. Buried beneath all the confusion was a simple but critical distinction between the "conditional" property law that supplanted slavery in the early Middle Ages, and the "absolute," or private, property that in turn supplanted medieval law with the rise of capitalism. Private property rights emerged in my mind as the Pandora's box of modern history, simultaneously unleashing the permanent revolution of capitalism and the total subordination of slavery.

For whatever reasons, the influence of these studies on the analysis of slavery in the Old South has remained unfortunately limited. The singular, outstanding exception is David Brion Davis. In the opening chapters of *The Problem of Slavery in Western Culture* Davis developed through intellectual history many of the categories and themes that guide my own analysis of the social history of southern slave society.[5] But Davis's contribution only highlights the massive conceptual barrier that still separates historians of New and Old World slavery. As an intellectual divide, the Atlantic Ocean makes little theoretical or historical sense. Chapter 1 tries to bridge the gap by integrating the conceptual framework developed by students of European and African slavery with some of the themes that have been developed among historians of New World—and especially southern—slavery over the past generation.

My larger hope is that a clearer definition of slavery will in turn clarify its relationship to liberal capitalism. This is the burden of Chapter 2, wherein the book's central thesis emerges. Stated in brief and oversimplified terms, the thesis runs like this: Because slavery is always defined as *the denial of freedom*, the way any given society defines freedom is inescapably tied to the way it defines slavery. Southerners took their definition of freedom from the liberal capitalist world which produced them and of which they remained a part, and this could only mean that *southern* slavery was defined as the denial of the assumptions of liberal capitalism. This makes the slave South's relationship to liberal capitalism at once closer and yet far more complicated than most studies have hitherto indicated.

This interpretation can be read in very different ways. Some will see in it confirmation of the thesis that the Old South was fundamentally "liberal," while others will see it as affirming slavery's intrinsic incompatibility with liberalism. This is not because of a deliberate obscurity on my part, and I certainly have no desire to create confusion. On the contrary: the ambiguous relationship of slavery and liberal capitalism has been a classic theme in western thought for more than a century. Both Marx and Weber appreciated the critical significance of wage labor, both recognized the "irrational" characteristics of slavery, and yet both saw that the "calculated and calculating" spirit of modern slavery located it firmly within the world of liberal capitalism. Only in recent years have American historians shied away from this ambiguity and portrayed the slave South as a society whose internal character was unequivocally different from, and virtually untouched by, liberal capitalism. At the risk of complicating this attractively elegant formulation, I have revived an older question: How did a social order that contradicted liberal principles as flagrantly as slavery did nevertheless accommodate itself to a liberal political culture? My short answer is that in the long run the slave South could neither escape from nor accommodate itself to liberalism, and that this was the central dilemma of slavery in the United States. A fuller answer is contained in the chapters that follow.

Did the problematical relationship between slavery and liberal capitalism make any difference to the men and women who together made the history of the South? Chapters 3 and 4 are designed to show that it did. Slavery and liberal capitalism, not individually but in concert, shaped the way southern men and women lived their lives and encountered one another in their various social capacities as slaveholders and yeomen, husbands and wives, masters and slaves. That the relationship between slavery and liberalism invested southern society with peculiarly explosive tensions became evident in the 1860's. That slavery's abolition therefore constituted a revolutionary transformation is clear as well. In a sense, then, this book is my attempt to do what every southern historian must ultimately do: come to terms with the Civil War. If I am right, the events of 1861–1865 were, in the most meaningful sense of the term, a civil war. Why that was so is this book's underlying question, and in my answer lies its overarching theme: that the pathway from the American Revolution to the Civil War begins at the intersection of slavery and liberal capitalism.

Beyond the subject matter of individual chapters, I also hope to suggest the relatively straightforward proposition that the problem of slavery is the problem of freedom—as Greek civilization well understood but as the twentieth century has had some difficulty remembering. We live in a political world dominated and perhaps overwhelmed by capitalism's extraordinary productive energies. "Freedom" has come to mean access to goods and services—Daniel Boorstin once labeled American consumer society a "democracy of cash"—and the quality of life is casually equated with levels of physical comfort.[6] We regularly judge the worth of other societies by the quantity and quality of their material possessions or by their standards of personal health. This is by no means a universal reflex, of course. Yet even when we focus our attention on the problem of human or civil rights, there is a disturbing tendency to "prove" the superiority of liberal society by references to the relatively depressed standards of living elsewhere. In such ways public discourse has moved away from the central political issues of obligation and consent, democracy and autonomy, power and freedom.

Inevitably, this evasion of the political has penetrated our scholarship. In recent decades it has sometimes seemed as though one's attitude toward slavery hinged on the difference of a few hundred calories a day in the slave diet, on the number of slaves who came down with pellagra, or on the square-footage of the average slave cabin. Purely relative facts—that slaves in the South did not die as readily as slaves in Brazil, that Russian serfs starved more often, or that physical growth was more stunted among the wage-earners of Dickensian London—were mistaken for evidence of something fundamental about slavery in the Old South.

I have no desire to dismiss the benefits of longevity or the importance of decent standards of material comfort in the alleviation of human misery. But I do wish to emphasize that these have little to do with slavery. To some degree the standard-of-living issue is universal: it applies to feudalism as well as to capitalism, to slave as well as to free societies. But a slave was a slave, whether he lived a healthy hundred years or a sickly forty, whether she was better fed than a Polish peasant or more miserably housed than an American yeoman. Nineteenth-century opponents of slavery sometimes made the same point. "Though the Negroes are fed, clothed, and housed, and though the Irish peasant is starved, naked, and roofless," Frances Kemble wrote in 1838, "the bare name of freemen—the lordship over his own person, the power to choose and will—are blessings beyond food, rai-ment, or shelter; possessing which, the want of every comfort of life is yet more tolerable than their fullest enjoyment without them."[7] We can only measure the substance of such criticism if we understand why "slavery" and "freedom" do not refer to material well-being.

To be sure, food, clothing, and shelter are never trivial matters, and it is good that we care to investigate them in the slave South. But they must be put in proper perspective. To the extent that southern masters defined themselves by how "kindly" they treated their slaves, they merely revealed the degree to which they had absorbed the assumptions of a society that was learning to mea-sure unfreedom by quantities of material deprivation and physical suffering. We are obliged to take such assumptions seriously; we are not obliged to make them our own. Above all, we must resist the temptation of our age to mistake such matters for the central problem of slavery: freedom.

FREEDOM AND SLAVERY are at bottom political categories; they refer to the distribution of power in society. This is perhaps the most important premise of *Slavery and Freedom*, but it is also one of the most difficult to communicate. A contemporary illustration may help. A while back the business section of the *New York Times* ran a series of articles exploring the legal problems raised by the growing number of unmarried couples forming single households. The author discovered, along with the couples, that marriage is much more than a romantic expression of love and fidelity: it is a profoundly significant legal relationship that rests at the very base of our society. By not marrying, for example, couples disrupt established patterns of property distribution. Die on the day before you marry and your property will go one place; die on your honeymoon and it belongs somewhere else. Unmar-ried partnerships raise the question not simply of child custody but of who and what a parent is. Moreover, as a legal relationship marriage defines the relative power of most men and women in society. For in the end, what a married woman can own and what she can do with her property are fixed in the laws of wedlock. And this makes marriage not only emotional but political. To get married is to alter one's basic relationship to society and posterity.

If we bear this in mind, the full meaning of the Louisiana slave code of 1824 becomes clearer. "Slaves cannot marry without the consent of their masters," the law declared, "and their marriages do not produce any of the civil effects which result from such contract." The implications of this sentence can hardly be exaggerated. Marriage among slaves did not determine the distribution of property. It did not define the relative power of men and women in society. Indeed, the "depoliticization" of marriage radically altered the family's role in defining the individual's relationship to society and posterity. To be sure, slaves got married; they developed strong feelings about the relative power of men and women and of their relations with family and society. But without legal sanction everything was different. All the political problems the *Times* reporter saw in the rise of unmarried couples were multiplied many times over by the fact that slave marriages could "not produce any of the civil effects" of marriage among free people. The difference was more than quantitative, for while the law can find solutions to the problems raised by unmarried free couples, the problem of slave marriages resided in the fact that the law did not recognize them at all.

The legal conundrum of slave marriages is an example of a more general problem that I am concerned with throughout this book: the degree to which relationships we take for granted are in fact deeply political, are in fact grounded in carefully developed laws regulating the power of the persons involved. I am not alone in this concern. For many years now scholars have pointed to the danger posed by social history's abandonment of the study of politics and power. The long tradition of narrative political history, too often written as though politics were a self-contained force, also helped give rise to the impression among social historians that politics are more or less irrelevant to everyday life.

But the separation of social from political analysis is not the unique affliction of the historical profession; it reflects a larger problem of twentieth-century intellectual analysis. Rather than study the structure of society, social scientists have increasingly zeroed in on particular groups. Rather than observe the shifting boundaries of society at large they studied small communities and peasant villages. Most recently historians have retreated all the way to biography—not of the great and powerful but of the ordinary and the powerless. This completes the repudiation of the grand tradition of "macro-analytical" social science from Marx and Weber to Durkheim and Parsons.[8]

By lowering its sights from the nation to the community, from society to the individual, contemporary scholarship has accomplished a great deal. It is now clear that the values that Durkheim and Parsons thought held societies together and allowed them to function smoothly were at the same time the basis for the articulation of conflicting meanings. By studying the culture of small groups we can now see that shared languages facilitate conflict as much as consensus. This is an important insight; it is another premise of *Slavery and Freedom*. But by narrowing our focus to the subgroup, by divorcing the individual from society or the village from its larger context, micro-analysis often loses sight of the political structures within which all men and women have always exercised and negotiated their power in society. Having lost sight of the negotiations—between men and women, slaveholders and nonslaveholders, or masters and slaves—we have lost sight of the process of historical change.

Southern history has not been immune to these trends. The splintering of the profession into various subspecialties has left a wide gulf between political and social historians of the Old South. And while students of southern politics have tried in recent years to incorporate the problem of slavery into their analyses, social historians have largely failed to make the appropriate political linkages.[9] There are significant exceptions, of course, but one is particularly important to my own work. In *From Rebellion to Revolution*, Eugene Genovese establishes the significance of the changing political context within which slave revolts took place in the New World. An earlier generation led by C. L. R. James and Herbert Aptheker had made initial inquiries along this line;

Michael Craton and Robin Blackburn have done so more recently for the British West Indies.[10] But among recent studies of the Old South, *From Rebellion to Revolution* is almost alone in linking the history of the slave community to the age of liberal revolution. My own analysis of the political significance of slave resistance, as well as of the relations between slaveholders and nonslaveholders, builds upon Genovese's insight—and no doubt takes it where he would not want it to go. Nevertheless, this book is in large part an effort to resolve what Genovese has quite properly labeled the "political crisis of social history."[11] I have tried to unite politics and society by focusing on some (though by no means all) of the most important negotiations over the distribution of power in the Old South. My central concern is with the political history of the relationships between slaveholders and yeomen, masters and slaves, and implicitly North and South.

A FEW FINAL POINTS. First, although the interpretation of the South presented in these pages is my own, this is also a work of synthesis. I have relied heavily on the scholarship of others, sometimes for information, sometimes for interpretation, and sometimes for the questions that determine the very direction of my analysis. I owe a special debt to those upon whom I have relied, whether I agree or disagree with their specific conclusions. Yet I was taught, and I still believe, that historians should write about the past and not about one another. With only rare exceptions, my text is therefore free of references to the scholars whose books and articles form the background for so much of what I have to say. I hope that my footnotes offer some compensation by indicating my reliance on this wealth of scholarship, and in a few instances by clarifying my relationship to it.

Second, having opened this introduction with a deceptively brief statement of what this study is about, I am compelled to state in somewhat more detail what had to be left out of a book so small on a topic so large. What, then, is this book *not* about? To begin with, it is not a history of slavery, nor of liberal capitalism. And while its subject is the nineteenth-century South,

I have repeatedly overstepped those temporal and geographical boundaries by going back before the nineteenth century and out beyond the borders of the southern states. Nevertheless, this is neither a work of comparative history nor anything like a world-historical analysis. Last, this is not a study of the origins of the Civil War so much as the "southern road" to it. Any complete examination of the breakup of the Union would require a far more comprehensive analysis, particularly of the northern route, than I attempt in the following pages.

These, then, are essays in interpretation, frankly exploratory and by intent suggestive rather than definitive. They cover a big place over a long period of time, yet they are—once again intentionally—brief and telescopic in organization. The goal is not to *prove* my thesis but to render it plausible and coherent. Still, these essays are the product of more than a dozen years of research and writing in and around the subjects under consideration. In a few cases, notably Chapters 3 and 4, the basic outlines of my interpretation were formulated years ago while I was a graduate student at Berkeley, learning from Charles Sellers about the conflict between slaveholders and yeomen, discussing with Reid Mitchell the revolutionary aspects of the slaves' behavior during the Civil War. For several years after I left graduate school I focused on developing and clarifying the analysis of liberal capitalism that now forms the second chapter. Intellectually, the definition of slavery in Chapter 1 is of the most recent vintage, though it precipitated a substantial reformulation of everything else. Yet, regardless of their age and origins, each chapter was written in a spirit not of conviction but of curiosity. The interpretations remain in my own mind far more tentative than the prose within which they are sometimes rendered. They will provoke disagreement but not, I hope, anger. If I am very lucky, they will stimulate discussion.

* * *

ACKNOWLEDGMENTS come last, and they will be brief—although this unjustly reverses their true importance. Princeton and Northwestern universities, the National Endowment for the

Humanities, and an Arthur Cole Grant from the American Economic Association provided the time and funding I needed to conceptualize and finish the book. John Matteson, Michele Gillespie, and Tim Hall did sturdy service as research assistants at various points. Chapter 1 benefited from a discussion at a History Department seminar at Northwestern; the section on Russian serfdom could not have been written without the advice and suggestions of John Bushnell and Richard Hellie. Chapter 2 was initially prepared at the invitation of John Boyer and Michael Geyer for presentation to a History Department colloquium at the University of Chicago. Chapter 3 appeared in very different form as "From Republicanism to Liberalism: Ideological Change and the Crisis of the Old South," *American Quarterly*, 37 (Fall, 1985). The latter portion of Chapter 4 appeared in slightly different form as "The Political Significance of Slave Resistance," *History Workshop*, 22 (Autumn, 1986). An "eccentric" version of the Epilogue was initially published as a chapter in Robert H. Abzug and Stephen E. Maizlish, eds., *New Perspectives on Race and Slavery in America* (Lexington, Ky., 1985).

For comments so apt that they slowed the completion of the manuscript by several months, I would like to thank Michael Bernstein, Timothy Breen, Felix Gilbert, Jan Lewis, Louis Masur, Martin Mueller, Daniel Rodgers, Kenneth Stampp, David Watt, Robert Wiebe, and Harold Woodman. As for Joe Barton—acknowledgment is a paltry repayment for the time, energy, and enthusiasm he gave this book. He listened endlessly to my formulations and reformulations, prodding me deeper and further than I could possibly have gone myself. Finally, my wife, Deborah, proved once again to be my severest critic and most enthusiastic supporter. Her faith in me has kept this project going; it has allowed me to finish, and it inspires me to go on.

SLAVERY AND FREEDOM

CHAPTER I

Outsiders

We have no property! We have no wives! No children!
We have no city! No country!
　　　　—New England slaves' petition for freedom

*T*AKE AWAY all of someone's freedom and you have a slave.
It was that simple. Slavery is the complete denial of freedom. Which is to say, it is not simple at all. For what is freedom,
and what does it mean to take all of it away? To address the question is to confront a great paradox. In western history slavery and
freedom are so closely intertwined that the very origins of freedom are sometimes said to have depended on the emergence of
slavery as its negative frame of reference. Every society that has
ever called itself free, even as it enslaved men and women, necessarily redefined slavery in its own image. For to be a slave is to
be, quite literally, unfree.

Freedom and unfreedom are experienced most directly in the
few basic human relationships that men and women must enter
into if society is to survive—the relationships in which they produce what they need to live on and in which they reproduce themselves. Society itself is largely shaped by how people work and
how they organize their families. We are most "free," therefore,
when we can form and dissolve our work and family relationships
without coercion, and when the relationships themselves are eq-
uitable. We are least free when we are coerced into an absolutely
inequitable relationship from which we cannot escape.* Because

---

*Liberal societies, for example, define freedom through a series of formal and
informal rights which, though vested in the individual, in fact serve to define
the individual's relationships with others. Someone has a "right to move"
only when he or she is bound to no one who has the power to hinder this
mobility.

3

no society is completely free of coercion or inequity, it is possible to define slavery as the furthest point on a spectrum of social relationships ranging from the most to the least free.

But to be a slave, whether in the American South or in classical Athens, was to suffer a deprivation of freedom so extreme as to be qualitatively distinct from all other forms of unfreedom. Except in rare cases, the master-slave relationship began in violent coercion and was so inequitable that the slave was incapable of entering into any other socially recognized relationships. This is what it means to say that the slave's subordination to the master was *total*: the slave could form no work or family relationships of which the master disapproved and which the master could not dissolve. "The slave is entirely subject to the will of his master," the Louisiana code announced, thereby excluding the slave from social relationships with anyone other than the master.[1] A slave could not make contracts, own property, or form legal partnerships on his or her own. By law the slave had no brother or sister, no husband or wife, no son or daughter, no ancestors and no posterity. This "kinlessness" and "natal alienation" meant that among slaves spouses had no legal obligations to one another and parents could exercise no formal responsibilities toward their children.[2]

Since kinship is the basis from which human beings normally establish their ties to the larger society, the slaves' legal kinlessness effectively deprived them of the most important relationships to the surrounding community. The law recognized little beyond the slave's relation to the master. Slaves had no formal powers to exercise over anyone else—they were utterly powerless. They could make none of the commonplace claims on family and community for economic support or physical protection, claims we take so much for granted that we mistakenly see them as natural. It was in this sense that the slave was an outsider—not because of geographic origins or ethnic differences, but because the slave was cut off from society, making slavery itself a form of social death.

By extension, slaves could only exist outside of the polity: it could not demand the slaves' allegiance nor could they expect any legal and political rights within it. A similar sense of political ex-

polity: political organization

clusion led many colonists to conclude that they were "slaves" of Great Britain and that England therefore had no claim on their allegiance. But the distinction between "slave" and "citizen" extends back far beyond eighteenth-century Anglo-America. In Ancient Greece, where active citizenship in the polis was seen as man's greatest source of self-fulfillment, the slave was virtually defined as the permanent noncitizen, and slavery's essence rested on the degrading exclusion of the slave from all public life.

Only by severing all of the slave's formal ties to society and polity could the master exercise powers that we generally think of as "property rights." Indeed, the western concept of absolute property may well derive from the legal codification of the slave's powerlessness beginning in the late Roman Republic. Most often we think of slaves as property because of the master's ability to exercise powers usually associated with the possession and use of inanimate objects or animals. In particular, slaves could be alienated—bought and sold, bequeathed and inherited, won or lost. The Greeks spoke of the slave as a "living tool," and modern historians similarly use the term "chattel slavery." But this did not mean that slaves were anything less than flesh-and-blood human beings. It meant, rather, that the master exercised a degree of power over the slave that had no counterpart in other systems of social organization.

If property rights in slaves were a manifestation of the master's power, the slaves' powerlessness was symbolized by the fact that they did not legally "own" anything themselves. Unlike the feudal peasant, for example, the slave had no legal claim on the land, or to the fruits of his or her labor. Put differently, the slave had none of the feudal peasant's legal powers that limited the power of the lord. And unlike the wage worker, the slave had no legal capacity to make a contractual arrangement to sell his or her labor power to an employer. Everything the slave could produce, every task the slave could perform, and indeed the slave's very physical body, were the "property" of the slaveowner in the sense that the master had the power to take what the slave produced, to compel the slave to labor, and to buy and sell the slave at will.

Slavery was also permanent. Unlike the subordination of children to their parents, slaves could not normally grow out of their condition. Unlike indentured servitude, enslavement did not end after five or six years. Prisoners never bequeathed their status to their children, whereas a substantial proportion of slaves throughout human history inherited their bondage at birth. This does not mean that masters never freed slaves. On the contrary, individual grants of freedom—manumission—were common to slavery in many societies and virtually automatic in some. In such instances manumission was usually generational in character: the slave's children would be freed, but the slave would remain a slave for life. In most cases manumission was the prerogative of the master, and until the master exercised that prerogative the slave's condition was perpetual. Judge Thomas Ruffin of North Carolina seized upon perpetuity in his famous *Mann* decision, to distinguish master-slave from parent-child relations. "There is no likeness between the cases," Ruffin asserted.[3]

> In the one, the end in view is the happiness of the youth, born to equal rights with that governor, on whom the duty devolves of training the young to usefulness, in a Station which he is afterwards to assume among freemen. . . . With slavery it is far otherwise. The end is the profit of the Master, his security and the public safety; the subject, one doomed in his own person, and his posterity, to live without knowledge, and without the capacity to make anything his own, and to toil that another may reap the fruits.

Like permanence, violence was a universal characteristic of slavery. For good reason, the master's whip has long served as a ubiquitous symbol of slavery everywhere. "If the law was to forbid whipping altogether," one southern slaveholder explained, "the authority of the master would be at an end."[4] It was not that slave systems alone used force, or that the force used against slaves was uniquely barbaric. We need not romanticize the history of serfdom or wage labor to appreciate that slave systems depended heavily on the widespread and continuous use of sheer physical force. Lacking the economic compulsions of a market relationship or the de facto distance between lord and serf, slavery was distinguished by its inescapable reliance on highly personalized mechanisms of coercion. No slave society has ever existed without a degree of systematic, often ritualized violence.

Perpetuity, violence, and kinlessness were joined in the master's legally unrestricted access to the slave's sexuality. The widespread castration of Roman slaves epitomized their violent separation from both ancestors and descendants, much as the nonexistence of the rape of a slave in the criminal law of Brazil, the antebellum South, and elsewhere revealed the legal irrelevance of marital and familial ties.[5] To claim open access to a slave's sexuality was to undermine, both violently and figuratively, the social significance of human reproduction and kinship relations.

In every society where men and women enslaved one another there was a paradoxical anarchy to the totalitarianism of the master-slave relationship. For slaves the daily conditions of life could vary as widely as the personalities of the slaveholders themselves. There were relatively few restraints on the masters, and this made any accommodation with the slaves less reliable and far less predictable. The daily experience of slavery, therefore, differed from culture to culture and from one century to the next as the cultural standards that defined the proper behavior of a master varied over time and place. Slavery changed from plantation to plantation and from day to day on the same plantation, as different masters succeeded or failed to live up to prevailing cultural standards, disregarded those standards entirely, or were simply moody and inconsistent in their behavior. Perpetual uncertainty was an unwavering constant of slavery. It was one of the master's most potent weapons and one of the greatest horrors of slave life.[6]

This does not mean that in practice slaves never owned property, had no families, or were absolutely dehumanized. As we shall see, the legal kinlessness of the slaves created special problems in the Old South precisely because the slaves did form strong family ties, and because those family ties formed the nucleus of a slave community and culture that resisted the intrinsically dehumanizing tendencies of slavery itself. Thus social death did not mean that the slaves had no bargaining chips at their disposal as they established a working relationship with their masters. Like every ruling class, the masters had to reach a reciprocal accommodation with those over whom they ruled.[7]

Nevertheless, the balance of power in the master-slave relationship was uniquely lopsided. The extent to which slaves owned anything, formed any families, or were treated with any humanity was subject almost entirely to the prerogative of the master. Masters could and did recognize slave marriages, but they could and also did sexually abuse slave women, castrate slave men, and destroy slave families at will. Masters could reward slaves for work well done, but they could and did brutalize slaves into submission. Masters could grant slaves privileges, but they could and did renege on their promises. In every slave society masters could even free their bondsmen, but in the nineteenth-century South they rarely did.

Slavery, then, was not simply the furthest point on a spectrum of statuses ranging from free to unfree; it was also a qualitatively distinct form of subordination. We can appreciate the subtleties this distinction sometimes raises by briefly examining a form of serfdom so extreme that it is often said to have been "slavery" in everything but name. In eighteenth- and nineteenth-century Russia, peasants were subordinated so thoroughly that they scarcely resembled medieval serfs. Until recently the consensus among historians was that as Russian serfdom grew ever more severe it became, in effect, slavery.[8] Yet even at their most degraded Russian serfs were embedded within a network of formal obligations to the family, the community, and the state, each of which made it difficult for the lord to claim the total subordination commonly demanded of a slave.[9] The point here is not that slavery and Russian serfdom cannot be compared, but that in pursuing the question of their comparability the distinctiveness of slavery may become clearer.

As extreme forms of subordination, slavery and Russian serfdom shared many attributes. By the nineteenth century, serfs could be bought and sold away from their land. Subject to the extensive judicial authority of their masters, serfs could be legally brutalized and were often whipped into submission. Slaves and Russian serfs alike were compelled by the master to work without any claim to the fruits of their labors. And just as the slave was legally propertyless, so was the serf's property ultimately owned by the lord. On the spectrum from freedom to unfreedom the differences between slavery and the most extreme forms of serfdom are difficult to distinguish and it is perhaps not worth the effort.[10]

Yet in important ways slavery remained a categorically distinctive form of subordination, even in comparison to Russian serfdom at its most oppressive. Consider the implications of serf marriages. Like earlier feudal lords, Russian masters could restrict the serf's right to marry, especially someone from a different estate—though there were ways of escaping this restriction, and within the bounds of a given estate serfs were more or less free to select their own mates. But, more important, the serfs' marriages were legally recognized. The church formally sanctified serf marriages and kept careful lineage and ancestral records. Although some masters did break up serf families, such actions were always illegal.

In certain ways the contrast with slavery, therefore, remains critical. No major slave society respected the integrity of slave families. Even where slave families existed, masters regularly broke them up. In Brazil, for example, the Church "sanctions and legitimizes" slave marriages, Agostinho Malheiro explained in 1866, but the "Civil Law grants these unions little practical effect. . . . [H]usband, wife, and children remain the property of the master."[11] For a legal marriage normally established formal obligations between spouses and between parents and children that were frankly incompatible with the slave's total subordination to the master.[12] In many cases slaves could not even form families, much less gain legal recognition of them. In Rome, Brazil, and Saint-Domingue, for example, scattered evidence suggests that slaves often lived not in family units but in sex-segregated barracks. Even in the American South, where family units were the norm, slave families had no legal security. What little statistical evidence we have indicates that as many as one in three slave families in the South was broken by the force of the master—suggesting that perhaps 600,000 slave families were shattered between 1820 and 1860. While some Russian lords violated the law by dividing serf families, there is no evidence that the rates of family breakup in Russia even approached the levels reached in the Old South.[13]

The serfs also enjoyed far more claims to property than did slaves in most places. The formal rules of Russian feudalism held that all property was ultimately the master's, but in practice serfs were required to own the draught animals and tools with which they met their feudal obligations. In addition, Russian peasants claimed customary ties to the land that remained powerful even in the face of the masters' abuse. "We are yours," went a well-known aphorism among the serfs, "but the land is ours."[14] Thus, even in the nineteenth century, Russian masters were unsure of their legal right to sell serfs away from the land, though they did so regularly.

With ambiguous claims to property and legally secure families, the serfs could organize their lives not on plantations but in peasant communes that had no counterpart in any slave society. In the South, for example, the customary division of the plantation among the heirs—a practice known as partible inheritance—resulted in the periodic destruction of the slave community and the breakup of slave families. Though Russian lords also practiced partible inheritance, it generally resulted in the sharing of control over an estate that remained intact. Peasant communes in Russia were far more secure than slave communities and had important legal and political responsibilities, including the mediation of the demands made by the master and the state. Every peasant, for example, was obligated to pay a yearly tax, and serfs were required to provide military service to the central government. But the obligation was levied through the commune, which decided collectively how best to fulfill the military demands of the state. Democratically organized, with treasuries of their own, serf communes served above all to maintain a relatively equal distribution of land among the local peasants through a process of periodic reapportionment that the masters almost never questioned.

The commune also mediated the masters' demand for labor and rent, giving serfs a degree of autonomy over their working lives that was largely alien to slavery. Under the traditional *barshchina* system—a holdover of the medieval *corvée*—masters commanded a certain amount of the serf's labor time. In the course of the eighteenth century these labor obligations reached their extreme limits, with serfs devoting all but their Sundays and holidays to the lord. But the master's demands were made on the commune, not on the individual serf, and it was the commune that decided how much time each family was capable of devoting to the fulfillment of the village's obligation. There was a second pattern of obligations distinct from the *barshchina* system: the *obrok*, or quitrent, in which serfs met their obligations by paying the lord not in time but in kind or, increasingly, in cash. The *obrok* gave peasants still more autonomy over the labor process by making the serfs' time their own and allowing them to meet their cash payments by going to work in factories and cities. By relieving them of most of their supervisory functions, it freed lords to live away from their estates—and their serfs. In a variety of ways, therefore, serf labor was largely self-directed. This degree of independence, however limited, was enough to allow the state to claim ownership of a huge proportion of Russian serfs—perhaps half by the late eighteenth century. For without self-governing communes such widespread state ownership would have been difficult to sustain.

There are few comparisons in plantation slavery. The state used only small numbers of slaves in limited ways that were of no general significance to slave economies, particularly plantation societies. The most autonomous working conditions in the Old South—excluding the exceptional individual slave—were found on plantations where the "task system" was in practice, primarily in low-country South Carolina. But even in such areas, where the slaves were assigned a certain number of tasks to perform on their own each day, their labor was still closely supervised by resident masters or overseers. On most plantations slaves worked in gangs under the direct supervision of the owner or his representative. No slave community enjoyed the power of the peasant commune to distribute the lands, for no slave enjoyed any claim to the land comparable to the serf's.

Thus, Russian serfs occupied a social world held together by the legal bonds of kinship and extensive ties of community. These

ties meant that the serf could not fulfill the most elementary requirement of slavery: total subordination to the master. For in the
serf's world wives were also subject to their husbands, children
were subject to their parents, and families were subject to the village commune. This crisscrossing of authority and obligation located the serfs within the complicated network of social and
political obligations that together made up Russian society.

The point is not that the serfs were free, or that their burdens
were not oppressive, or that their lives were anything better than
nasty, brutish and short. Horror stories abound in the annals of
Russian serfdom. In his late-eighteenth-century *Journey from St.
Petersburg to Moscow*, A. N. Radishchev told the story of "a certain
man" who so ruthlessly exploited his hundreds of serfs that they
came to "resemble tools that have neither will nor impulse." To
increase the produce of his estate he "took away from his peasants
the small allotment of plough land . . . forced all his peasants and
their wives and children to work every day of the year for him . . .
doled out to them a definite quantity of bread" and a bare minimum of clothing. "Naturally, these serfs had no cows, horses,
ewes, or rams." In short, they were treated like slaves.[15] S. T.
Aksakov told the more gruesome story of Mikhail Kurolesov,
whose "instinct of cruelty and lust of blood" created a living hell
for the peasants on his estate. On drunken binges Kurolesov
would issue "outrageous commands," and at the slightest hint of
disobedience order the offending peasant "to be chained, knocked
about, as often as not soundly flogged, and then locked up in the
cellar." The reign of terror ended only when Kurolesov was poisoned by two of his servants.[16]

The parallels with slavery are obvious. What is hard to duplicate is the commentary both these stories provoked. For both
Radishchev and Aksakov considered the behavior of the serf owners extreme and, in fact, illegal. "The wealth of this bloodsucker
does not belong to him," Radishchev asserted. "It has been acquired by robbery and deserves severe punishment according to
law." For Aksakov, Kurolesov's tortures were possible because he
had terrorized and corrupted the local officials who might otherwise have intervened. "There is not the slightest doubt that this

sudden death of Kurolesov would have been followed by a strict judicial enquiry," Aksakov wrote, had it not been for the fact that one of Kurolesov's own appointees "succeeded in hushing up the affair."[17] Yet what both masters did to their serfs slaveholders commonly did to their slaves, ordinarily and quite legally.

As brutal as Russian serfdom was, then, can we properly call it slavery? After all the differences between slavery and Russian serfdom have been explored, the answer is still unclear. Except for the legality of serf marriages—an unambiguous distinction—most of the remaining evidence suggests differences of practice rather than of formal status. The serfs thought of the land as their own, but the law did not recognize their ownership of it. The serf owner recognized the peasant commune, but not because the peasants had any legal right to organize their villages as they commonly did. By law the taxes paid by peasants were levied on the master and it was the master who was legally responsible for meeting the draft quotas. Thus, while the serfs lived in a social world that was different in important ways from that of the slaves, they had almost no legally secure ties to their community beyond those of the family. The spectral analogy placing Russian serfs together with slaves at the extreme of unfreedom therefore retains much of its validity. But we must be careful to draw the proper inferences. Slavery was always a qualitatively distinct form of subordination, at best comparable only to the most extreme forms of serfdom known to western history.

Even at that, the comparison remains ambiguous. For kinlessness was fundamental to the very nature of slavery, while the family ties of Russian serfs halted their slide into degradation just short of the complete unfreedom of the slave. This was a distinction that pressed to the very core of slavery as a way of life and as a day-to-day experience. Much of what it felt like to be a slave derived from the inability to form enduring family ties or from the intrinsic insecurity of whatever ties slaves succeeded in forming.

If Russian serfdom—one of slavery's closest historical analogues—remained different from slavery in critical ways, all the more different were the myriad forms of subordination with which slavery is too often confused, including indentured servitude, imprisonment, wage labor, and in some cases marriage and childhood. Because each of these involved some limitation on freedom, each inevitably shared many of slavery's characteristics. But slavery was different from all of them. For the slave's freedom was not merely restricted or limited; it was denied altogether. Only the slave's subordination was total; only the slave was cut off from society, a permanent outsider, socially dead.

And only emancipation could return the slave to society. "Through manumission," a Brazilian legal authority wrote in 1866,

> the slave is restored to his natural condition and state of manhood, to that of a *person*. He enters the social community, the *city*, as the Romans said, without any indication of his former slave status. It is then that he appears in society and before the law as a person (*persona*), being able under the law, properly speaking, to freely exercise his rights and activities like other citizens.

Beneath these abstractions, however, the real meaning of freedom rested in the fundamental transformation of the life of the former slave:[18]

> He may establish a family, acquire a full right to property for himself, pass on a *legacy* even when dying intestate, make contracts, dispose of property through sale or trade or through his last will and testament; in other words, like the minor child who upon reaching adulthood acquires his *full freedom*, he can practice every act of civil life. He may even become a guardian or protector.

This is what it meant to make a slave free.

AS THERE IS no greater dishonor than to be denied all standing in society, so there is no condition more completely dishonored by society than the social death of slavery. Yet the symbols of dishonor are perhaps the most complicated of slavery's defining features. Slavery's brutality is manifest; its permanence is easily grasped; and even kinlessness had legal and social consequences that are readily documented. But "honor" and "dishonor" are not patterns of behavior, nor are they codified in statute law—though both law and behavior reflect prevailing standards of honor and dishonor. Like racial superiority and inferiority, honor and dishonor are powerful cultural constructs, not intrinsic characteristics. In everyday language, however, black slaves were often said to *be* inferior, just as certain persons were said to *be* honorable or dishonorable. Yet the analogy breaks down quickly. For where racism as an ideology posits the innateness, and therefore the universality, of superiority and inferiority, honor and dishonor are far less tangible and by no means universal. Superiority may be a gift from God, but honor and dishonor are bestowed by society at large—and what society giveth society taketh away. One's honor is one's own, but only so long as it is recognized as such. In a sense, honor and dishonor refer chiefly to reputation, to one's public persona, and as such they are expressed in symbols more than ideas. Thus awards or titles are often said to be "honorific," symbolic expressions of community esteem. But where formal expressions of recognition are the most tangible badges of honor, dishonor is symbolically expressed through ridicule and humiliation.[19]

Honor and dishonor are the cultural siblings of power and powerlessness. As symbolic expressions of inequality in human relationships, exalted standards of honor necessarily accompany exaggerated symbols of dishonor. Hence a paradox. On the one hand, no honor is more esteemed than that which is bestowed by one's peers, one's colleagues, in essence one's equals. All classes may expect deference from their subordinates, but members of the same class may covet honor among themselves even more. For the highest honor is that which is given without coercion by those who are in no sense inferior to the beneficiary of an honorific gesture. On the other hand, the concern for honor appears to be most pronounced in those societies where the gulf separating the upper from the lower classes is widest. Because the inequitable distribution of power reached its extreme in slavery, the masters' obsession with honor reached corresponding heights. And because the slaves could exercise no power, because they were completely subordinated, they were necessarily dishonored. Thus, where honor among equals is especially prized, dishonor attaches itself ever more firmly to inequality and subordination.

In recent years there has been increasing awareness of some of the means by which free men in the Old South displayed a heightened concern for honor. Historians have focused in particular on the elaborate ritual of the duel, the quintessential "affair of honor," and while their analyses have given us a more sophisticated understanding of dueling than ever before, we nevertheless lack a clear sense of the ritual's larger significance. For although dueling was probably more common in the slave states than elsewhere, it was scarcely common even in the South. Few Southerners dueled to begin with, and over time the number of duels declined as planter-dominated legislatures, possessed by the spirit of antebellum reform, outlawed dueling altogether. The Louisiana constitution went so far as to prohibit those convicted of dueling from holding seats in the state legislature.

Was there an overriding concern for honor in the symbols, rituals, and ceremonies that accompanied the passage of everyday life within the planter class: child-rearing, adolescence, marriage, aging, and death? Such passages were in no way distinctive to the South; in many cases planter families took their cultural cues on such matters from family-practice manuals written by and for the northern middle class. Precisely what such guidebooks obscure is the distinctive sense of honor that slavery imparts. The same is true of the *code duello*: regardless of how widespread or uncommon duels were, the ritual's connection to slavery was indirect at best. Nor do any of these rituals provide a wide enough window through which to view both honor and dishonor, and to examine them not as discreet entities but as related opposites reflecting some of the symbolic aspects of the interaction between master and slave. More revealing than child-rearing treatises, and certainly more widespread than duels, were the commonplace symbols of honor and dishonor embedded in the normal workings of the master-slave relationship.[20]

The very process of enslavement was replete with the symbols of dishonor. Slavery most often began in an act of violence, typically an act of war in which the slave who might otherwise have perished was instead made one of the spoils of battle. But the demand for slaves often stimulated the very acts of war that presumably justified slavery in the first instance. When the New World's thirst for labor reached the staggering proportions of the Atlantic slave trade, for example, it provoked widespread political disruption and endemic warfare across vast stretches of the African continent over several hundred years. "Nothing reigns nowadays but confusion and anarchy," Philip Quaque wrote from the Gold Coast in 1786, "dissipation and discontent throughout the country."[21]

Samuel Ajayi Crowther's narrative of his own enslavement in Africa vividly captures the violence of enslavement along with its symbolic importance. The context was the Yoruba wars of the early nineteenth century, which "for some years" had brought "much devastation and bloodshed" to Crowther's Oyo country. In early 1821 Crowther "was violently turned out of [his] father's house, and separated from relations; and . . . was made to experience what is called to be in slavery." Crowther's account of the invasion of his village emphasizes the disruption of family relations. Mothers clung to their infants as they ran for protection into the bush, only to be "overtaken and caught by the enemies with a noose of rope thrown over the neck of every individual, to be led in the manner of goats tied together." "The last view I had of my father," Crowther remembered, "was when he came from the fight, to give us the signal to flee." As the twelve-year-old boy was led away from "the place of my birth, the play-ground of my childhood, and the place which I thought would be the repository of my mortal body in its old age," Crowther caught a last glimpse of his grandmother being led away with several of his cousins. And in the hours and days that followed, Crowther "passed several towns and villages which had been reduced to ashes." His sense of chaos is balanced by a corresponding sense that African warfare had become an efficient mechanism for the mass production of slaves.[22]

If these were not so much "wars" as organized kidnapping raids, they were sufficiently war*like* to sustain the traditional justification of enslavement as an alternative to death for prisoners taken in battle. The same theme reappeared where enslavement replaced capital punishment, or when individuals enslaved themselves during famines to avoid starvation. In each case slavery replaced a violent or untimely loss of life.[23] For this reason, the slave was often said to live under a suspended sentence of death. Thus the very process of enslavement generated the ruling metaphors that appeared again and again in the discussion of bondage. The separation from parents, the disruption of communal ties, the sense of chaos and confusion—all of these became for captured Africans, as for the subsequent generations who read their narratives, the most potent emblems of enslavement.

Where slavery was an inherited condition—as it was in the nineteenth-century South—the degradation of enslavement was symbolically reenacted with each new generation of masters and slaves. Childhood in a slave society was, therefore, unusually rich in the symbolism of power and powerlessness. Thomas Jefferson's eloquent evocation of the fearful implications of raising a child to be a master of slaves is deservedly famous. "The whole commerce between master and slave," he wrote, "is a perpetual exercise of the most boisterous passions, the most unremitting despotism on the one part, and degrading submissions on the other. Our children see this, and learn to imitate it. . . . The parent storms, the child looks on, catches the lineaments of wrath, puts on the same airs in the circle of smaller slaves, gives a loose to the worst of passions, and thus nursed, educated, and daily exercised in tyranny, cannot but be stamped by it with odious peculiarities."[24]

Jefferson's concern was chiefly with the effects of slavery on free men, and it was a concern that even the slaves shared. In the 1850's Solomon Northup vividly recalled being forced by his master to administer a particularly vicious beating to another slave while the mistress "stood on the piazza among her children, gazing on the scene with an air of heartless satisfaction." This prompted Northup to consider "[t]he effect of these exhibitions of brutality on the household of the slave-holder." The master's oldest son, he wrote,

> is an intelligent lad of ten or twelve years of age. It is pitiable, sometimes, to see him chastising, for instance, the venerable Uncle Abram. He will call the old man to account, and if in his childish judgment it is necessary, sentence him to a certain number of lashes, which he proceeds to inflict with much gravity and deliberation. Mounted on his pony, he often rides into the field with his whip, playing the overseer, greatly to his father's delight. Without discrimination, at such times, he applies the rawhide, urging the slaves forward with shouts, and occasional expressions of profanity, while the old man laughs, and commends him as a thorough-going boy.[25]

Like Jefferson's, Northup's concern was with the rearing of the slaveholder's children: the brutalization of the young boy's sensibilities and "the father's delight" in it. But Northup's memory captures another aspect of this distinctive child-rearing pattern— its humiliation of the slaves.

Few things symbolized the slave's degradation as thoroughly as the spectacle of a small child flogging a helpless adult. "One of the most trying scenes I ever passed through," a North Carolina slave recalled, was the whipping his mother received at the hands of the master's child, whom she herself had raised. The free child, a "young girl, came into the kitchen one day, and for some trifle about the dinner, she struck my mother, who pushed her away, and she fell to the floor." When the master returned and his daughter complained, he beat the slave woman with a hickory rod "and then called his daughter and told her to take her satisfaction of her, and she did beat her until she was satisfied."[26]

The special poignancy of such memories rests on their symbolism as much as their brutality. The usual relations of adult and child are radically altered: parents abandon their traditional role as disciplinarians and instead encourage their children to humiliate adults with physical abuse. In effect, the child is made the equal of the adult, and as such the honor of the youth must be defended by the parent. Moreover, the parent must recognize the child's equal right to punish the slave for transgressing accepted social boundaries. At the same moment the child is made the superior of the adult slave. The youth is thus simultaneously invited into a world of freedom, where honor depends upon the recognition of one's equals, and a world of inequality, where slaves are dishonored by means of humiliation.

For the slave there is a powerful moment of recognition: the sudden assertion of the young master's authority becomes at the same time a symbolic act through which the slave child is made to understand the extremes of power and powerlessness intrinsic to his or her condition. Lunsford Lane recalled that moment vividly. As a young slave in antebellum North Carolina he remembered "playing with the other boys and girls, colored and white, in the yard. . . . I knew no difference between myself and the white children; nor did they seem to know any in turn." But when he was put to work at the age of ten or eleven, Lane recalled, "I discovered the difference between myself and my master's white children. They began to order me about and were told to do so by my master and mistress. I found, too, that they had learned to read, while I was not permitted to have a book in my hand."[27] In ways that Jefferson had scarcely considered, the education of the master coincided with the education of the slave.

Clearly such incidents were turning points in the lives of slave and free children alike. If the master's child was learning to wield power, the slave child was learning the meaning of parental powerlessness, and by extension his or her own subordination. For many, this was a profound realization. William Wells Brown, for example, never forgot the day he heard his mother crying in pain as the overseer whipped her in a distant field. Though he "could hear every crack of the whip, and every groan and cry of my poor mother," Brown later wrote, he remained in his cabin, "not daring to venture any farther." Instead, he went back to his bed "and wept aloud."[28]

To appreciate the symbolism of such events is to recall that kinship is the primary system of authority in society and the first link between the individual and the community. It is not surprising, then, that kinlessness figures prominently in symbolic expressions of the slave's dishonor. If African culture retained any saliency in the slave community—and there is considerable evidence that it did—it taught the slaves that status in society rested on one's place in the lineage system and that there was no greater disgrace than the denial of one's bonds of kinship. The slaves remembered the physical abuse of their parents because it taught them the meaning of parental powerlessness and because they associated that condition with dishonor. Kinlessness was not simply frightening to the child, it was deeply humiliating.

The distinctive rites of passage among southern children were by no means the only occasions for displays of honor and dishonor. Whipping, for example, took on ritualized form as masters used the lash not only to punish presumed transgressions but to humiliate the victim—to dishonor the slave. Once again, kinlessness, the legal irrelevance of the slave family, figures prominently in such episodes. "Who can imagine what could be the feelings of a father and mother," one ex-slave asked, "when looking upon their infant child whipped and tortured with impunity" while the parents themselves were "placed in a situation where they could afford it no protection." The same slave, Henry Bibb, remembered being "compelled to stand and see my wife shamefully scourged and abused by her master; and the manner in which this was done, was so violently and inhumanly committed upon the person of a female."[29]

Through the ostentatious display of the master's power and the slave's subordination such episodes transcended their immediate rationale. They captured much of the essence of slavery: the violence, the sexual abuse, and the dishonoring of the slaves through the explicit disregard for their kinship relations. Parents were denied the power to protect their children. Spouses watched helplessly as their mates were brutalized. The slaves were not simply punished for their putative transgressions, they were humiliated and dishonored besides.

At other times masters proclaimed their own sense of honor by distancing themselves from the actual use of the lash. To brutalize a slave was to risk one's reputation within the community. And so intermediaries—overseers or slave drivers—were charged with

the task of whipping the slaves, a device that had the dual advantage of simultaneously representing the master's honor and the
slave's dishonor, the power of the one and the subordination of
the other. "I rarely punish myself," one southern slaveholder explained, "but make my driver virtually an executive officer to inflict punishments."[30] The brutal behavior intrinsic to slavery, and
the ill repute that such behavior could engender among one's
peers, was thus culturally transferred from the slaveholders themselves to the drivers and overseers, whether or not the latter
groups deserved the slight.

Masters likewise recoiled from the spectacle of the slave auction, even though the purchase and sale of human beings was built
into the very structure of slavery. Their disdain was itself part of
the symbolism of slave sales—it demonstrated the master's sense
of honor even as he sent the slave off to be sold. Though slavery
was inconceivable without a slave trade, masters frequently—
though by no means always—faced the necessity of selling slaves
with sincere if effusive hand-wringing. Consider Thomas Chaplin, a South Carolina planter who in 1845 bemoaned the "unpleasant extremity" to which he had been "driven." Faced with debts
that had to be paid, Chaplin decided to sell "ten prime Negroes,"
or as he himself put it, "to separate families, mothers and daughters, brothers and sisters—all to pay for your own extravagances."
Chaplin's use of the second person, "your," instead of the more
accurate first person—"*my* own extravagance"—was a brief gram-
matical illustration of the master's attempt to distance himself
from the whole business. Yet in the end Chaplin honorably took
responsibility. "I cannot express my feelings on seeing so many
faithful Negroes going away from me forever," he wrote, "not for
any fault of their own but for my own extravagance." With such
expressions men like Chaplin extracted a modicum of dignity
from the ultimate exercise of their power.[31]

For the slaves, however, being sold was a degrading experience
infused with the symbols of their powerlessness. It so often involved the breakup of a family that slave auctions became the
quintessential expression of the slaves' kinlessness as well. Such
demonstrations were sufficiently vivid so that even slaves whose

families were preserved saw their implications. "After my master died," one slave recalled, "my mistress sold a number of her slaves from their families and friends—but not me. She sold several children from their parents—but my children were with me still. She sold two husbands from their wives—but I was still with mine. She sold one wife from her husband—but mine had not been sold from me. The master of my wife, Mr. Smith, had separated members of families by sale—but not of mine." Thus even in the relative security of unbroken families slaves had no trouble drawing the lesson from the sale of others: "We knew and, what is more, we *felt* that we were slaves."[32]

Nothing made slaves *feel* more like slaves than the financial transaction by which they were actually sold. Auctions were so much a part of slavery, they evinced such distinct patterns, that we may speak of them as having become ritualized. Slaves were often sold in the same places: at well-known markets in cities like New Orleans and Charleston, or on the front steps of the local courthouse. They were often sold at the same time of year. "Of all days in the year, the slaves dread New-Year's day the worst of any," one southern slave explained. "For folks come for their debts then; and if anybody is going to sell a slave, that's the time they do it."[33]

The symbolic meaning of the auction was especially clear in the treatment of the slaves being sold. William Chambers's description of a Richmond, Virginia, auction in 1853 is at once dispassionate and evocative. A man up for sale was brought forward and asked to step behind a screen for examination. He was then

> ordered to take off his clothes, which he did without a word or look of remonstrance. About a dozen gentlemen crowded to the spot while the poor fellow was stripping himself, and as soon as he stood on the floor, bare from top to toe, a most rigorous scrutiny of his person was instituted. The clear black skin, back and front, was viewed all over for sores from disease; and there was no part of his body left unexamined. The man was told to open and shut his hands, asked if he could pick cotton, and every tooth in his head was scrupulously looked at.[34]

In many cases slaves were greased to enhance their appearance or forced to dance to make them seem happy. Humiliating inspections lapsed easily into a form of public sexual abuse. In the worst cases, the auction block was the actual site of harrowing family breakups.

Scenes like this were intrinsic to the economics of slavery, but they were much more than that. Slave auctions were ceremonies of degradation, symbolic reenactments of the violence of original enslavement, potent reminders of the slave's powerlessness and dishonor. Auctions brutally represented the legal irrelevance of the slave's kinfolk, the totality of the slave's subordination, the violence of enslavement, and the hard, practical reality of social death. Even more than the whip, the auction block was a symbol of the slave's dishonor.

Many more questions would have to be raised and addressed in a complete analysis of the symbols of honor and dishonor in the master-slave relationship. The sensibilities of free children as they assumed the authority of the master; of slave children as they were made to understand their powerlessness; of parents as they saw their children through such transitions—each of these situations was rife with cultural and psychological connotations unique to slavery and deserving of far more detailed examination than they can be given here. The way slaves were sold, how the masters rationalized auctions, how the different experiences each slave carried onto the auction block altered the personal meaning of the event, and what went on in the minds of the buyers as they watched and participated in the sale of the slave—these questions, too, demand fuller exploration than is possible or appropriate here. What seems clear even from so brief a sketch as this one, however, is the importance of the relationship between honor and dishonor to the culture and psychology of slavery.

NEITHER SLAVERY nor any other social relationship is capable of determining the ideology necessary for its defense. Instead, whenever masters took up their own cause they followed the time-honored practice of ruling classes everywhere: they appropriated the words, phrases, and ideas already available in the wider culture, reformulating them in their own interests. The ideology of slavery, therefore, has tended to shift according to its specific historical context. Most often defenders of slavery resorted to dualisms—related opposites that could parallel the distinction between outsiders and insiders and, in so doing, could justify the coexistence of slavery and freedom. Indeed, ever since antiquity slavery and freedom have served as the paradigm for all other polarities. "The principal distinction made by the law of persons is this," a Roman jurist declared in the second century A.D., "that all human beings are either free men or slaves."[35] Western thought has been rich in such dichotomies: the natural world and the world of society, the citizen and the foreigner, civilization and barbarism, honor and dishonor, public and private, black and white. These are not gradations of hierarchy so much as categorical antitheses. They do not connect the high and mighty to the low and degraded through a series of escalating statuses but, on the contrary, radically separate the sinner from the saved, the citizen from the foreigner, and so on. Slavery thrived on such polarities. Proslavery ideology virtually required them.[36]

Among the ancient Greeks and Romans it was considered natural for a man or woman to find freedom within society, making the slave's place outside of society "unnatural." In his *Digest* of Roman law, Justinian articulated the common proposition that while liberty was "the natural ability to do whatever anyone pleases," slavery put a person "into the ownership of somebody else" and was therefore "contrary to the natural order."[37] But once the slave's condition had been defined as unnatural, it was perhaps inevitable that some men would declare that slaves were made "by nature" for their status. This paradox—that slaves were naturally suited for a condition that was essentially unnatural—first emerged in the writings of Aristotle. They established an enduring precedent.

Ever since then, dehumanizing cultural stereotypes have defined slaves as different from free people and therefore deserving of their condition. The most extreme formulations depicted the slaves as alien "by nature," and often subhuman or animal-like. In a notorious passage in *The Politics* Aristotle declared that "a slave is a sort of living piece of property. . . . The use made of slaves hardly differs at all from that of tame animals: they both help with their bodies to supply our essential needs. It is nature's purpose therefore to make the bodies of free men to differ from those of slaves."[38]

There was an underlying political purpose to such reasoning. Cultural stereotypes were widely invoked to justify the slave's political exclusion, for, as Joseph Vogt has explained, "slaves count for nothing in the community of citizens." Even Aristotle's assertion of a natural physical distinction between slaves and free men served chiefly to introduce a proposition about the nature of citizenship and the polity. While the bodies of slaves were "strong enough to be used for necessary tasks," he argued, the bodies of free men were "well suited for the life of a citizen of a state, a life which is in turn divided between the requirements of war and peace." What was true for Aristotle was true for the authors of Mississippi's antebellum constitution: the slave was by nature unfit for citizenship.[39] The distinction between the natural and the unnatural was only one of the recurring polarities of proslavery thought from antiquity onward.*

But it is not clear that Aristotle was representative of Greek thought. Although Plato questioned whether members of the "Greek race" should be enslaved, for example, he did not posit distinctions grounded in nature. Instead, Plato invoked a classic dichotomy between civilization—which he equated with Greeks —and the "barbarism" of non-Greeks, which presumably suited them to slavery. A passage in the *Republic* asks, "Do you think it just that Greek cities should enslave Greeks? or should they make it their rule, and enforce the same in other cities, to spare all of the Greek race, fearing their own enslavement by the barbarians?"[40] For Plato the polarity of slave and free became, almost explicitly, the distinction between outsiders and insiders.

---

*The polarities upon which slavery thrived extend beyond slavery itself. Louis Mazur notes that foreigners who become citizens are still said to be "naturalized."

The Romans, who were even less likely than Greeks to attribute the slave's character to nature, nevertheless assumed that slaves were morally inferior. A Christian writer in the later Roman Empire had to go to some lengths to refute the commonplace myths about the character of slaves. "Among our slaves there are thieves and runaways," the prevailing wisdom held. "They are also called liars. . . . They are accused of being dominated by their appetites and by greed." And when Roman masters, under the pressures of civil war and economic dislocation, began to free their slaves in large numbers, Dionysius of Halicarnassus complained that "great infamy and filth which cannot be cleansed should not be allowed to be introduced into the citizen-body." At certain points the Roman government, believing "it very important that the people should be kept pure and uncorrupted by any taint of foreign or slave blood . . . set limits on the number of slaves that might be manumitted."[41] Superiority and inferiority, morality and immorality, cleanliness and filth—these are among the many polarities that slavery has relied upon over the centuries.

Christianity, however, has provided Westerners with the most bountiful collection of dualisms that could be used in defense of slavery. The Augustinian Cities of God and of Man, Luther's Christian Liberty and Christian Slavery, the faithful and the heathen, the sinner and the saved, the worldly and the spiritual, the sacred and the profane—most of these became, at one time or another, useful dichotomies for proslavery writers. In late Rome Christians joined in the defense of slavery fairly quickly. The Pauline epistles, Augustinian catholicism, and, much later, evangelical Protestantism all posited a separation of the worldly from the spiritual that rendered irrelevant the earthbound distinction between slave and free, and this undoubtedly facilitated an explicit Christian defense of slavery. There are few more enduring themes in the ideology of slavery than that which consigns the infidel to the punishment of absolute bondage.

But if the slave was a permanent outsider, could one enslave a fellow Christian, a member of the community of believers? Just as Plato wondered whether Greeks could enslave Greeks, there were always nagging doubts about the propriety of Christians enslaving one another. A residue of ambiguity appeared, for example, in the persistent belief that to free a slave was to perform an act of Christian piety, even though slavery itself had long since been pronounced compatible with biblical sanction. A paradigmatic theme in the early literature of conversion has the wealthy slaveholder forsaking worldly riches by *selling* his or her estate while *freeing* the slaves.[42] In the New World, "heathenism" loomed so large in Englishmen's initial rationale for the enslavement of Africans that seventeenth-century Virginians worried about the legality of holding Africans in slavery after they had been baptized. For as long as religious identity and community membership remained linked, just so long would the converted slave present an ideological problem for the master class.[43]

The same distinction between believers and unbelievers appeared with even more consistency in Islamic writings on slavery, which may mean only that Islamic practice diverged more sharply from prevailing norms. A Borno king in medieval Africa insisted that enslaved captives should be asked about their religious beliefs. "If they say, 'We are free men and Muslims,' " the king insisted, ". . . release them and return them to their liberty and Islam." Even as the African slave trade expanded, Islamic scholars sustained the principle. The "reason for slavery is non-belief," Ahmad Babr wrote in 1614. "Whoever is captured in a condition of non-belief, it is legal to own him."[44] By the nineteenth century Islamic slavers evaded this injunction by simply declaring slaves to be "unbelievers" by definition. At that point, at least one Muslim slave trader could invoke the Koran to justify wars of enslavement "in order to carry out more fully the commands of a true Mohametan to destroy all unbelievers."[45]

Through all of these theological peregrinations, Christians continued to enslave Christians and Muslims enslaved Muslims. Yet religious hypocrisy is not the issue. The point is that the powerful impulse to define slaves as outsiders had conflicting implications for religious dogma. The absolute servility of the heretic was explicitly justified and perfectly compatible with basic theology. But where co-believers were enslaved, the same distinction between the faithful and the infidel presented special ethical problems because in so many societies religious ideals proclaimed the spiritual unity of the faithful within a community of true believers.

Slavery usually required a more clear-cut dichotomy than religious doctrine alone provided, and New World slaveholders developed one. Brazilian masters, for example, not only appropriated most of the ideological traditions that justified slavery in antiquity and Christendom, they went further than their predecessors by naturalizing the distinction between slave and free with a theory of race. The basic proposition was startlingly simple: "that the Negroes are not people like ourselves," as one Brazilian miner put it. Nature itself had determined the place of the African in Brazil. "When the Author of Nature drew from nothing the precious continent of Brazil," one defender of slavery insisted in 1823, "it seems that through an act of His special Providence he also created just opposite Brazil in the interior of Africa men who were deliberately constructed to serve on this continent."[46] With similar arguments endlessly duplicated, the distinction between black and white became the most powerful dualism in the history of proslavery thought.

But Brazilians neither invented racism nor carried it further than anyone else.[47] The latter distinction belongs to the slaveowners in the United States. Thomas Jefferson reveals the depth of racism in the American South, not because he was an extremist but, on the contrary, because he was so moderate. He thought slavery an evil and he held blacks and whites equal in certain qualities of the heart that he viewed as essential to a virtuous republic. It is in the light of such moderation that Jefferson's racism seems all the more significant. The difference between blacks and whites "is fixed in nature," he explained, "and is as real as if its seat and cause were better known to us." Among the differences Jefferson pointed to were the "eternal monotony" of black color, the distinctive hair and inferior "symmetry of form" that made black people prefer whites "as uniformly as . . . the Oranutan [prefers] the black woman over those of his own species." Jefferson also detected in blacks a "very strong and disagreeable odor," a greater tolerance for heat, and less need for sleep than was true for whites.

On and on he went, the racial distinctions piling up. Blacks were as brave as whites, but more reckless; they were more emotional, but their "griefs are transient" and "their existence appears to participate more of sensation than reflection." In memory, Jefferson wrote, blacks "are equal to the whites; in reason much inferior." Hence black intellectual and artistic achievements were "destitute of . . . merit." Whatever the origins of this "distinct race," he concluded, blacks were "inferior to the whites in the endowments of both body and mind," and this "unfortunate difference of color, and perhaps of faculty, is a powerful obstacle to the emancipation of these people."[48]

As we shall see, the views Jefferson set down in the 1780's grew even harsher in other men's hands until, by the middle of the nineteenth century, the tenets of racism achieved the status of a science. Here and there a southern slaveholder would reject the most extreme formulations, especially the theory that God had created blacks and whites separately. But compared to Greek, Roman, African, and even South American slaveholders, southern masters would come to rely more consistently on racism, and their racism itself would become far more intense. Even so, the distinction between black and white began from premises about the natural distinction between slave and free that had sources outside of racism itself. Ancient philosophy, Christianity, and racism combined in the American South to sustain the traditional dualism between freedom and slavery.[49]

Alfred Taylor Bledsoe, Thomas R. R. Cobb, and other proslavery writers, for example, gave prominent display to quotations from Aristotle's Politics. Bledsoe was especially severe with abolitionists for their failure to recognize that blacks were "unfit" for civil society, just as Aristotle had explained.[50] Cobb opened his inquiry into the law of slavery with a reverent citation to the Greek philosopher's conviction that "some men were slaves by nature, and that slavery was absolutely necessary to a perfect society." Thirty-five pages of evidence from science and history followed, all tending toward Cobb's central conclusion regarding the fate of the Negro: "[A] state of bondage, so far from doing violence to the law of his nature, develops and perfects it; and . . . in that state, he enjoys the greatest amount of happiness, and arrives at the greatest degree of perfection of which his nature is capable."[51]

Whereas the Greeks held that slaves were naturally suited to an unnatural condition, racist ideologues held that slavery was the natural condition of inferior blacks, and this latter conviction was by no means universal to slavery. Antebellum Southerners were apparently more receptive to Aristotle's extreme pronouncements than were the philosopher's fellow Athenians. Ancient Romans may have believed that slaves were greedy, stomach-driven thieves and liars, but there is little to suggest that masters believed such characters were the product of the slaves' inherent nature. And when many traditional African societies defined the slave as kinless they did not look upon that condition as evidence that slaves were unfit for freedom. On the contrary, kinlessness within the context of African "lineage ideology" actually made the slaves and their descendants available for gradual assimilation.[52] Barbarians could be civilized, sinners could be saved, and slaves could be freed. But the logic of racism held that the difference between black and white was beyond human control—decreed by the laws of nature. In the New World, especially in the American South, "black" slavery and "white" freedom produced the most extreme dualism in the long history of proslavery ideology.

SLAVERY IN the American South shared the basic characteristics of slavery everywhere. Perpetual outsiders, noncitizens stripped of virtually all legal rights, southern slaves were totally subject to the authority of masters, who could be kind or cruel or, perhaps most terrifying, kind and cruel by turns, arbitrarily and without warning. Southern slavery epitomized the anarchy of absolutism characteristic of slavery everywhere. Socially dead and symbolically dishonored, slaves in America experienced their degradation and powerlessness within a legal system that defined the master's authority as a right of property. Slavery in the South was violent, and it was permanent. For the slaves and their descendants, freedom was a hope and a prayer, but for those who could not break from the system entirely, it could never be an aspiration.

In important ways, however, slavery in the United States was unlike slavery in other times and places. In the South, for example, the slave was not only a slave for life, so too were the slave's children and grandchildren, all of them, forever. The permanence of slavery was always one of its defining characteristics, but in most societies manumission was also a common feature. Nor was the inescapable inheritance of slavery in the United States universal to all slaveholding societies. For slaves in most times and places there have been avenues to freedom that were not normally available to slaves in America.

When slavery still existed in early modern Russia, for example, running away was so difficult to prevent that perhaps one in four slaves ended his or her bondage simply by abandoning the master.[53] Throughout Africa, alternatively, slaves could often anticipate the gradual assimilation of their descendants into the social mainstream. Though they numbered in the millions over several centuries, African slaves did not automatically bequeath their completely subordinated status to their offspring. Rather, with each passing generation many people shed some of the social stigmata of their enslaved ancestors, were transformed from outsiders to insiders, and moved from kinlessness to incorporation within the established lineage system.[54] Though recent scholarship suggests that generational assimilation was less common than African historians once thought, the contrast with the American slaves' prospects for manumission remains stark.

Nor could American slaves pursue the option open to many of their counterparts in ancient Rome: self-purchase through an agreed-upon arrangement with the master. The highly developed Roman *peculium* gave to slaves with exalted status the ability to earn and save enough to offer their masters a good price in return for manumission. The masters—always interested in a lucrative proposition—were doubly rewarded with slaves who were motivated to work hard for their freedom and to pay a good price for it. Furthermore, manumission did not necessarily free the Roman slave from all obligations to his former master. Through an elaborate network of patron-client relations Roman masters continued to claim certain prescribed obligations from the slaves they freed.[55] In colonial Peru, slaves were often allowed to purchase their freedom with the proviso that they continue to work one or two days each week for their former masters.[56] Similarly in Brazil, a small but steady stream of slaves moved out of slavery and into a subordinate form of freedom.[57]

Why, when compared to the many societies with slaves, do the prospects for individual manumission seem to have been so limited in the United States?[58] One hypothesis holds that in the United States the absence of an aristocratic hierarchy so widened the gulf between slavery and freedom as to make manumission all but impossible. As one Georgia writer concluded after examining the manumission statutes of the southern states, "There is no middle ground between slavery and freedom; no such thing as qualified freedom, or qualified slavery. If the negro is a slave he cannot enjoy any of the rights of a freeman, denied to other slaves. If he is free, he cannot be forced to submit to any bonds, not imposed on other free persons of color."[59] But the discriminations against free blacks, women, and a host of other groups amply demonstrated that the American political system was perfectly capable of establishing a social hierarchy, if not by the construction of a formal aristocracy then through the inequitable distribution of rights. Indeed, throughout much of our history, the majority of the American people occupied the space between slavery and freedom, vested with far more rights than slaves yet lacking the full citizenship privileges of propertied white men.

Still, the distinction between slave and free in the South was powerfully reinforced by a racist ideology that seemed to intensify as the cultural legitimacy of political inequality among free men eroded, and this may have inhibited southern masters from freeing slaves more often. Historically, such cultural obstacles to individual liberation had by no means been insurmountable: other nations had overcome their ethnic and religious biases against manumission, even where a strong democratic ethos raised the possibility that with emancipation would come social, or at least political, equality. This was true of certain periods of Athenian history, and it was also true of the United States during the revolutionary era, the very moment when democratic politics were becoming respectable.

The origins of the South's distinctively low rate of manumission probably lie not in the distance from slavery to freedom or the power of cultural prejudices but in the traditional causes of individual emancipation in other societies: economic or military disruption. Whether it was the fragile base of consumer demand in ancient Rome or the stagnation of large segments of the Brazilian slave economy, masters most often freed slaves when there were sound economic reasons for doing so. Whether it was the Peloponnesian War between Athens and Sparta or the civil wars of the late Roman Republic, military disruption occasioned numerous offers of manumission.[60] In the United States the War for Independence and the stagnation of the slave economy coincided in the late eighteenth century to promote the largest wave of manumissions in American history. In those same years the northern states set in motion plans for slavery's gradual abolition.

But the return of peace and the spectacular rise of cotton after 1790 brought manumission to a rapid end in the southern states. Thus, except for the brief but significant spurt of emancipations following the Revolution, southern slaves were rarely freed. On the contrary, the slaveholders themselves tightened the legal restrictions on manumission in the nineteenth century, making it difficult, though not impossible, for individual masters to free individual slaves. American slaves could count on no gradual acquisition of freedom for their descendants, no realistic opportunities to run away in large numbers or to purchase their own freedom, and no enduring tradition of private manumission by individual masters.

Severely restricted access to freedom was both a cause and a consequence of perhaps the most distinctive characteristic of slavery in the United States—the ability of the slave population to reproduce itself and, in fact, to grow rapidly on its own even after access to the Atlantic slave trade was closed off in 1808. A naturally growing slave population meant that the United States, alone among New World slave societies, could withdraw from the Atlantic slave trade without undermining slavery. There is no single explanation for this distinction, but once again the Brazilian comparison suggests an important possibility. In Brazil women of child-bearing age were freed in disproportionate numbers, leaving the slave population heavily dependent on the importation of adult males and therefore unable to grow naturally. By the time slavery ended in Brazil, the freed people and their descendants were more numerous than the slaves. By contrast, the paucity of manumissions in the British colonies of North America meant that great numbers of women—and all of their children—were held in perpetual slavery. Over time, therefore, the sex ratio of slaves in the South evened out and the slave population as a whole began to grow on its own, unlike any other such community in the New World.[61]

There are other possible reasons for the distinctive growth rate of slavery in the South. Given the relatively salubrious climate and geography of North America compared to the tropics, the expanse of unhealthy lowland swamps where crops might be cultivated was quite limited. Moreover, the health of the free population was by the late eighteenth century extremely high by historical standards and was largely, though not fully, shared in by the slaves.

Whatever its causes, however, the consequences of a naturally growing slave population were far-reaching. It endowed North American slavery with unique and painful ironies. By facilitating America's withdrawal from the Atlantic slave trade, the natural growth of the slavery only reinforced the pressures to restrict private manumissions once the external source was gone. Because they were born enslaved and survived into old age, North American slaves lived without freedom longer than most slaves in human history. And most tragic of all, because a balanced sex ratio allowed American slaves to create a family life for themselves, the consequences of their legal kinlessness were uniquely appalling. For it made the disruption and breakup of slave families one of the endemic features of slavery in the American South.[62]

Southern slavery was also distinguished from many, though by no means all, societies in the degree to which the slaves' functions were restricted to agricultural labor. In Athens, Brazil, and colonial Peru, large numbers of slaves worked as miners. In ancient Rome they performed the manual labor on the Italian latifundia, but they also taught the classics and built many of the engineering marvels. In Islamic Africa and the Near East, slaves staffed the civil bureaucracies and stocked the harems of local notables. The Portuguese navy used slaves as oarsmen. In Russia slaves served in the military and as domestics in upper-class households. Slaves throughout history have been a source of prestige, of military strength, of higher learning, of wise counsel, skilled craftsmanship, domestic service, sexual release, and manual labor. In some societies slaves were a source of great wealth; more often they were a sign of it.

But slavery in the United States "was above all a labor system," as Kenneth Stampp pointed out some years ago, and the bulk of the slaves' labor was performed on rural plantations.[63] To be sure, slaves in southern society served in many other capacities that were common to slavery everywhere. They were a source of prestige, an indication of wealth; they worked as domestic servants on family farms, in plantation houses and urban residences. They were skilled craftsmen, factory operatives, nurses, and sometimes plantation managers. On the other hand, they did not serve in the military, they were not teachers, they did not staff the government bureaucracy. Rather, slaves in North America were primarily field hands on farms and plantations.

The significance of such plantations has varied according to how important slavery was in the larger society. There were slave plantations in colonial Peru and in eastern Africa, but in neither instance did slave labor dominate the economic structure of society.[64] In the South, slave plantations were the lifeblood of the economic system. When we speak of the plantation South as a "slave economy," we are therefore making a distinction of tremendous historical importance—the last, though perhaps the most critical, distinction that must be made.

While dozens of societies have had slaves, there have been by some counts only five genuine slave societies in all of human history: Greece, Rome, Brazil, the Caribbean, and the American South.[65] Genuine slave societies have been as rare as societies with slaves have been common, for slavery has never been an ideal basis on which to construct a social order. While slave economies could be immensely profitable—it is difficult to imagine an unprofitable slave system staying "in business" for any extended period of time—they nonetheless presented serious obstacles to dynamic development. Slavery hindered technological innovation even where its profitability depended on the latest techniques for processing and transportation. It slowed the development of cities and industry, hampered the growth of a consumer market, reduced the flow of savings, and promoted soil exhaustion and demographic instability by dampening interest in long-term improvements on the land.[66]

To be a "slave society" meant many things, not least of them a relatively high percentage of slaves in the population. Where slaves in most times and places counted for little more than 5 or 10 percent of the population, full-scale slave societies were perhaps one-fourth to one-half slaves. But these numbers are misleading insofar as they divert our attention from the more important qualitative characteristics of a true slave society. For, in such rare cases, slaves were not merely present in large numbers, their presence dominated the economic, social, and political history of their age.[67]

A better way to envision a slave society is to construct what economic historians call a "counterfactual." Imagine the Old South without slaves. Everything is different. The proverbial social pyramid—slaveholders on top, nonslaveholders in the middle, slaves on the bottom—does not simply change with the hypothetical removal of slaves, it collapses altogether. However oversimplified the pyramid undoubtedly is, its mere plausibility demonstrates how thoroughly slavery defined the entire structure of southern society before the Civil War. Do the same thing with the northern colonies of British North America in the middle of the eighteenth century, and the results are very different. In every colony slavery was legal, and in places like New York City slaves were at times surprisingly numerous. In colonial New England a substantial proportion of the most prominent leaders were slave-holders. Yet if all the slaves had hypothetically been removed from the northern colonies, the structure of society would not have fundamentally altered. The basis of the economy, the organization of politics, and the social hierarchy might have changed somewhat, but they would not have been radically transformed. The difference between the northern and southern colonies in the eighteenth century was the difference between a society with slaves and a slave society.

A slave society, then, was one in which a relatively high proportion of slaves signaled the central place of slavery in the social hierarchy, the economic structure, and the political system. Social standing was determined by whether one was slave or free and, if free, whether one owned or did not own slaves. The most important economic activities, the basis of a society's wealth, derived from slavery. "It is in truth the slave labour in Virginia which gives value to her soil and habitations," Thomas R. Dew explained in 1832; "take away this and you pull down the atlas that upholds the whole system."[68] So overwhelming was slavery's presence in the economy and society that the preservation of the slaveholders' power became, directly or indirectly, the guiding force of the most significant political activities.

But where does one draw the boundaries of a slave society? If they are coterminous with political borders, it follows that the southern slaveholders never erected a central political system they could call their own. Rather, the masters went from being colonists subject to the political authority of London to being citizens subject to the federal Constitution. Only in 1861 did the slaveholders attempt to bring political borders more into line with the boundaries of their society. And even then they took it for granted that the political borders of the southern states, which encompassed a growing majority of politically active nonslaveholders, were proper lines of demarcation separating free from slave society.

Herein lay the fatal anomaly of southern slavery. Unlike Greece and Rome, the Old South emerged within a larger political system in which the slaveholders' influence could not be permanently guaranteed. Southern slavery had the added distinction of operating within a social and economic setting—capitalism—that inevitably altered the way slavery developed and functioned. Thus southern slave society grew up in a liberal capitalist world and never for one moment escaped its influence. Indeed, the obscurity of its political and social boundaries raises the question of whether the American South can be conceived of as a "slave society" at all. It has been argued, for example, that the dominance of liberal capitalism was so overwhelming that the antebellum South was not a slave society in the strictest sense of the term. To view it as such is, by this reasoning, to assume into existence the very political and economic independence that the slaveholders attempted (and failed) to claim for themselves in 1861.[69]

Yet this was not a dilemma unique to southern masters, for in some ways slavery was always overshadowed by its context. Everything about slavery presumed the existence of something else—a world of insiders, of citizenship, and of social life. Slavery was a series of negations, denials, and exclusions, all of which put the slave outside society but, in so doing, could not help but reveal the contours of the society from which the slaves were excluded. Where there was unfreedom there had to be freedom. And with each new conception of freedom, of citizenship, and of society, the very definition of slavery shifted as well. In short, slavery assumed, even required, a larger context. If we are to understand the history of *southern* slavery, we must therefore look to the liberal capitalist world within which it developed, flourished, and finally died.

CHAPTER 2

Slavery and Liberal Capitalism

The declaration in the first article of the bill of rights that all men are by nature equally free and independent was opposed by Robert Carter Nicholas, as being the fore-runner or pretext of civil convulsion. It was answered, perhaps with too great an indifference to futurity, and not without inconsistency, that with arms in our hands, as-serting the general rights of man, we ought not to be too nice and too much restricted in the delineation of them; but that slaves not being constituent members of our so-ciety, could never pretend to any benefit from such a maxim. —Edmund Randolph, *History of Virginia*

SLAVERY TOUCHED everything in the Old South. Southern-ers grew up, took spouses, reared children, worked, and died in the shadow of human bondage. It dominated the social struc-ture, drove the economy, and permeated the political system. This was what it meant to be a "slave society." But slavery was also prominent in Periclean Athens, ancient Rome, and colonial Brazil, and so slavery alone cannot explain what made each of these civilizations distinct. Despite all that the few genuine slave societies had in common, each one was shaped by the specific his-torical circumstances within which it developed. Slavery itself has been so widespread in human history that it can scarcely be stud-ied without reference to the various contexts within which it emerged. It was as heavily influenced by its setting as it was in-fluential within its own world.

One way to grasp the significance of the larger context of slav-ery in the Old South is to consider how much of southern culture was actually inherited from the world beyond the Mason-Dixon

Line. The evidence is well known: The literature Southerners read was the literature Northerners, and sometimes Britons, published. Prosperous planters and mistresses reared their children according to the precepts laid down in guidebooks written by and for the northern middle class.[1] Statistics reveal the paltry number of printing presses in the Old South; the annual flood of southern youngsters who migrated North for their education; the reverse migration of northern educators who filled the faculties of the South. Southern jurists followed the precedents of northern courts.[2] Southern and western doctors alike complained that the dominance of New England medicine failed to meet the specific needs of their respective regions.[3] With more success than is generally appreciated, southern intellectuals kept up with the latest European ideas.[4] The South's finest plantation homes and public buildings were often copied from architectural plans drafted in Europe (especially in the colonial era), or were renderings of the same neoclassical fashion that swept the world of Atlantic republicanism in the eighteenth and nineteenth centuries.[5] And the great mass of Southerners, free and slave, rich and poor, counted themselves among the heirs of northern and western European Protestantism, in particular the evangelical strains of the Methodists and Baptists.[6]

North and South were in large measure the products of a specific set of western historical traditions. If we were to line up all the cultures of the globe in 1860, beginning with those most similar to the antebellum North and ending with those least like it, the Old South would surely stand close to the front of the line, if not first. Southerners and Northerners spoke the same language, prayed to the same God, read the same books, voted for the same sets of presidential candidates. It is no wonder that some historians have been impressed by the traditions the South shared with the United States in general.

If this perspective is finally inadequate, it is largely because it lacks a reasonable appreciation of slavery's special character: its social, cultural, economic, and political influence, and the rare and distinctive nature of slave societies in human history. By 1860 countless Americans believed that the North and South had evolved into two profoundly different, perhaps even incompatible civilizations, and that the source of this division was, somehow, slavery. But there were just as many Americans who were quite unable to believe that slavery could possibly matter enough to justify all the tensions dividing the sections. Ever since then historical interpretations have tended to duplicate the insights as well as the shortcomings of each of these positions. In recent decades, for example, our justifiable sensitivity to slavery's significance has nonetheless obscured the degree to which southern slavery was influenced by its larger setting.

If slavery everywhere evinced certain basic characteristics, what made slavery *southern* was precisely its intersection with the world beyond the South. Only after situating the South in its larger historical setting can we understand the economic dynamics, political tensions, and ideological divisions that developed in southern slave society. Only after tracing the powerful influence of liberal capitalism within the South can we understand, first, how the slaveholders exercised and negotiated their extraordinary powers and, second, how the capitalist economy, the liberal state, and western political culture placed equally extraordinary limitations on the slaveholders' power.

IT IS BEST to begin where the South itself began: in a western European world just emerging from the so-called "age of crisis," or "crisis of the seventeenth century."[7] This was a period of widespread economic stagnation marked by low agricultural productivity and depressed commerce. Different nations responded to the economic doldrums of the 1600's in radically different ways, but the states that best survived the crisis—England, Holland, and to a lesser extent France—were those whose economies had gone furthest toward capitalist methods of production and exchange. These changes shaped Holland's entire culture, for example, and radically altered the basic patterns of consumption.[8] The growth of the urban economy in the Low Countries had the most profound economic consequences of the age, for it rested on unprecedented agricultural specialization and the growth of the world's first wage-earning proletariat, which together sustained a spectacular leap in the productivity of the Dutch economy beyond all others on the continent.[9]

In the long run, however, the revolution of the rural economy went further in England than anywhere else, largely because a powerful landed aristocracy successfully reorganized its estates, freeing itself from the restraints of peasant agriculture. Large portions of the English countryside had already been enclosed by the end of the sixteenth century. The Civil War of the 1640's precluded the growth of absolute monarchy and with it an important ally of peasantries elsewhere.[10] The combination of a powerful landed élite, enclosed farms, and the specific advantages of English soil allowed estate owners to respond to the crisis of the seventeenth century by completing the rationalization of their landholdings. A unique pattern of agricultural labor emerged: huge farms were divided up into rented plots cultivated by tenant farmers with no claims to ownership of the land. Unusually responsive to shifts in the market, English estate owners and tenants alike proceeded to implement agricultural improvements—crop rotation, row planting, the fencing of livestock—that substantially increased the productivity of the rural labor force.[11]

England emerged from the crisis of the seventeenth century as the world's first fully capitalist society. But it is important to understand what this means, since there are almost as many ways of defining capitalism as there are social scientists who write about it. The definition used here focuses on the way property is held in society. The development of capitalism, while underway for hundreds of years, was not complete until "absolute" property rights had fully replaced the feudal system, in which customary rights to the use of land were held "conditionally" by serf, lord, and ultimately the king. This seemingly simple shift in the way property was held in fact implied a wholesale revolution in the way labor was organized throughout Europe and its colonies. With private property came various forms of free labor as well as an extraordinary revival of the ancient system of slave labor. Not for another two centuries would the industrial revolution bring this process to its culmination with the spread of a wage-labor economy. But long before then free laborers—whether independent yeomen, self-employed shopkeepers, or tenant farmers—had become the most important source of productivity and economic dynamism. Absolute property had been secured by the English Revolution of the 1640's and, thereafter, decisions about what should be produced and how goods should be distributed in society were increasingly determined by the impersonal forces of the market.[12]

The economic effects of these developments were dramatic. As agricultural productivity rose, English estates needed fewer and fewer tenants to keep up with the growing demands of the market. Rural workers unable to find employment in agriculture began spilling into the nascent manufacturing economy as wage laborers. At the same time, a process of social differentiation proceeded among independent small farmers. As the least successful farms failed, they were taken up by the most successful entrepreneurs —who were, in many cases, the most resourceful members of the old landed aristocracy. And this, too, swelled the labor pool for a growing manufacturing sector. By the middle of the eighteenth century, self-sufficient farmers were a quaint anachronism in England, and in another fifty years only one in three English workers was employed in agriculture. Britain's social structure had been radically transformed. These developments proceeded more slowly elsewhere in Europe, but they proceeded nonetheless. West of the Elbe, a growing proportion of Europeans depended on the market. Rising taxes forced more and more peasants to produce cash crops. Peasants were becoming petty producers; petty producers were becoming tenants; tenants were becoming wage earners.

For a century after 1650, as a rapidly growing proportion of English working people sold their labor for wages and purchased the basic commodities they needed to survive, productivity increases helped keep prices down enough to allow real income to grow. So, while men and women were more dependent than ever on cash for their survival, they had more money than ever before. Yet such were the workings of this novel economic organization that even its most impoverished victims had come to rely on wages and consumer purchases for their meager survival. The result is easy enough to imagine: a steady increase in the purchasing power of the growing body of wage earners, independent or tenant farmers, artisans and tradesmen.[13] Above the "plebeians" grew a prosperous new middle class, which by 1760 included perhaps one million out of England's seven million citizens—and these men and women began to purchase "luxury" items that far surpassed their subsistence needs. Thus began the process of self-generating consumer demand so characteristic of capitalism. A consumer-oriented economy was in view by 1750, laying the groundwork for the spectacular industrial revolution to follow.[14]

With the growth of purchasing power, retail stores proliferated, offering an ever greater variety of consumer goods. Ale and coffee houses sprang up everywhere, catering to new consumer wants. Improved transportation networks and a rationalized financial system sped the flow of capital and the extension of credit, further facilitating the growth of consumer demand. But demand also grew from more pressing concerns. For quick comfort and inexpensive calories, for relaxation and for warmth, the new wage-earning classes of London and elsewhere, together with prosperous farmers in Old and New England, generated an unprecedented demand for tobacco, sugar, cocoa, coffee, rice, and cotton.

New World slave societies came into existence to serve the needs of this exploding population of consumers stretched along the rim of the North Atlantic basin. The tea and rum consumers grew to love and to need required the sugar and molasses produced by slaves. A new set of clothes, once a rare event in a person's life, had become for many men and women a periodic necessity, and for still others public evidence of being "in fashion." By the nineteenth century everybody wanted cotton. Both consumer demand and the Atlantic slave trade, therefore, followed a similar curve of slow growth over the sixteenth and seventeenth centuries, followed by a spectacular leap beginning in the late 1600's.

It is possible to see the first signs of New World slavery as a mere extension of the commercial network that had been spreading across Europe since the Middle Ages. We know that slavery did not simply disappear from the West after the slave societies of the ancient world had collapsed. Just as wage labor existed long before wage economies prevailed, so too did slave labor persist long after ancient slave societies declined. From this perspective the first phase of the Atlantic slave trade, from roughly 1450 to 1650, appears as a mere expansion of slavery's geographic scope which logically coincided with the commercial expansion of Europe itself.[15]

It is not possible to see the sudden extraordinary growth of slave societies in the late seventeenth and eighteenth centuries in that same light. Around the mid-seventeenth century commercial *expansion* became substantive economic *change*. Slaves were no longer merely present in European outposts; rather, European colonies became slave societies—the first in western history since the decline of Rome. Early attempts to exploit the labor of indigenous Indian populations or to encourage the migration of a European work force were abandoned as one New World colony after another switched to the labor of imported Africans. The development of New World slave societies made the years after 1650 the most active for the Atlantic slave trade.

We can simplify the connection between the social transformation of England and the emergence of New World slave societies by focusing on the rising popularity of a single commodity: sugar. In 1660 the English people consumed one thousand hogsheads of sugar and exported twice as much. Within forty years they were consuming over thirty thousand of the fifty thousand hogsheads of sugar they were importing. By 1730 exports of sugar had not increased at all, while imports had leaped to 100,000 hogsheads a year. Between 1650 and 1800 British consumption of sugar increased by an astounding 2,500 percent.[16] Who was consuming all this sugar, and who was producing it? The relationship between slavery and capitalism is neatly summarized in the answers to these two questions.

Sugar had long been a luxury item coveted by wealthy Europeans, who paid dearly for it. But trade in luxury items is one of the universal prerogatives of the wealthy, and by itself such commerce does not signal the level of consumer demand characteristic of capitalism. Though we can trace the growing popularity of sugar in the centuries before 1650, we cannot find anything comparable to what happened thereafter. The popularity of sugar spread dramatically with the emergence of a prosperous, capitalist society. The middle class could now begin in earnest its tireless habit of mimicking the aristocracy by indulging in traditionally élite luxuries. At the same time the poorest wage workers found in sugar a source of inexpensive, and mildly addictive, calories. The rise of sugar consumption certainly required the development of a taste for sweetness, and Englishmen acquired that more avidly than any people ever had. But the taste itself could only flourish in a society that could afford it, or at least had the money to indulge it—as only Englishmen and, to a lesser but significant extent, other western Europeans could through the eighteenth century.[17]

The sugar habit also needed a supplier—and New World slavery proved exceedingly useful to Europeans at this critical point. Brazilians, for example, had been shipping sugar from Bahia to northern Europe from about 1510 onward, but until the early seventeenth century they relied chiefly on the labor of indigenous Indian populations. By 1600 northern European buyers of Brazilian sugar eclipsed all others, and Holland eclipsed all other European buyers. Even after 1620, when an economic crisis interrupted Brazil's steady growth, the strength of the European sugar market could still generate a huge increase in the number of slave imports. From 1450 through 1600 perhaps 275,000 Africans were sold to Brazil, but twice as many were sold in the next hundred years, nearly 2 million during the eighteenth century, and 1.2 million more between 1800 and the abolition of slavery in 1888.[18] Yet, this explosive growth notwithstanding, Brazilian sugar plantations actually fared relatively badly after 1650, for by then the British colonies of the Caribbean were taking control of the sugar market.[19]

It began in Barbados. Plantation slavery was already in place among the English settlers by the 1630's, but not until planters switched from tobacco and cotton to sugar in the two decades after

1640 did the island's economy take off. The sugar boom, Richard Dunn writes, "created a massive demand for laborers in Barbados." It was in the years of transition to sugar that British planters ceased to import English workers and came to rely almost exclusively on the labor of African slaves.[20] But this was only the beginning. As the European demand for sugar exploded, the slave economy burst the bounds of Barbados. Sugar and slaves spent the eighteenth century leapfrogging across the Caribbean to the Leeward Islands, then to Jamaica, on to the French colony of Saint-Domingue, before finally overtaking Spanish Cuba and Puerto Rico in the nineteenth century.[21] In each case a floundering, moderately productive colony was suddenly overwhelmed by a "sugar revolution" that transformed the islands into roaring slave societies.

Because it was tied so closely to the sugar boom, the chronology of the Atlantic slave trade inevitably reflected the influence of the European economy. The men and women exported from Africa in the century and a half beginning in 1450 amounted to little more than 3 percent of all the slaves who eventually passed through the Atlantic trade, and the majority of those earliest slaves went to Europe rather than to the New World. During the worst years of economic crisis, approximately 1600 to 1650, the slave trade stagnated. The number of slaves exported to the New World actually fell in the second quarter of the seventeenth century. The bulk of the slaves shipped from Africa across the Atlantic in the 1600's—some 16 percent of the entire Atlantic slave trade—were sent in the latter half of the century. In fact, all the slaves exported in the Atlantic trade from 1450 through 1650 did not match the number sold in the next five decades. The return of western European prosperity after 1650 set in motion a steady rise in slave exports that would not subside for more than a hundred years. Though the slave trade had existed for centuries before 1650, 95 percent of the African slaves brought to the New World came *after* that date.[22]

Africa could scarcely remain immune to these developments. Though an Islamic trade had carried slaves across the Sahara since the Middle Ages, the rapid growth of the Atlantic trade transformed African slavery from a marginal to a central institution and introduced several new elements into the continent's history. By extending a powerful trading network deep into the African mainland, European commerce provided local slavers with a novel outlet for the sale of slaves while at the same time creating unprecedented incentives to pursue wars of enslavement. Commercial networks were consolidated at the expense of indigenous African polities. Organized lawlessness spread across much of the continent after 1650, radically disrupting the traditional balance of power among contending groups.[23]

If the slave trade politically fragmented much of Africa, it also tied distant parts of the continent together within a vast, efficient Atlantic trade network. If it radically increased the number of slaves within Africa, it did so in a way that limited slavery's long-term significance. A disproportionate number of African slaves were women, while men were overwhelmingly shipped to the New World. Because slave women in Africa traditionally served not as a labor force but as concubines to local chieftains, their children often benefited from the custom of gradual incorporation within African lineage systems. Thus slavery disrupted an entire continent without fundamentally altering the basic structures of society.[24]

Slavery and capitalism had the opposite effect on the New World: it was less disruptive than in Africa, yet it altered the structure of society in far more radical ways. The consumer revolution, for example, transformed daily life throughout the British colonies of North America. What English workers manufactured in exploding quantities American colonists purchased with increasing alacrity. One scholar has charted the spectacular growth of commercial advertisements in the New York press. Where fifteen or so imported items were offered to potential customers each month in 1720, by the 1770's there were advertisements for some nine thousand manufactured items. In the quarter century after 1750 alone, the demand for imported goods leaped by 120 percent. Where once consumers had had access only to a limited supply of generic items—paper, cloth, or carpets, for example—buyers were now increasingly able to select from a variety of colors, styles, and price ranges.[25]

Nothing demonstrates the significance of this development as effectively as the emergence of the consumer boycott—the non-importation agreements—as a weapon of American revolutionary politics in the 1760's and 1770's. By then it had become clear that producers and consumers alike were enmeshed in a world of commercial interdependence, and that where there was dependence there was also power. "A vast demand is growing for British Manufactures," Benjamin Franklin had noted in 1751, "a glorious Market wholly in the Power of Britain."[26]

The colonial South was inescapably swept up in all of these changes.[27] Yet if it followed the general pattern evident in the Caribbean, it was not by any simple correlation of rising consumer demand with rising slave imports. By 1620 Virginians had discovered that Europeans could now afford to develop a fondness for tobacco even as they were growing attached to sugar. All the colonists had to do was get the land and labor to cultivate it. As part of the "headright" system Virginia planters were rewarded with a fifty-acre tract for each indentured servant brought to America. This system facilitated the growth of a tobacco economy in the seventeenth century by allowing planters to build up large plantations and at the same time providing them with the necessary workers. Thus the Chesapeake area's dependence on the growing consumer demand for tobacco was established at a time when the bulk of the labor was performed by British servants.[28]

But indentured servitude could only be a short-term solution to the labor problem of the seventeenth century. Over the long run the system put itself out of business—in general because laborers were released from their indenture after five or six years of service, and in the Chesapeake in particular because so many servants died before their service was completed. In these circumstances the labor shortage would never disappear and could actually intensify over time. Perhaps the most significant effect of the headright system was that it actually helped create the three major preconditions to the emergence of a slave society: a well-developed commodity market; the inequitable distribution of land; and a severe labor shortage. By the late seventeenth century the wealthiest planter families had amassed large tracts of land. They cultivated a crop for which Europeans were developing an avid addiction. But their economic strength rested on a labor force that was intrinsically temporary; they were perilously dependent on a steady stream of new arrivals from England. The return of prosperity in the late seventeenth century sharply curtailed that stream. And with that all the preconditions for the growth of a slave society were in place.[29]

By then slavery was the obvious alternative to indentured servitude, although that alternative never appeared to Englishmen as something they might consciously decide to pursue or reject. Rather, free Virginians steadily acquainted themselves with the resources of the Atlantic slave trade even as the tobacco plantations were developing. Slowly they established the legal distinction between slave and free, reconstructing absolute bondage in their own world without ever stopping to ask whether or not this was a wise thing to do. When, after 1680, the flow of British servants slowed down at the same time the growth rate of tobacco demand slowed, the colonists had little trouble finding a solution: slavery and, ideally, crop diversification. Slave labor would allow planters to stay in the tobacco market, while crop diversification would afford some measure of protection from the fickle demands of the buying public.[30]

In the forty years from 1680 to 1720, Virginia was transformed from a society with slaves into a slave society. The first Africans had arrived in Virginia in 1619, but their numbers were small and grew only erratically until the closing decades of the seventeenth century, when slave imports to the Chesapeake region skyrocketed. Around the turn of the century South Carolina also blossomed as a slave economy. Georgia followed soon thereafter, for by 1750 the antislavery policy of the colony's utopian settlers had been vanquished. Across the southern colonies, slave imports grew through the first half of the eighteenth century, declining in the latter decades only because by then the slave population was beginning to grow rapidly on its own. By the middle of the eighteenth century, four out of ten Virginians were slaves, while in South Carolina there were more slaves than there were free men and women.

Clearly the demand for slaves grew in complex relation to the rising demand for consumer goods. Just as clearly, consumer demand was itself a product of a fundamental transformation of western society. A new mode of production necessarily implied new patterns of consumption. As Marx explained in the *Grundrisse*, "production mediates consumption; it creates the latter's material; without it consumption would lack an object. But consumption also mediates production, in that it alone creates for the products the subject for whom they are products." It was through this same pattern of mediation that consumption bound slavery to capitalism.

Thus, each of the modern slave societies had at least this much in common: their very being was inconceivable except as a function of capitalist development. And this is what set New World slaveholders apart from their most important predecessors in western history. Where slavery dominated the economy of the ancient world, New World slavery was itself the servant of the driving force of capitalism.

Throughout antiquity consumer demand was severely limited —in Greece, to whatever local markets could be generated by a population of subsistence-oriented peasants and to the limited export trade; in Rome, to the urban populations displaced by slavery's expansion in the countryside or to the large numbers of state-owned slaves. Except for extractive industries like silver mining, the economic security of slavery in both societies required that masters take care to limit production, lest the fragile base of consumer demand be overwhelmed.[31] But New World slave societies were tied to a developing capitalist society with a seemingly insatiable demand for slave-produced goods, and in such circumstances slaveholders could reverse the historic incentive to limit production. The force of capitalism thus generated one of the great paradoxes of slaveholding culture in the Americas. Slavery limited the opportunities for increasing productivity, yet productivity increases were clearly in the slaveholders' interest. Although slave labor inhibited technological development, restricted capital accumulation, and encouraged soil exhaustion, the slaveholders nevertheless stood forth in politics and society as the great advocates of scientific farming, transportation improvements, efficient management, and state-sponsored development projects.[32]

For historians of modern slavery, this presents a special challenge. Slavery is what distinguished southern society, separating it off from the North, pushing southern history along its own path of economic, political, and social change. Yet capitalism is what set New World slave societies apart from their predecessors in antiquity. American masters were the first in history whose power depended on commercial relations with a capitalist world that was ultimately more powerful than all the slave societies put together. But in what ways did capitalism's influence manifest itself within the South?

To scan the diaries and letters left by hundreds of slaveholders is to approach an answer to that question. Throughout such documents one finds evidence of that rationalized pursuit of sustained profit which Max Weber labeled the "capitalist spirit" and which he so carefully distinguished from the commonplace greed of ruling classes everywhere.[33] If double-entry bookkeeping had yet to reach the antebellum plantations, the irrational pursuit of quick riches that nearly destroyed the earliest settlement at Jamestown had long since given way to a more calculating ethic which alone could ensure the survival of a slave economy in a capitalist world. Every tedious journal entry recording the weather, the condition and whereabouts of the field hands, or the number of rows planted, weeds dug, or bales packed was sparked by the capitalist world's demand for cotton. Behind every task assigned to every slave every day stood the mill owners and factory hands of Old and New England. At the root of every systematic attempt to sustain the slaves' productivity—including the bribes, the whippings, and the crude efforts to encourage breeding—was the growing consumer demand of free laborers, dependent and independent, on farms and in cities on both sides of the Atlantic. Thus was the rationalizing force of capitalism fused with the irrational substance of slavery.

The slave's subordination to the master was total, yet the masters had masters of their own, and they loom in the slaveholders' letters and diaries, ominously but invisibly, like the bondsmen whose personalities are rarely mentioned but whose presence is always felt. To live the life of a slaveholder was to live in close but dependent relation to the capitalist world, to live in need of cash, in need of credit, in need of markets. Above all, the accelerated economic environment of capitalism demanded of New World slaveholders a far more rationalized ethos than was necessary among the ruling classes of antiquity or the Middle Ages. Successful slaveownership generally required an acute concern for the details of labor management and an obsession with the vagaries of a market over which even the wealthiest planters had no control whatsoever. To be a slaveholder was to live in a world of relentless westward migration driven less by the supply of cotton or land than by erratic fluctuations in world demand. In such circumstances sheer economic survival required the most rational organization of labor that was possible in a slave economy.

A highly developed market economy was a precondition to the emergence of any slave society. Yet master and slave formed what was, at bottom, a nonmarket relationship. Capitalism therefore multiplied the tensions already intrinsic to slavery, for it required that the slaves sustain a reasonable level of productivity but without the powerful incentives of a wage system. To be a slave in the Americas was to spend a lifetime feeding capitalism's demand for cotton fibers, coffee beans, sweeteners, and snuff. But how could such productivity be sustained? Slaves could be whipped, but they could not be fired; they could be bribed but not paid wages; they could be sold but not laid off; rewarded but not freed. Slavery offered few incentives to work hard, yet the demand for the slaves' labor never ceased so long as free consumers wore cotton clothing, smoked or chewed or snuffed tobacco, and chose to drink coffee sweetened with sugar.

We are thus confronted with a difficult paradox: capitalism's influence was sufficient to transform the daily lives of master and slave in profound ways, yet capitalism did this without transforming the system of slavery itself. Some scholars believe that the influence of the world market was so powerful that modern slavery was capitalist in every way that matters.[34] Others argue, in contrast, that a social system founded upon the labor of slaves could never be truly capitalist, and that slavery was in fact tied to a historically ubiquitous "merchant capital" that was never strong enough to overturn the social basis of any society.[35] Yet neither proposition seems wholly adequate to the task. Where the former underestimates the distinctive economic consequences of slave labor, the latter misses the powerful force of capitalism within the slave system.[36] Marx captured the essence of the problem when he wrote of capitalism as having been "grafted" onto slavery in the Old South. With the Civil War fresh in his memory, Marx argued that "as soon as peoples whose production still moves within the lower forms of slave labour . . . are drawn into a world market dominated by the capitalist mode of production, whereby the sale of their products for export develops into their principal interest, the civilized horrors of over-work are grafted onto the barbaric horrors of slavery." In the American South, he concluded, slavery's "moderately patriarchal character" had long since given way to the calculated "over-working of the Negro" in order to meet the worldwide demand for cotton.[37]

In fact, the South's close ties to capitalism were forged well before the cotton boom of the early 1800's. By the end of the eighteenth century the South was inextricably integrated into the Atlantic economy. The economic relationship that had impressed Franklin in the 1750's came to frighten many slaveholders during the debt crisis of the late 1760's. "The planters," Thomas Jefferson explained in 1784, "were a species of property annexed to certain mercantile houses in London." Long after the American Revolution, perceptive observers continued to see the slave economies of the New World as anything but independent. "These are hardly to be looked upon as countries, carrying on an exchange of commodities with other countries," John Stuart Mill wrote of the sugar islands of the Caribbean, "but more properly as outlying agricultural or manufacturing estates belonging to a larger community." Mill's vision of the relationship between Britain and the West Indies could as easily apply to the ties that bound the cotton South to Old and New England. They "cannot be regarded as Countries with a productive capital of their own . . . [but are, rather,] the place where England finds it convenient to carry on the production of sugar, coffee and a few other tropical commodities."[38]

To be sure, there were slaveholders who were seduced by their own productive capacities into attributing regal powers to the cotton crop itself. But cotton was pawn, not king—and it is clear now if it was not at the time that the slaveholders needed capitalism far more than capitalism needed the slaveholders. Modern slave societies had come into existence to serve capitalism; they could not survive without capitalism; they went to their graves at the behest of capitalism.

SOUTHERN SLAVEHOLDERS might have buffered themselves more effectively against the demands of the Atlantic economy had they fashioned a political system that placed the law of slavery above all others. But no such system existed, either in the British colonies of North America or in the independent United States. Perhaps it could not exist anywhere. Masters and slaves form "an aggregation, but not an association," Rousseau explained in *The Social Contract*, "for they have neither public property nor a body politic." The master, "had he enslaved half the world, is never anything but an individual; his interest, separated from that of the rest, is never anything but a private interest."

Where the law in general establishes the rules by which men and women organize their social, personal, and political relations, the law of slavery merely declares those rules irrelevant to the slaves themselves. To be a slave was to be deprived of any "legal personality." Slave law thus required something other than itself: a legal structure establishing the framework of a society separate from slavery and from which the slaves were excluded. Slave societies have flourished in a variety of political formations—the autocracy of the Roman Empire, the royal bureaucracies of Spanish-America, and the representative democracies of Periclean Athens and the Old South—but nowhere did the polity simply reflect the assumptions of the master-slave relationship. For no society can be built on a body of law whose purpose is to negate society itself.

The political history of southern slave society therefore begins in its larger political context: the fundamental legal and philosophical transformations that accompanied the emergence of capitalism. Even as the southern colonies were being settled, the divine right of kings and many of the aristocracy's inherited privileges were under attack in England. By the eighteenth century, rights were no longer secured by a monarch to whom all men were grateful and, more important, obedient. Increasingly, rights preceded all obligations, and they were inherent in the individual rather than conferred from on high. Liberalism was overtaking the ideal of an organically unified social hierarchy patterned on the model of the patriarchal family. In short, the primacy of duty and obligation was being replaced by the primacy of individual rights. This was the "age of revolution," and the slaveholders were not only its products, they were among its leading architects. If we are to understand the relationship between slavery and politics, we must therefore begin with the patriarchal structures the slaveholders helped overturn.[39]

Patriarchalism grew slowly but logically out of the medieval understanding of society as a hierarchy of orders so thoroughly interdependent as to be "organically" unified, like the various parts of the human body itself. In the twelfth century John of Salisbury explored the duties and obligations incumbent upon earthly princes, who took "the place of the head in the body of the commonwealth" and who were "subject only to God and to those who exercise His office and represent him on earth." The bodily metaphor encompassed religious authority, which was said to take "the place of the soul in the body of the commonwealth." But John of Salisbury's *Policraticus* extended the metaphor to include the lowliest men and women within the organically unified social order. Where the Senate functioned as the heart, judges and governors as the eyes, ears, and tongue, and soldiers as the hands, he wrote:

> The husbandmen correspond to the feet, which always cleave to the soil, and need the more especially the care and foresight of the head, since while they walk upon the earth doing service with their bodies, they meet the more often with stones of stumbling, and therefore deserve aid and protection all the more justly since it is they who raise, sustain, and move forward the weight of the entire body.[40]

Four centuries later Jean Bodin reiterated John of Salisbury's conception of organic unity, but with some critical differences. Where the *Policraticus* emphasized the subordination of the prince to religious authority and his responsibility to his subjects, Bodin's *Six Bookes of a Commonweale* argued for the divine right of kings to exercise absolute power over their subjects. And where John of Salisbury was silent on the question of slavery, Bodin attacked it. Christianity continued to provide the dualisms that could justify the enslavement of the infidel, but Bodin's organicism made it hard for him to imagine the traditional place for slaves outside society, for even the most degraded men and women occupied an assigned place *within* the body politic. "There be in mans bodie," Bodin explained, "some members, I may not call them filthie (for that nothing can so be which is naturall) but yet so shamefull, as that no man except he be past all shame, can without blushing reveale or discover the same: and doe they for that cease to be members of the whole bodie?"[41] Because slaves were always outsiders, there was no place for them in Bodin's scheme.

Bodin's leading disciple in England was also patriarchy's last great Anglo-Saxon defender, Robert Filmer. He imagined the organic unity of society through the metaphor of the patriarchal family: the authority of the father became the divinely ordained model for authority throughout society. As "Adam was the lord of his children," Filmer wrote, "so his children under him had a command and power over their own children, but still with subordination to the first parent, who is lord-paramount over his children's children to all generations, as being the grandfather of his people." Fatherhood became, in Filmer's rendering, the ruling metaphor for all political and social relations on earth. The subjection of children to their parents was "the fountain of all regal authority" and, finally, of all civil power. "If we compare the natural rights of a father with those of a king," he explained,

> we find them all one, without any difference at all but only in the latitude or extent of them: as the father over one family, so the king, as father over many families, extends his care to preserve, feed, clothe, instruct, and defend the whole commonwealth. His war, his peace, his courts of justice, and all his acts of sovereignty, tend only to preserve and distribute to every subordinate and inferior father, and to their children, their rights and privileges, so that all the duties of a king are summed up in an universal fatherly care of his people.[42]

In theory, the power of kings was an extension of the power of the father, and it was absolute (though when James II tried to act on this assumption his subjects sent him packing). "The lordship which Adam by command had over the whole world, and by right descending from him the patriarchy did enjoy," Filmer proclaimed, "was as large and ample as the absolutest dominion of any monarch which has been since the creation." To allow the rule of any but the fathers was to subject mankind to the reign of children—a clear perversion of God's law. "For as kingly power is by the law of God, so it hath no inferior law to limit it."[43]

This was *Patriarcha*, a world where hierarchy was as natural to the political order as it was to the family itself, where the distinction between family and society was blurred to the point of irrelevance. Children were reared to accept without question the station into which they were born. Obedience to the father became the paradigm for obedience to all authority. And in the patriarchal world no man was an island. Individuals could only be defined by the relationships that tied them to particular places in society. They could no more alter those places than they could undo the very circumstances of their births. The burdens and obligations of society were clearly superior to the inherent rights of the individual. Indeed, there was no such thing as the "natural liberty of the people," Filmer insisted. For "all those liberties that are claimed in parliament are the liberties of grace from the king, and not the liberties of nature to the people."[44] Against the spreading ideology of liberal individualism, Filmer protested that "There never was any such thing as an independent multitude who at first had a natural right to a community."[45]

For all his extremism, Filmer represented a classic vision of society, in which duty and obligation took precedence over the rights of individuals. It was not that men had no rights, but that the rights they enjoyed were bestowed from on high, a gift from patriarchal authority. And it was this latter assumption that was under attack in the seventeenth century, when Filmer launched his defense. With the Revolution and the beheading of the King, England firmly repudiated absolutism by pushing the organizing principles of political life away from the primacy of obligation. The rights of Englishmen were proclaimed a gift of nature, bestowed on every individual, and taking precedence over the obligation to authority. Instead, authority came into existence to protect individual rights, particularly the right of property.

This was liberalism—what philosopher Charles Taylor calls "the primacy of rights"—and its implications for the organization of society were revolutionary.[46] In liberalism the most important social relationships were legally defined by a series of individual rights. A family, for example, was constructed out of the respective rights of the husband and wife, the parent and child. The individual's place in civil society was defined by each citizen's right to speak, to live in privacy, to profess a creed. Liberal ideology even defined capitalism as a set of economic relations in which each individual had the right to dispose of his or her property and labor however he or she chose. With liberalism, freedom was defined in the rights of individuals.

Liberalism's origins were as varied as its consequences. Locke, Hobbes, and Rousseau were indisputably important. Despite their differences, each grounded the organization of society in the interests of the individual, each repudiated the patriarchal premise of organic unity and the natural subordination of the child to the father as the model for political life. But liberalism had other sources as well. Anglo-American republicanism undermined patriarchal principles by its emphasis on individual independence and the social benefits of the pursuit of self-interest. Scientific rationalism glorified reason over religion. Protestantism stressed the individual's personal relationship to God, unmediated by a clerical hierarchy. All of these and more established the priority of the individual over the collectivity, the science of politics over divine injunction, universal rights over reciprocal obligation. Liberalism thereby threatened the ideological pillars of absolute monarchy, noble privilege, religious orthodoxy, and the established church —the institutional mainstays of patriarchal government in the West.

Slaveholders throughout the New World were receptive in varying degrees to ideological attacks on patriarchy. Enlightenment ideals captured the imagination of the most important intellectual movement in Brazil in the early nineteenth century. In Colombia, the slaveholders articulated a liberal-constitutionalist critique of Simón Bolívar. In Cuba, the pervasive influence of Enlightenment deism was reflected in the declining authority of the clergy throughout the years of the island's great sugar boom.[47] And in the British colonies of North America, southern slaveholders took the lead in translating Anglo-American republicanism into a revolutionary movement for colonial independence.

The French Revolution and the slave rebellion it inspired in Saint-Domingue substantially dampened enthusiasm for liberalism among western élites, slaveholders included. Nevertheless, the slaveholding classes throughout the Caribbean and most of South America remained sufficiently influenced by Enlightenment republicanism to overthrow patriarchal government sometime in the late eighteenth and early nineteenth centuries.[48] Even in Brazil, where the Portuguese royal family for a time preempted political transformation by installing itself physically in the New World, liberal revolution eventually triumphed. The "final disintegration of the patriarchy in our society," Gilberto Freyre wrote somewhat dolefully many years ago, "coincided with the

abandonment of the monarchial form of government for the republican."[49] In Brazil republicanism and emancipation came together, but in other slave societies patriarchal government was
overthrown by the slaveholders themselves.

Of all New World slave societies, the southern United States
was most powerfully shaped by liberalism, and of all the founders
of liberal philosophy no one was more influential in the South
than John Locke. Of course, what Americans took from Locke
was not distinctive to him, and what was distinctive to Locke was
not what made him influential. But among the numerous philosophers who formulated the principles of liberalism, Locke was
echoed most often. Through his influential critique of Robert Filmer, often filtered through the writings of the Scottish Enlightenment, Locke set the tone for much of the political discourse of
the eighteenth-century South.

Where Locke's well-known *Second Treatise* of government
sketched the outlines of a liberal state, his entire *First Treatise* was
a sustained attack on *Patriarcha*. "It is impossible that the rulers
now on earth should make any benefit," Locke wrote, "or derive
any the least shadow of authority from that, which is held to be
the fountain of all power, *Adam's private dominion and paternal jurisdiction*." Far from equating the power of the father with the
power of the magistrate, Locke insisted on their radical disjunc-
tion. And far from granting the father absolute authority over his
offspring, Locke argued, "reason and revelation" both showed
that the mother "hath an equal title" in the rearing of children.
Parents were responsible for training the child not to dependency
and obedience but to rational independence. They should "inform
the mind" of the child, Locke explained, "and govern the actions
of their yet ignorant nonage, till reason shall take its place."[50] As
with Filmer, Locke's larger point concerned the legitimacy of authority. Whether private or public, he argued, authority derived
not from patriarchal privilege but from the social compact with
which civil society came into existence.

Locke's most famous formulation was the "state of nature," the
hypothetical place wherein all men were born equal in their rights
to life, liberty, and property. Because the equality of property

rights tended to produce disparities of wealth and the jealousies associated with such inequality, the state of nature inevitably degenerated into a "state of war," in which no rights were safe. Men therefore fled from the state of nature into the security of society, by means of a social compact, precisely in order that they might better protect their natural rights. Thus, while rights were derived from the state of nature, freedom—the enjoyment of rights—was only possible in society. For Thomas Hobbes the tyranny of the state of nature not only compelled men into society but also demanded their strict obedience to the governmental Leviathan—a line of reasoning that would find some support in the postrevolutionary South. But in the Lockean scheme of things, which was generally more influential among the slaveholders, government occupied an ambiguous position: it was necessary to protect and defend individual rights, yet the state was itself the greatest threat to those rights.

The writings of eighteenth-century Southerners were steeped in Lockean premises, never more thoroughly than during the American Revolution. "Men in a State of Nature are absolutely free and independent of one another as to sovereign Jurisdiction," Richard Bland of Virginia wrote in 1766. They enter into society "by their own consent," he explained, just as "they have a natural Right to quit the Society of which they are Members . . . [to] recover their natural Freedom and Independence." Thomas Tucker of Charleston, South Carolina, also invoked the metaphor of a "social covenant" to explain why men who were equally endowed with "natural freedom" would enter into society. They form governments, Tucker explained in 1784, for "protection both in person and property against the evil disposed part of his fellow citizens."[51] In its insistence that rights were distributed equally among all citizens liberalism carried a latent egalitarian impulse. "*Rights* imply *Equality* in the Instances to which they belong," Richard Bland argued, "and must be treated without Respect to the Dignity of the Persons concerned in them."[52]

The "rights" Southerners were prepared to defend as natural or inherent varied slightly. Locke's triad of "life, liberty and property" was the most widely invoked, but under the influence of

Scottish common-sense philosophers the wording was sometimes changed or the list was expanded. Thomas Jefferson replaced "property" with "the pursuit of happiness," though some of the most influential Scottish writers used the terms interchangeably. In 1783 an anonymous Charlestonian declared that "The Rights of individuals from society by Natural Law, are, Safety, Liberty, Kindness, and Due Portions of Common Property, of Political Consequence, and of Social Emoluments."[53] There was a whole host of less-than-natural rights retained by men as they entered into society. Jefferson listed many of them in one of several letters to James Madison urging that the new federal constitution contain "a bill of rights, providing clearly and without the aid of sophism, for freedom of religion, freedom of the press, protection against standing armies, restriction of monopolies, the eternal and unremitting force of the habeas corpus laws, and trials by jury."[54]

However the lists of rights were constructed and whatever their philosophical origins or specific wording, Southerners uniformly presumed the primacy of individual rights. It was only "in order" to protect rights that men even bothered to form governments, as one state after another declared in the preamble to its constitution. The purpose of Kentucky's 1792 constitution, its authors declared, was "to secure to all citizens thereof the enjoyment of the right of life, liberty, and property, and of pursuing happiness." And in nearly identical language, the first constitution of the state of Louisiana was written "in order to secure to all citizens thereof the enjoyment of *the right of life, liberty and property*."[55]

Southern slavery grew up in a political world that was learning to speak not only in Lockean terms but in the language of classical republicanism as well. Both strands of thought contributed to the philosophy of liberal individualism which the slaveholders would eventually have to confront. But where Locke and his sympathizers focused on the origins of individual rights, republicanism stressed the importance of individual independence and virtue to the preservation of rights. For this reason republican ideology has been interpreted as a secular version of the Protestant ethic: both were racked by a tension between the release of individual energies and an ascetic fear of the consequences of accumulated wealth. The temptations of luxury tended to undermine virtue, thereby corrupting government, and in the republican scheme of things corruption threatened the rights of the people. Southern leaders were particularly convinced that the best way to preserve those rights was to keep the material self-interest of each citizen in harmony with the interests of the community at large. "Let individuals then be but true to their common interests," the Charleston *Tribune* explained in 1766, and the virtue of the republic "will always be secure." Fifteen years later another Charleston writer repeated the theme. "It is fatally prejudicial to accustom yourselves to consider the interests of society and the rights of individuals as distinct."[56]

The point was not that the interests of society should take precedence over those of the individual. Rather, on the premise that "the interests of the people of the same community are necessarily mutual in some particulars," the "law of interest" would work to the betterment of the community as a whole. And this could not help but lead to the kind of argument made by a South Carolina essayist in 1789. Echoing one of the central themes of the Scottish Enlightenment, he declared that individual ambition was the principal reason "we have been wafted from a barbarous, to an enlightened age. . . . The human system is a machine; ambition the spring that puts it in motion."[57]

To pursue self-interest was to be free to exercise one's basic rights. But the same pursuit generated social inequalities and with them personal interests that could threaten the virtue of the polity. "Interest" was thus ambiguous in the republican mind—it had to be unleashed and restrained at the same time. In both cases this meant that government should be limited: first, to stand clear of the rational pursuit of self-interest, and second, to diminish the opportunities for corruption. Ideally men would eschew greatness so as to preserve "that equality on which the security of the government depends," Carter Braxton of Virginia wrote in 1776. Unfortunately, he added, men would "always claim a right of using and enjoying the fruits of their honest industry, unrestrained by any ideal principles of government," and this would create the accumulations of wealth that distorted men's "interests" as they entered into public life.[58] In that case, the locus of public life—government itself—had to be restrained, and Braxton, like other eighteenth-century Anglo-Americans, had a clear idea of how to assure that it was. Just as rational self-interest worked to the good of the whole, so too would the clashing of interests within the government restrain its excesses and so leave the people free in the exercise of their rights. This was the point of England's glorious "mixed government," in which the monarchy, the aristocracy, and the democracy served to check each other's power, thereby preventing the dangerous slide into anarchy and tyranny.

But to many North American eyes England's mixed republic had failed the colonists, it had become mired in luxury and corruption, and in consequence it had threatened the rights of the American people. Having rejected the mixed constitution in 1776, Americans spent the next decade developing an alternative liberal state. In this new political structure the rights of the individual took precedence over everything else. No one interest or faction was singled out for special treatment; no class of men was granted formal control over any branch of government. Quite the contrary, the very equality of rights presumably generated a ceaseless clash of competing interests in a government too centralized to feel the sway of any one faction and too weak to endanger the liberties of any other. "The great desideratum in Government," James Madison explained, "is such a modification of the sovereignty as will render it sufficiently neutral between the different interests and factions, to controul one part of society from invading the rights of another, and at the same time sufficiently controuled itself, from setting up an interest adverse to that of the whole Society."[59]

By the late eighteenth century these were the ideological presuppositions of state governments across the South. Virtually every southern state constitution rested on the assumption that although rights were a gift of nature men were only free where they could enjoy their rights, and that this is what impelled men to form political systems. Maryland's revolutionary constitution of 1776 declared that "all government of right originates from the people [and] is founded in compact only." In the same year Virginia enacted a constitution whose Bill of Rights opened with the declaration "that all men are by nature equally free and independent, and have certain inherent rights, of which, when they enter into a state of society, they cannot, by any compact, deprive or divest their posterity."[60] Mississippi's 1832 constitution announced that "all freemen, when they form a social compact, are equal in rights." Floridians used nearly the same wording in their constitution six years later. And even Alabama's secession constitution of 1861 retained the standard "declaration of rights" that opened with the commonplace assertion that "all freemen, when they form a social compact, are equal in rights."

With the spread of liberalism the attack on patriarchal government marched triumphant across eighteenth-century America.[61] For in the starkest sense, liberalism was everything patriarchy was not. Where Filmer saw society as the working out of social relations grounded in the patriarchal family, liberalism held that society was a compact of solitary individuals. Where patriarchy emphasized the duties and obligations within an organically unified social and political hierarchy, liberalism posited the primacy of rights that protected the individual from the threats of society and the depredations of the state. The one presumed an inherent inequality of all men, while the other posited the universality of rights. The maintenance of order was the chief purpose of the patriarchal state, and complete obedience was its modus operandi. For many liberals, however, the state was an unfortunate necessity (a "badge of lost innocence," in Thomas Paine's words) brought on by the need to preserve the individual's rights to life, liberty, and property—and many Southerners persisted in the belief that any state that failed to protect those rights risked losing its claim to allegiance. Absent this tradition, secessionists in 1861 would have had no clear justification for their action.

Of course, the threats to order implicit in such reasoning generated a distinctly liberal defense of strong government. Duty and obligation could be demanded in the liberal state, conservatives would increasingly argue, precisely because liberal government's chief purpose was the protection of individual rights. Working from such premises, one Southerner pronounced the "state of nature" a preposterous abstraction riddled with revolutionary implications, while at the same time he insisted that "the right of property, as well as those of life and liberty, are the gifts of nature. The end of civil society," he wrote, "is to guard them by stronger sanctions" against an overbearing democratic majority.[62] Disorder was conceived in the liberal imagination as a threat to rights, especially property, without which there could be no freedom.[63]

In some ways, then, liberalism was as vague and unpredictable as it was historically specific. Over a lifetime of several centuries liberal thought has proven itself perfectly equipped to launch attacks on popular democracy as well as corporate capital, on universal suffrage as well as special privilege. Yet across this political spectrum, Americans almost always assumed the primacy of rights. The more emphatically radical Jeffersonians argued that a democratic franchise was itself an inalienable right the more worried conservatives grew about the security of their property rights. In nearly all instances, however, freedom itself was defined as the primacy of rights, and it was upon this assumption that a peculiarly southern definition of slavery developed.

For if slavery was the denial of freedom, in liberal societies that meant, primarily, the denial of rights. In the simplest cases, this appeared in the law as the mere "exception" of the slave from the rights of free citizens. A 1638 "act for the liberties of the people" of Maryland located the slaves, literally, in parentheses: "[A]ll Christian inhabitants (slaves excepted) to have and enjoy all such rights, liberties, immunities, privileges and free customs, within this province, as any natural born subject of England hath or ought to have or enjoy in the realm of England." South Carolina's slave code of 1712 likewise excluded the slaves from civil society. Given their "barbarous, wild, savage natures," the statute declared, the slaves were "wholly unqualified to be governed by the laws, customs, and practices of this province."[64]

By the nineteenth century, when liberal government was far more developed in the United States, the statutes regulating slavery became ever more specific. The Louisiana slave code of 1824 was unusually detailed—a veritable laundry list of the rights that, in their explicit denial, defined the essence of slavery. Much of the statute reads as a series of negations:

> [The slave] is incapable of making any kind of contract . . . he possesses nothing of his own. . . . They can transmit nothing by succession. . . . The slave is incapable of exercising any public office, or private trust; he cannot be tutor, curator, executor nor attorney; he cannot be a witness in either civil or criminal matters. . . . He cannot be a party in any civil action. . . . Slaves cannot marry without the consent of their masters, and their marriages do not produce any of the civil effects which result from such contract.[65]

The Alabama code of 1852, like Louisiana's of a generation before, also defined slavery in a litany of rights denied. Those "having charge of a slave" were directed to ensure that the slave not exercise the rights of a free person. The slave was not permitted "to hire himself to another person, or to hire his own time, or to go at large. . . . No slave must go beyond the limits of the plantation on which he resides, without a pass. . . . No slave can keep or carry a gun. . . . No slave can own property. . . . Not more than five male slaves shall assemble together at any place off the plantation." Slaves were forbidden to make speeches to other slaves without a license, even in church.[66] It was like turning the Bill of Rights upside down.

To argue, then, that the common law made no allowance for slavery or that the South was not liberal because slavery negated the premises of liberalism is to misunderstand the nature of the problem. For slavery was, by definition, the negation of whatever principles defined freedom in any given society. As the Maryland statute made clear, a mere parenthetical expression—"slaves excepted"—made the common law substantially compatible with the development of slavery. There was a curious irony in this, for slavery actually revealed the boundaries of freedom by specifying what it meant to be unfree.

Southerners could define slavery only in the terms they used to define freedom. That is what Thomas R. R. Cobb, one of the antebellum South's best legal scholars, did when he declared: "Of the three great absolute rights guaranteed to every citizen by the common law, viz., the right of personal security, the right of personal liberty, and the right of private property, the slave, in a state of pure or absolute slavery, is totally deprived." Only in a society where freedom was understood as the primacy of rights could "*absolute or pure slavery*" be defined in simple Lockean terms as "the condition of that individual, over whose life, liberty, and property another has the unlimited control."[67]

This is how southern law put the slave outside of society. Without rights, the slave could form none of the basic economic, political, or personal relationships that together bring society into existence. Slaves could not hire out their labor; they could not enter into economic contracts; they could not own property; they could not participate in politics; they could not exercise the rights of marriage. The slave everywhere was the perpetual outsider; in the liberal South the slave was made an outsider through the specification of rights denied. Where the patriarchal ethos held that even the lowliest persons were part of an organically unified social hierarchy, the denial of rights placed the slave outside society altogether. Thus the inversion of liberalism was very different from a reversion to patriarchalism.

Liberalism had a robust variety of linguistic devices for imagining the slave's place outside of society. The first was the state of nature, where no one's rights were secure and where life degenerated into a Hobbesian nightmare, a perpetual state of war. The "social compact" invoked by southern state constitutions presumed the existence of a world where no compact had been made prior to man's entrance into society. In this "uncivilized State," one South Carolinian wrote in 1784, every man "has a right to consider himself or his family as independent of all the world." But in that case, he continued, "it is evident that he is not intitled to the assistance or protection of his neighbours under any circumstances whatever, and therefore must be exposed to every injury which the malevolence or avarice of wicked men may prompt them to commit. There cannot be a moment secure of property, liberty or life."[68] Where there was no compact there was no society, and without society no one's rights were secure.

This is where liberalism sometimes put the slave—outside society, banished forever to a state of nature that had degenerated into the chaos of perpetual war, thereby destroying the security of all rights, beginning with property. Because the slaves were "not capable of any property," John Locke wrote, they "cannot in that state be considered as any part of civil society; the chief end whereof is the preservation of property." Slavery, he concluded, "is the state of war continued." The obvious problem posed by this line of reasoning is the implicit license it gave slaves to use whatever means were necessary to regain their freedom. In the state of war there was no authority. Where "the state of war subsists" between master and slave, Rousseau explained, "the exercise of the rights of war supposes that there is no treaty of peace."[69] Hence the slaveholders—like most Americans in the nineteenth century—dropped the language of the state of nature, fearful of its revolutionary implications.

More often, liberalism recognized the master-slave relationship by retaining a language of property rights stripped of its origins in the state of nature. This only made sense. After all, the vesting of rights in every individual is, at bottom, a method of codifying the basic relationships that together constitute society. In this sense property rights define some of the limits beyond which one person may not interfere in someone else's life. In capitalism, where those limitations are considerable, property rights are said to be "absolute." In a similar way, the distinctive attribute of the master-slave relationship was that no one outside of it could interfere with the slave's total subordination to the master. Just as a piece of "private property" was held beyond the reach of society by its owner, so was the slave removed from society by his or her total subordination to the master.

Notwithstanding the enormous moral and political difficulties raised by the definition of humans as property, southern states fell into the habit of doing so from their earliest slave codes. Virginia's 1705 statute declared that all slaves "shall be held to be real estate and shall descend unto heirs and widows according to the custom of land inheritance."[70] Other colonies and subsequent states followed Virginia's lead by defining slaves as either real or personal property. Once this was done, the way was clear for a defense of slavery on the grounds of property rights. One southern constitution declared in 1850 that the "right of property is before and higher than any constitutional sanction." The point of the article was to legalize slavery, so in the very next phrase the constitution announced that "the right of the owner of a slave to such slave and its increase is the same and as inviolable as the right of the owner of any property whatever."[71] Slavery, the Alabama legislature declared in 1852, confers "on the master property in and the right to the time, labor and services of the slave, and to enforce obedience on the part of the slave, to all his lawful commands."[72]

The language of property rights provided southern masters with a justification of slavery most compatible with liberal political culture. When hundreds of Virginians petitioned their legislature in 1784 hoping to thwart serious consideration of a gradual emancipation bill, they openly invoked the liberal ideology of the recent Revolution. "We were put in the Possession of our Rights of Liberty and Property," they declared. "But notwithstanding this, we understand a very subtle and daring Attempt is made to dispossess us of a very important Part of our Property."[73] By the nineteenth century this was commonplace logic among southern masters. "As an owner of slaves (and one whose income is derived almost entirely from their labor)," one slaveholder wrote, "I assert an unquestionable right to my property, and protest against every attempt to deprive me of it without my consent." It was the right of property that led many Southerners to question the constitutionality of all laws restricting the importation of slaves into western territories. "A man's slave is his property, so recognized by the constitution," A. G. Brown complained in 1848, "and a citizen of Mississippi may settle with his slave property in the territory of the United States, with as little constitutional hindrance as a citizen from any other state may settle with any other species of property."[74]

There were still more sophisticated attempts to place southern slavery under the rubric of liberalism, but they almost always came back to the rights of property. "We go out of a state of nature into a state of society, to render certain our personal liberty, our personal security, and the right to acquire and enjoy private property," William O. Goode explained. Because "the right of property exists before society . . . the Legislature cannot deprive a citizen of his property in his slave. It cannot abolish slavery in a State. It could not delegate to Congress a power greater than its own."[75]

In the most sustained effort to integrate liberal ideology and the defense of slavery, Alfred Taylor Bledsoe pursued a somewhat different line of reasoning. He focused on the distinction between the "state of tyranny" and the "state of society" throughout his exhaustive critique of abolitionism. While he explicitly accepted many of the philosophical premises of slavery's opponents, Bledsoe insisted that what they failed to realize was that black people were inherently unfit for life in civil society. The "state of tyranny" was their natural abode.[76] This was the great burden of proslavery thought in the nineteenth-century South. It was easy enough to show that the Bible and history alike sanctioned slavery. What the slaveholders had to do was demonstrate that slavery was compatible with freedom and that *black* people were inherently suited for the state of tyranny, rendered unfit for the freedom of society by the immutable laws of nature, and as such justifiably reduced to the status of human property.

Here the rhetoric of "natural" distinctions proved crucial, for it provided liberalism with a powerful justification for distributing rights unevenly across society. All men may have been created equal, but through much of American history the liberal tradition interpreted this precept with a literal-mindedness that afforded women fewer civil and property rights than men. The severest legal discriminations suffered by Native Americans and free blacks were the restrictions on their rights to participate as equals in civil and political society. And as with the assumption that children are by nature unfit for the full rights of adulthood, the maldistribution of rights among women and ethnic minorities rested on presumed differences in "nature."

It was to this line of reasoning that the slaveholders ran for defense, along with so many nineteenth-century Westerners who recoiled from liberalism's egalitarian claim of universal rights.

Rights imply equality, Richard Bland of Virginia had written, but only "in the Instances to which they belong." This allowed for vast differences of opinion on a variety of fundamental issues, among them democracy, capitalist development, and slavery. But underlying all of these differences was a question that could only arise from shared liberal assumptions: Were the inequalities that clearly existed in society the product of *natural* distinctions—of talent, intelligence, or perhaps "race" and gender—or were they caused by *artificial* distinctions perpetrated by government?

Thus racism, though partly an expression of the universal political exclusion of slaves, was also a reflection of its particular historical context in the modern nation-state. It is worth remembering that southern slaveholders not only played a leading role in the first great nationalist revolution that created the United States, but that the American Revolution was also a major turning point in the development of scientific racism. The connection was not simply fortuitous, and Benedict Anderson's important distinction between racism and nationalism suggests why it was not. Nationalism is a language of *inclusion* within what Anderson calls the "imagined community" that constitutes the nation. By contrast, racism is a language of *exclusion* that *"erases nation-ness* by reducing the adversary to his biological physiognomy." Thus it is not entirely surprising that the birth of the "first new nation" was accompanied by the disturbing articulation of a racist ideology. For the emergence of nationalism generated novel pressures to reaffirm the slave's place outside the "imagined community" of the modern American nation.[77]

These various efforts to fit slavery into the liberal scheme of things can be read in very different ways: as evidence of the harmony of slavery and liberalism or as proof that slavery represented a major irritant within the American political tradition. In a sense both views are correct, for while liberalism had several philosophical boxes within which slavery could be fitted, none of them offered a perfectly comfortable abode. If anything, slavery pushed its advocates to conflicting extremes in their search for more congenial quarters. Some writers bluntly rejected all of liberalism's egalitarian implications, even to the point of belittling

Jefferson himself. Others held that slavery bolstered the equality of all free men through the democratization of southern politics. There was praise for slavery as the bulwark of industrial progress, but it was also defended for shielding the South from capitalism's worst ravages. Even within liberalism there was no one way to construct a proslavery defense. The same ideology embraced populists and élitists, free-traders and protectionists, libertarians and statists, and each group had its spokesman among proslavery ideologues. At best, liberalism was no more than a center of gravity for proslavery thought. Yet every proslavery ideologue worked either within liberalism or against it. None could escape its influence.

Counteracting the tendency toward ideological extremes, the liberal state sustained a politics that muffled the most exotic proslavery formulations or isolated them at the fringes of respectable public opinion. Historians have correctly pointed to the myriad ways the slaveholders succeeded in tilting the American political system toward the defense of their interests. But in return for that support the slaveholders thoroughly accommodated themselves to the liberal state itself, and this restrained as much as it protected the master class. In the nineteenth-century South the liberal state did not grant to slaveholders—as slaveholders—noble privileges within the larger polity. It did not establish separate branches of government to recognize the distinct political personality of the slaveholding class. Neither the federal government nor any state in America, North or South, ever recognized slaveownership as a qualification, much less a requirement, for either voting or officeholding. Even the U.S. Constitution's notorious "three-fifths" clause (which counted 60 percent of the slave population in determining the size of a state's congressional delegation) increased the representation of each slave state as a whole, benefiting slaveholders and nonslaveholders alike.

The political power of the southern slaveholders is not in dispute. By 1860, when the proportion of white families owning slaves had slipped to 25 percent, virtually every southern governor was a slaveholder, as were nearly all the justices of the various state supreme courts. Wealthy slaveholders dominated the structures of the two major political parties throughout the antebellum years. In almost every southern state the slaveholders, especially the planters, filled the legislatures in numbers far beyond their proportion in the general population. Indeed, as the percentage of slaveholders in the South fell more rapidly than ever during the 1850's, their numbers in the legislatures rose all across the region. There is no question that the slaveholders exercised a degree of political power that far exceeded their proportion of the electorate, both nationally and regionally.

But no matter how powerful the slaveholders became in executive offices and legislatures across America, no matter how many ways the Constitution protected slavery, and no matter how far the Supreme Court was willing to go to accommodate the slaveholders' interests—the fact remained that governors' mansions, the presidential office, Senate chambers, Houses of Representatives, and Supreme Courts were political institutions whose provenance was at best tangentially related to the history of slavery. They sustained the slaveholders' power not by any formal preference for the master class but, in most cases, by their susceptibility to the influence of wealth in almost any form.

The slaveholders' politics might have been easier to understand had the South preserved a patriarchal state on the European model, complete with a formal aristocracy and a powerful monarch. In that case we could simply look to the legal basis of the slaveholders' political influence: the judicial indemnities that protected them from public prosecution for crimes against citizens; the fiscal privileges that immunized them from certain forms of taxation; the labyrinth of land and inheritance laws ensuring that estates would stay in the same families over succeeding generations; the political offices that could be filled only by those who were to the manor born; the formal titles that separated them from all other citizens; the monarchy that dispensed those titles; and the established church that legitimized them. These were the legal trappings of the European aristocracy, and they survived into the late 1800's even after centuries of diminution.[78]

In aristocratic societies the nobility defined itself by carving out a body of legal and political privileges that it alone could exercise.

The slave South did the reverse. A body of "universal" rights was established and a class of slaves was carved out and excluded from the enjoyment of those rights. In Europe the law created nobles. In the South the law created slaves. Aristocrats were distinguished not simply from their tenants but from all other free men. By contrast, southern law established a powerful relationship between masters and slaves that implied no formal distinctions among free men and no automatic access to political power. As the separation of public from private authority emerged in early modern Europe, the nobility lost many of its private juridical rights while retaining important political and legal privileges. Here again the southern pattern was nearly the reverse of the European. The private rights of masters were preserved in a polity that guaranteed them no public offices. No southern governor held office by virtue of his birth. No planter was guaranteed his seat in the legislature for life. No southern judge inherited his bench. The Old South had neither a monarchy nor an established church. The planters could boast of no formal titles. Their plantations were not entailed. Their status could not be legally passed on to succeeding generations. There were no legal restrictions on popular access to land and slaves among free men.

It was precisely this distinction between liberalism and aristocracy that allowed so many Southerners to speak of their society as egalitarian—on the assumption, of course, that slaves were not part of society. As one South Carolinian explained, the "dignity of the commonwealth does not consist in the elevation of one or a few, but in the equal freedom of the whole."[79] State constitutions in the South explicitly prohibited the aristocratic tradition of distributing privileges to a select class of free men. "No man or set of men are entitled to exclusive or separate public emoluments or privileges from the community," the Kentucky constitution of 1792 declared.[80] Only by defining slaves as "outsiders" could such pronouncements appear the least bit plausible to any substantial body of free Southerners.

Even among free men and women, however, slavery generated tremendous inequalities, and there were more than a few planters who fancied themselves as aristocrats of a sort. Yet the political context simultaneously compelled the slaveholders to emphasize the least aristocratic aspects of their society. One of the recurring themes of proslavery ideology was that abolitionism was actually fomented by the English aristocracy. In a stinging rebuke to Scottish abolitionists, James Henry Hammond held Britain's landed élite up to scorn. "Doubtless you all boast of being ideally free," he wrote in 1844, "while the American citizen counts *your* freedom slavery, and could not brook a state of existence in which he daily encountered fellow mortals, acknowledged and privileged as his superiors, solely by the accident of birth."[81]

The fact that the slaveholders exercised their political power within the confines of the liberal state had profound consequences for southern history. Rather than repudiate the principle of checks and balances, the tradition of mass-based representative government, or the concept of judicial review, the slaveholders clung to them as the source of their political authority. Slaveownership was explicitly protected in early American law. But it was sanctioned primarily as a property right and protected through the means and mechanisms of the liberal state. And this put the slaveholders in the paradoxical position of legitimizing the very political structures that would ultimately be used to destroy slavery.

IN THE CENTURY before 1776 the southern colonies had been thoroughly transformed into a full-scale slave society. At the moment when Americans declared their separation from Great Britain the South was as dependent on slave labor as it would ever be, while the northern economy was grounded in the labor of free farms, independent artisans, and mercantile enterprises. The South's economic reliance on staple crops, its demographic profile of a self-reproducing slave population, and its plantation system —all of this distinguished the southern from the northern colonies in 1776. Although present in the northern colonies, slavery played no comparably significant role. And yet North and South joined in a successful rebellion against the British, and together formed one of the world's first modern nation-states.

Shared experience was thus strong enough to overcome already profound differences. By the late eighteenth century all the colonies, northern and southern, had developed commercially oriented rural economies; each had been transformed by the consumer revolution of the eighteenth century. The intrinsic insecurities of commercial agriculture, the newly discovered dangers of luxury and corruption, and the anomalous conjunction of de facto political autonomy and colonial subordination—all of this had nourished among Americans a political culture that would eventually justify their rebellion against England, notwithstanding all the social divisions within the colonies. For a brief but critical moment in American history, all that the slave South and the free North shared—in economics, in politics, and in culture—took on tremendous historical importance. That unity was as significant as the American Revolution, no more and no less.

This does not mean that the slave South was, at bottom, a liberal capitalist society. Nor does it mean that liberal capitalism was thoroughly compatible with slavery. In the end the universalization of rights and the dynamic force of free labor overwhelmed and destroyed slavery. But southern slave society emerged within rather than apart from the liberal capitalist world, and that made a crucial difference. For the ambiguous relationship between slavery and liberal capitalism thereby became intrinsic to the Old South, not merely the basis of sectional animosity. And herein lay the greatest of all the ironies that mark southern history. The slaveholders had emerged triumphant from the American Revolution, wielding considerable influence in a new and unified nation, but in their very triumph they had helped to unleash forces over which they would eventually lose control.

CHAPTER 3

Slaveholders
and Nonslaveholders

In this country alone does perfect equality of civil and social privilege exist among the white population, and it exists solely because we have black slaves.—Freedom is not
possible without slavery.
—Richmond (Va.) *Enquirer*, 1856

J. C. KEYSAER'S recollections of class relations in the Old
South were unusually bitter. A yeoman farmer from Bell
Buckle, Tennessee, Keysaer complained that before the Civil
War the "Slave holders always acted as if they were of a better
class and there was always an unpleasant feeling between slaveholders and those working themselves." It was not that the slaveholder was "antagonistic" toward the yeoman, "just 'uppish.' "
Holding himself "above the working class," the slaveholder nevertheless "used money [to win votes] whenever he could. This fact
usually elected him." Although these were severe sentiments,
they were far more common among yeomen farmers than among
those who had owned slaves before the war. Indeed, owning
slaves apparently made a difference in the perception of class relations in the Old South. Thus the more prosperous of Keysaer's
fellow Tennessee veterans interviewed many years later remembered that relations between slaveholders and nonslaveholders
were grounded in "social equality." Over and over again former
masters remembered "no difference," "no antagonism," "every
body was equal."[1]

Keysaer himself inadvertently revealed one reason why memories of relations between masters and yeomen were so often contradictory: "Slaves were hardly known there," he said of his

boyhood community. Others agreed. "Not very many slaveholders in this section of the county," William Harkleroad told an interviewer. Andy Guffee remembered no slaveholders within "more than 5 miles of where I lived." The sons of wealthy planters often said the same thing. William Gordon, whose father owned over forty slaves, recalled that the classes were "not antagonistic," largely because they lived in "separate neighborhoods." There was "no social communication" between slaveholders and nonslaveholders that Gordon could remember. This was a product of physical as much as cultural distance, however. Slaveholders tended to live among slaveholders, yeomen farmers tended to live among slaveless farmers like themselves. For this reason, Edwin Garder could recall that in the area where he grew up "nearly every family owned slaves."[2]

What was true of the Old South was true of many slave societies: slaveholders and nonslaveholders did not live among each other. And the reasons were above all economic, for as slave economies expanded they tended to displace the peasantry. This is precisely what happened in ancient Rome. The last two hundred years of the pre-Christian era saw the transformation of Roman Italy from a society of yeoman farmers to one of large-scale, slave-based latifundia. As slavery expanded into the countryside, peasant farmers were steadily pushed off their lands. In some cases rising taxes made peasant agriculture insupportable; at other times slaveless farmers were simply evicted by force. Vast populations shifted as peasants moved first from the countryside to Rome and then to the provinces—with service in the army functioning as a medium of relocation. Slave-based agriculture thereby replaced peasant holdings in large parts of Italy. Not surprisingly, there was pervasive political conflict over land-distribution patterns in the Republic, especially since officeholders continued to rely on the citizenry for support. Julius Caesar began the policy of forced relocation, but not until the rule of Augustus were the political pressures relieved by the massive migration of landowners into the provinces of the Empire, usually outside of Italy.[3]

Slavery's tendency to displace the peasantry reemerged in the New World some fifteen hundred years later. It was particularly relentless in the Caribbean. The limited lands available for slave-based agriculture combined with an especially intense sugar boom to put unparalleled pressures on slaveless farmers. In Barbados the sugar explosion of the mid-seventeenth century undermined the island's self-sufficiency. Small farmers were pushed onto tiny plots of land, where they pursued a hand-to-mouth existence growing small amounts of cash and subsistence crops. The wealthiest planters steadily monopolized the island's best lands, concentrated around St. George's Valley. All the while, freed indentured servants, wage laborers, failed yeomen, and even slaveholders moved steadily off Barbados in search of opportunities elsewhere in the Caribbean or in the British colonies of mainland North America. In the century following the introduction of sugar culture, as many as ten thousand Barbadians moved to the Carolinas.[4]

But if the migrants did not bring slavery with them, it followed them across the Caribbean. As the sugar boom struck the Leeward Islands in the early eighteenth century, small farmers began to leave and the planters quickly took over. Nevis in 1706 struck Daniel Parke as "a rich little Island" with "but few people . . . divided among a few rich men that had a vast number of slaves, and hardly any common people, but a few that lived in the town." The same pattern duplicated itself in Jamaica. Large numbers of small farmers had migrated to escape the advance of the Barbadian planters only to discover that the planters could engross whole islands almost as easily as they could individual farms. Between 1689 and 1713, Jamaica's small planters were "pretty well wiped out." As in the Chesapeake region slave labor was replacing indentured servitude. But unlike Maryland and Virginia, the islands had no continent to the west where freed servants and displaced peasants could recapture their landed independence.[5]

Brazil's slaves and peasants shared a similarly close history. In the sugar-producing region of Bahia, for example, slavery literally produced its own peasantry, thanks to a long tradition of manumission. But it was a hungry and impoverished class, one whose growth so frightened the planter élite that by the nineteenth century "their numbers weighed heavily in political calculations."[6] In Vassouras, where coffee was the chief export crop in the mid-nineteenth century, the steady expansion of slave plantations all but destroyed the small, independent farmers. "They have been reduced to dependents of the big planters," one observer noted. "Today the best lands are denied them and they may no longer cut any forest lands."[7]

As slave plantations spread over parts of East Africa in the nineteenth century, a similar pattern emerged. Muslim clove planters on Zanzibar began to occupy lands that had probably been inhabited by the Wahadimu people. As the profitability of slave plantations was secured, the encroachment by Arab planters onto Swahili lands became far more aggressive. Much the same thing happened on the nearby East African mainland. Once again Arab slaveholders, concentrating on the production of rice and other grains for export, began to expand their plantations into areas traditionally occupied by subsistence farmers. In 1844 a local missionary, Ludwig Krappf, was astonished by how "systematically the Mahomedans encroach upon the Wanica [Mijikenda] land in this direction."[8]

Over time the displacement of peasants led to the physical separation of slaveholders from nonslaveholders. Zanzibar, for example, became divided into two regions: an Arab-dominated slave economy in the north and west and a Wahadimu economy of subsistence farms to the south and east. In the New World, those areas where slavery thrived have come to be known as "plantation belts" or, more commonly, "black belts." Sometimes a major crop gave the region its name, as in the South's "cotton belt." In these areas slaveholders always managed to secure near-monopoly control of the best soils, plantations were relatively large, the percentage of slaves in the population could reach as high as 90 percent, and the proportion of farms with slaves often hovered around two-thirds. By contrast, small farmers tended to concentrate in those areas where the soil or climate was incompatible with slave-produced staple crops: in mountainous terrain with too much or too little rainfall, relatively poor soils, and limited access to markets. In such areas, most farmers had no slaves, and most of those with slaves had few of them. Small farmers survived best where slavery could not flourish.

Thus the expansion of slavery often produced sharp regional divisions that coincided with fundamental social distinctions. Small farmers in Barbados were largely confined to the eastern and southern coasts, where rainfall was lighter and soil less fertile than in St. George's Valley. The nineteenth-century sugar boom in Cuba divided the island broadly into two halves. Slavery dominated the west. It was richer than the east, more politically influential, the farms were larger and the soil more fertile. The east was more mountainous, the farms were smaller, the soils poorer. Of course, this was not an absolute pattern; there were pockets of slavery in the east and small farms here and there in the west. Nevertheless, the political history of nineteenth-century Cuba reflected a social division that conformed to geographic realities.[9]

In this light, the social history of the Old South becomes somewhat easier to chart. Free settlers and indentured servants alike arrived in America possessed of the powerful heritage of the English yeomanry. They sought out land and clung to it as a source of independence and they were determined to protect that tradition as they moved into politics. But slavery limited the yeomanry's capacity to re-create itself and pulled the South's free farmers in contradictory directions. It left the yeomen alone in their pine barrens, hill counties, and mountain hollows. But as we shall see, slavery also expanded aggressively across the southern frontier, preventing an independent yeomanry from coming into existence through much of the eighteenth century and seriously threatening its independence in the nineteenth.[10] With the growing antagonism between the upcountry and the black belt, the battle lines of southern politics were drawn. The first major skirmishes between slaveholders and nonslaveholders in American politics erupted long before the secession crisis loomed.

DANIEL HUNDLEY argued in 1860 that the Jeffersonian reforms of the American Revolution "made it necessary for the Gentlemen

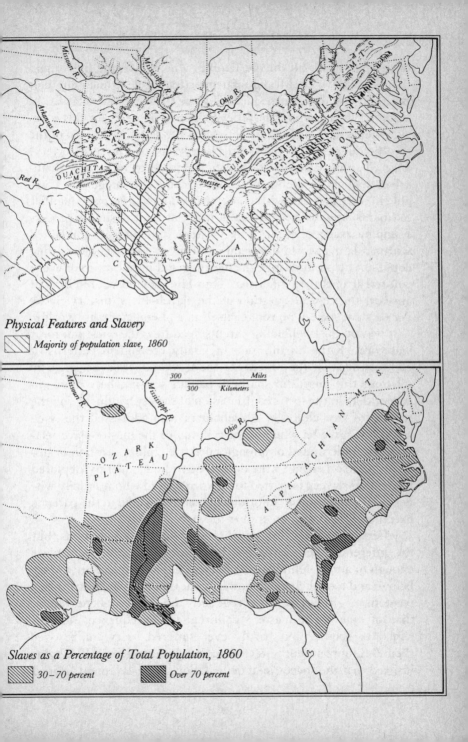

Physical Features and Slavery

▨ *Majority of population slave, 1860*

Slaves as a Percentage of Total Population, 1860

▨ *30–70 percent* ▨ *Over 70 percent*

of the South, for all the old families who had before lived upon their hereditary wealth and influence, to struggle to maintain their position, else to be pushed aside by the thrifty middle classes."[11] Whether the revolution or Jefferson deserved credit for this is beside the point, for Hundley was correct to link the survival of the slaveholding class to the political structure of southern society. Like all ruling classes, the slaveholders had to reproduce themselves anew with each generation. Lacking the safeguards available to the European aristocracy, they adopted a strategy familiar to liberal capitalist societies. But this was not the simple process Hundley made it seem. The masters were indeed embedded within a larger world of liberal culture, yet as slaveholders they could not help but change the meaning and implications of every cultural artifact they inherited. Thus Hundley raised, but did not answer, the central question of the slaveholders' history: How does a slave society reproduce itself in a liberal capitalist world?

It was up to slaveholding parents to address the question, for it was through the organization of family life and in patterns of childrearing that the process of social reproduction began. The dilemma this raised for southern parents was nowhere more apparent than in the tortured discussion of slavery's influence on the rearing of free children. Slaveholders who addressed the issue could not agree on whether the tyranny of the master-slave relationship undermined or strengthened the child's devotion to liberty. Jefferson engaged the debate when he eloquently deplored the lessons slavery imparted to a growing child who was daily witness to the notoriously unbridled passions released in the parent's exercise of despotic power over the slave.

Jefferson drew no clear conclusions from his observations, but the inferences he encouraged his readers to draw were clear enough to annoy John Taylor. Slaves, Taylor wrote, "are too far below, and too much in the power of the master, to inspire furious passions . . . [they] are more frequently the objects of benevolence than of rage." The master's children, in consequence, "are inclined to soothe, and hardly ever suffered to tyrannize over them." A more ardent Jeffersonian than Jefferson himself, Taylor insisted that the spectacle of degradation, of enslavement, placed constantly before the free child's gaze, nourished an unusually powerful commitment to freedom. "Vicious and mean qualities become despicable in the eyes of freemen from their association with the character of slaves." By seeing up close what it meant to be a slave, the child grew to appreciate in a unique way the full meaning of human liberty. "Instead therefore of fearing that children should imbibe the qualities of slaves," Taylor concluded, "it is probable, that the circumstance of seeing bad qualities in slaves will contribute to their virtue."[12] In later years leading proslavery ideologues, Thomas R. Dew and William Harper among them, would embrace Taylor's reasoning more often than Jefferson's.

Indeed, Jefferson himself seemed uncertain, for at times he came close to agreeing with his severest critic. Not five years after having written the passage in *Notes on Virginia* to which Taylor objected, Jefferson composed a letter to the English moral philosopher Dr. Richard Price, placing his hopes for the ultimate abolition of slavery on the rising generation. After noting the fate of slavery in the northern states, Jefferson wrote that Virginia "is the next State to which we may turn our eyes for the interesting spectacle of justice, in conflict with avarice and oppression; a conflict wherein the sacred side is gaining daily recruits, from the influx into office of young men, grown and growing up. These have sucked in the principles of liberty, as it were, with their mother's milk," Jefferson proclaimed, "and it is to them I look with anxiety to turn the fate of this question. Be not therefore discouraged."[13]

If the issue was unresolved, even in Jefferson's own mind, it was far from academic. Frances Kemble was terrified by the example slavery set to her young daughter. "I do not think that a residence on a slave plantation is likely to be peculiarly advantageous to a child like my oldest," she wrote in 1839. Watching as slave children followed her daughter about and "sprang to obey her little gestures of command," Mrs. Kemble was disturbed. "Think," she concluded, "of learning to rule despotically your fellow creatures before the first lesson of self-government has been well spelled over!"[14] And yet, only days earlier, Mrs. Kemble had recorded a conversation between an older woman and her three-year-old daughter that gave substance to John Taylor's observations about what children learned from their proximity to slavery. The woman went out of her way to make the little girl, Mary, aware of the distinction between slavery and freedom. "Some persons are free and some are not—do you know that, Mary?" she asked. Not only did the little girl understand the distinction perfectly, she had also picked up her mother's antislavery convictions. "Yes, missis, *here*," she answered. "I know it is so here, in this world." But when asked whether she thought it would "not always be so," Mary added: "Me hope not, missis."[15] In everyday conversations such as this, slavery's precarious dualisms were reintroduced to every generation.

The great challenge for slaveholding parents was to raise their young to the exercise of despotic rule and, at the same time, to a world of individual freedom and political equality. The simplest solution was merely to assert the distinction between the worlds of freedom and slavery. Hence Thomas Ruffin's firm rejection of the simile that likened the rearing of slaves to that of free children: "There is no likeness between the cases," he insisted. Whether slavery would encourage the child to "give loose to his worst of passions," as Jefferson feared, or "cause us rather to hate servility than to imbibe a dictatorial arrogance," as Taylor argued, remained unclear.

The source of this ambiguity is easy enough to trace: slaveholding families were strongly influenced by new Anglo-American ideas about how to order domestic life properly, and yet those same families were profoundly influenced by the presence of slaves within the household. The result was a master class whose culture was at once recognizably American and yet distinctively southern. Standing at the intersection of slavery and liberal capitalism, planter families were a paradigm in miniature of the larger history of the antebellum South.

At first glance, there is nothing distinctively southern about the "enlightened" attitudes toward marriage and child-rearing that made their appearance among planter families sometime in the middle to late eighteenth century. As early as 1750 Virginia planters began to express unprecedented concern for privacy, to idealize the affectionate companionship of husband and wife, and to

sentimentalize children. With the elevation of her role as nurtur-
ing mother, the plantation mistress increasingly nursed her own
children, abandoning the aristocratic tradition of wet-nursing that
still prevailed on the European continent.[16] Plantation homes
were constructed with a newfound concern for the solitude of the
individual. The evocative symbolism of southern family portrai-
ture was transformed: the father, no longer aloof and above his
family, instead assumed a loving pose beside his wife and among
his children. Gone, or at least substantially diminished, was the
image of the family as the domestic reflection of patriarchal government, with its emphasis on hierarchy and subordination, obedience, and intergenerational continuity. The new understanding
demanded that children be nourished on love more than filiopiety;
reared to individual autonomy rather than hierarchical interdependence. In this emerging image of the family, the world was
remade with each new generation.[17]

That the children of slaveholders were reared under the growing influence of liberal family values is further indicated by
changes in southern family law between the Revolution and the
Civil War. The economic insecurity of property holdings in the
antebellum economy sometimes compelled southern legislatures
to modify or abolish laws that restricted the property rights of
women. In many cases family property could best be protected
by giving women greater control over it. More and more women
therefore established "separate estates," sidestepping the "cover-
ture" laws that automatically transferred a bride's property to her
new husband.[18]

In still other ways the ancient custom of equating the family
with the husband and father weakened over time. Divorce was
never easy for women in the Old South, but it did become more
common in the years from the Revolution to the Civil War. If
South Carolina resisted the reform impulse, Virginia and Maryland were more representative of southern and national trends.
Both states made it easier for women to win legal separations from
their husbands. And as southern legislatures terminated marriages in increasing numbers, fathers steadily lost their presumptive right to custody of the children. In 1845, for example, the

Georgia legislature declared that in all disputes over the placement of children "the Common Law rule vesting said custody always in the father, shall be abolished." Thereafter, custody was to be awarded to whichever parent the court considered "most beneficial to the interest of said children." But this standard—the interests of the child—grew steadily into a presumptive bias in favor of the mother. The shift took most of the nineteenth century to complete, but by 1850 southern courts were as likely as not to award custody to the mother, thereby reversing a centuries-old patriarchal tradition.[19]

Certainly the Old South was no stronghold of sexual equality. Male-dominated families—what one scholar has recently termed "domestic patriarchy"—prevailed throughout nineteenth-century America, and perhaps more firmly in the South than elsewhere. Property laws continued to disadvantage women. Given the dangers of childbirth, large families continued to place southern women's lives and health in jeopardy.[20] Nevertheless, relatively egalitarian inheritance patterns, female literacy, property rights for women, and the legal recognition of the distinctive interests of wives and children, all represented major inroads of liberal political culture among slaveholding families.

Without entailed estates, with no tradition of primogeniture, and with none of the elaborate legal mechanisms that preserved the integrity of noble privilege in Europe, the slaveholders developed child-rearing and inheritance patterns that reflected the powerful force of liberal individualism. In the late eighteenth century every southern state abolished primogeniture, and long before then it had been abandoned in practice. Planters broke up their estates with each passing generation, distributing their property differentially but broadly among their children. Eldest sons could expect to take possession of the family home, but land and slaves were distributed among sons and daughters. Nathaniel Francis had built up his Virginia plantation from 137 acres and 7 slaves in 1827 to nearly 3,500 acres and 37 slaves some two decades later. But when he died in 1849, Francis's widow received one-third of the estate, while his four sons divided the remainder, leaving each of the children far less wealthy than their father had been. "In our republic, there is no law of primogeniture, there are no hereditary rights," Andrew Jackson Downing explained. "The man of large wealth dies to-morrow, and his million, divided among all his children, leaves them each but a few thousands."[21]

To be sure, "a few thousands" was quite a bit in the Old South. The practice of dividing estates among heirs may have slowed the accumulation of wealth in planter families, but it hardly reduced them to poverty. In North Carolina, for example, planters distributed their wealth among their children in a relatively egalitarian pattern that had contradictory implications for the subsequent generation. Only one in four children whose parents owned seventy slaves or more in 1830 held the same number a generation later in 1860. Yet if children of the largest planters could not individually recover all of their parents' wealth, the combined wealth of the new generation almost always surpassed its parents'. Sixty-two percent of 1860's wealthiest North Carolina planters were direct descendants of the wealthiest in the 1830 generation. And more than three out of four planter children remained within that select group of those who owned twenty or more slaves.[22] Thus the breakup and reconstruction of plantations was the prevailing pattern in the Old South.

For slaveholders the implications were far-reaching; for slaves they were devastating. Partible inheritance transformed the death of a master into one of the great horrors of slave life, the point at which the slave community was most consistently disrupted, when relatives and friends were separated, and when families were most threatened with breakup. As was so often the case in western history, the equality of free men, relative and incomplete though it was, rested on the distinctively brutal character of the master-slave relation.

Nor could the socialization of the masters' children escape the influence of prevailing inheritance patterns. This was especially obvious in the attitudes toward wealth and its accumulation that parents bequeathed along with the family property. The diaries and letters of slaveholders make clear that by the nineteenth century the advantages of the well-born were, by themselves, insufficient to ensure that the child would live in the same degree of comfort as his parents. Every young man was expected to make his own contribution to the social reproduction of the slaveholding class. Self-discipline, hard work, and the systematic acquisition of wealth became central ideals passed down from father to son in slaveholding families. "Without prudence, industry and a close attention to business," one father wrote his son in a typical letter, "you cannot expect to be successful." Another counseled "steadiness, sobriety, and attention to business" as the surest way to prosperity. "Industry, perseverance, prudence, economy, temperance," one master inscribed as a motto on the opening page of his diary. "Frugality and Industry," he wrote, "are the hands of Fortune."[23] These were the clichés of bourgeois culture grafted onto the distinctive institutions and relations of a slave society.

Given the prevalence of the bourgeois ideals of equal opportunity and individual achievement, it was the challenge for each new generation of slaveholders to reconstruct a society that distributed its wealth very unevenly. Forty percent of the people of the South were, as slaves, impoverished by definition. But there were also considerable distinctions of wealth among free men, the majority of whom remained slaveless at any given time. Even within the slaveholding class itself the majority of masters owned a relatively small fraction of the slaves. The richest 10 percent of the owners—2 or 3 percent of the South's free men—held 50 percent of the slaves. The majority of the masters owned no more than five slaves each; only one in four owned more than ten. And since land- and slaveownership patterns tended to coincide, those with the most slaves also had the best lands with the highest proportions of improved acreage.

For this pattern to remain constant in a society where estates were divided up every generation, at least some of the children of wealthy planters had to rebuild their parents' fortunes, and many others had to fail in that endeavor. Because the children of small slaveholders usually began their adult lives as slaveless farmers, most of them had to reenter the slaveholding class on their own, and some had to remain outside the master class throughout their productive lives. The statistical evidence bears this out. Upward —and downward—mobility were, almost by definition, characteristic of the life cycle within the master class. Because slave-ownership was something that came later in life, upward mobility was a normal experience for successful masters. Nor was this a rare experience in the Old South, for in 1860 one out of every four free families owned at least one slave, and the proportion had usually been higher than that. Most often slaveownership rates ranged from 30 to 35 percent, and in many parts of the South it was much higher, even in 1860. Over the course of a free man's lifetime there was probably a fifty-fifty chance of becoming a slaveholder for some period of time.[24]

On the other hand, if a master was very wealthy, the chances were that his parents had been as well. The advantages of education, connections, and an economic head start were as important in the South as they were anywhere else in America. Thus, even in the absence of legally entailed estates or other barriers restricting admission to the aristocracy, the slaveholding class successfully reproduced itself with each passing generation. The liberal strategy worked. The "classes of society remain; they are permanent," a prominent tobacco manufacturer in Virginia observed.

> But of the individuals that comprise them, many are constantly passing from one to another as changes occur in their circumstances and fortunes; and to secure such a change and transfer from a lower to a higher sphere is one of the great struggles of life. . . . Indeed there are but few of our prominent men . . . who if they undertook to trace their genealogy, would not soon run into the mud; while there are many imbeciles now in the mire who can easily trace their ancestry back to aristocracy.[25]

It would be a mistake to conclude from all of this that the history of the slaveholding class was a mere variation on a larger liberal theme. The South was, at bottom, a slave society, and the significance of slavery extended well beyond the relationship of master and slave. The ownership of even a single slave affected all the other relationships that made up the master's world. Slavery reshaped the ties between farmers and merchants; it transformed the relationship between slaveowners and their neighbors; and it profoundly influenced the bonds of marriage and the patterns of childrearing within the master's family. For all of liberalism's influence, slavery nevertheless reproduced itself in distinctive ways, beginning with the organization of family life.

Consider what could happen to the rhythm of daily life when a free farmer acquired a slave. We know that slaveless farmers relied extensively on the labor of their own families, that they divided up work in patterns based on age and gender, and that these patterns changed over time as the family grew and matured. The ownership of only a few slaves, perhaps even one, could subtly but profoundly alter these patterns. No doubt the effects multiplied as the number of slaves in the household increased. But the consequences appeared, and were perhaps most pronounced, with the ownership of the first few.

Clear-cut examples showing the effect of slavery's introduction into yeoman households are extremely rare, but circumstantial evidence provides some important clues. For instance, among those who owned only one slave—and more masters owned a single slave than any other number—there was a clear preference for adult males. This may simply have reflected the supply of slaves available for purchase. Planters in the eastern states, where breeding was most common and where most of the slaves on the market came from, tended to hold on to fertile women and sell off young men. Yet despite the fact that slave men were more available than women, buyers were willing to pay the much higher prices males generated at slave auctions. This preference among those acquiring their first slave implies that the consequences of owning a male rather than a female slave were potentially significant.[26] The difference deserves a brief examination.

With a slave on the farm, particularly a male, a father could more easily afford the labor lost by sending his son to school or by having his daughters tutored. "Laborers was respected" in the Old South, one yeoman farmer remembered many years later, but "the men that owned slaves did not work and did not have there children to do any work." However exaggerated such perceptions were, a survey of Tennessee's Civil War veterans nevertheless demonstrates that slaveholders' children were absent from school less frequently than were yeomen children. "When a boy, I was not expected to do manual labor, as I was at school all the time," a planter's son explained. During his college years "my entire time was occupied with my studies. I[t] was not necessary for me to work with a plow or a hoe."[27] Slaveownership thus enhanced the educational opportunities of the master's children. Despite the fact that public education in the South advanced more slowly than it did in the North, the children of slaveholders, girls as well as boys, were almost always educated. So widespread was literacy within the slaveholding class that the overall literacy rate among free Southerners was one of the highest in the western world.[28]

A female slave, perhaps only one, could relieve mistresses of some of the most onerous chores of housekeeping, from cooking and cleaning to gathering wood and tending the family's vegetable garden. The Tennessee veteran's survey revealed that nine out of ten yeomen women did their own chores at home, whereas less than a third of small slaveholders' wives did. Only 7.7 percent of the mistresses on large plantations performed their own household chores, for as the number of slave laborers grew the mistress was transformed into a domestic manager.[29] "My father occupied his time in general management of the place," J. A. Pickard remembered of his youth on a very large Tennessee plantation, while "my mother . . . looked after the house and overlooked the work of the negro women who spun, wove and made clothes for themselves and the other negroes."[30] Such tasks could be difficult on large plantations, but the transformation of the mistress's role began with the first slave. "The non-slaveholder knows," J. D. B. DeBow wrote in 1859, "that as soon as his savings will admit, he can become a slaveholder, and thus relieve his wife from the necessities of the kitchen and the laundry and his children from the labors of the field."[31]

By eliminating the planters' reliance on the labor of their own children, slavery may have made it possible for large slaveholders in the oldest states to respond to the limited supply of land by reducing the size of their families. Nearly all of the evidence—and there is not much of it—comes from the eastern seaboard in late antebellum decades. But two items stand out. First, black-belt families were consistently smaller than families in the "upcountry," where yeoman farms predominated. Second, the difference appeared in Virginia during the second quarter of the nineteenth century, when the average number of children in planter families began to decline. By 1860 planter families were still relatively large, especially so by the new standards being set by the northern middle class. On the other hand, the wealthiest Virginia families did follow the pattern common to long-settled regions throughout the United States, shrinking to a size consistently smaller than those of yeomen farmers.[32]

As children reached adulthood, slave labor could make it easier for their parents to subsist and prosper without the help of their own offspring. Bound labor often replaced child labor in the life cycle of the slaveholding family. Free men were most likely to own slaves when they were in their forties and fifties, when their children came of age and moved out on their own. Thus slavery loosened the bonds of intergenerational dependency that made older parents traditionally reliant on their grown children. In turn, children benefited from the age structure of the slaveholding class. The average number of slaves a master owned peaked in middle age but declined among those who reached their sixties. This may be why the slaveholders struck M. B. Goodrich as "a class of old men who had negroes and sons to take their place as they were beginning to get feeble."[33] Slavery made this possible by allowing the most prosperous parents to transfer some of their slave property to their grown children in the critical years of early adulthood.

Thus, slaveholding parents joined the physical reproduction of the family to the historical reconstruction of southern society. By reducing the size of their families, by educating their children, by impressing upon them the importance of middle-class values, by providing them with economic assistance at critical moments early in their careers, and above all, by recapitulating the dualism of slavery and freedom in everyday life, masters assured the survival of the slaveowning class over succeeding generations. But if the socialization of the slaveholders' children began with the individual's relation to the family, it was complemented by the slaveholding family's relationship to society. The communities in which the master's children were reared, and which they were expected to reconstruct, were even more distinctive than the families that prepared them for participation in those communities. And, as with relationships within the family, the ties between family and society began to change with the purchase of a single slave.

By systematically altering the farmer's links with the market economy, slavery in turn transformed the very structure of southern society. The sociological chain reaction was precipitated by the economic consequences of slaveownership. Most masters were farmers, and for most of them the cost of a slave was a significant expense, in fact a major investment. Whether a farmer borrowed the money to buy a slave or saved up the cash, he naturally expected the fruits of the slave's labor to repay the initial expense. Property taxes on slaves added to the burden. Since slaveholders monopolized the most productive soils, the taxes on their lands were often higher than those of yeomen farmers. To own even a single slave, therefore, was to be subject to periodic mortgage payments and yearly taxes that slaveless farmers did not have to meet.

Simply put, slavery required production for the market. The mere purchase of a slave was, in Gavin Wright's words, "an act which *ipso facto* implied a commitment to at least enough cash-crop production to cover the purchase price, debt payments and taxes involved." In most cases this meant that the slave's labor would be devoted primarily to the production of crops for which there was a relatively predictable consumer demand in the market. Statistical evidence shows a fairly clear correlation between slave-ownership and production of staples such as cotton, tobacco, sugar, and rice. The more slaves a master owned, the more land he was likely to devote to marketable crops.[34]

But slavery also made market production easier. By some estimates the average slave produced at least twice as much as was necessary for his or her subsistence, making slaveownership a source of considerable profit to masters for as long as the market in staples was flourishing. It was not that slave labor was intrinsically more productive than free labor—evidence of slavery's efficiency or of economies of scale in plantation agriculture is subject to tremendous dispute. But it is clear that a slave was normally expected to work longer and harder than were any members of the master's family. Slave children went to work in the fields at a younger age than did free children; slave women were expected to do field work, which few free women did except at harvest time. Slave men worked longer hours and had fewer holidays than did free men. In the slave quarters of large plantations, cooking and babysitting were frequently communal chores, often reserved for elderly slaves, and this too increased the labor power available in the work force. Slaves usually produced most of their own food, provided much of the diet for the master's family as well, and at the same time increased the farm's production of marketable staples. Thus the farm's potential productivity increased significantly with the acquisition of slave labor. That, of course, was the point of slavery in the Old South.[35]

For all the economic obligations slaveownership entailed, it also liberated masters from the heavy reliance on neighbors that was essential to successful yeoman communities. Slaveownership eased the settlement process by fulfilling at least some of the demands for labor that all farmers experienced. Slaves could clear the fields, build the barns, perfect the crafts, and perform the labors that normally impelled a yeoman farmer into cooperation with his neighbors. At the same time, superior access to markets made it easier to purchase inexpensive goods from distant manufacturers rather than from a local class of artisans, craftsmen, and merchants. Just as slave labor eased the settler's reliance on his neighbors, so did the combination of plantation self-sufficiency and dependence on international markets effectively limit the slaveholders' economic links to his own community. The larger the plantation, the more removed it was likely to be from the economic organization of the locality. A Natchez, Mississippi, newspaper editorial published at the height of the depression of the 1840's complained that "the large planters—the one-thousand bale planters—do not contribute most to the prosperity of Natchez. They, for the most part, sell their cotton in Liverpool, buy their wines in London or Havre; their negro clothing in Boston; their plantation implements and supplies in Cincinnati; and their groceries and fancy articles in New Orleans."[36]

This does not mean that slaveholders were thoroughly isolated from their localities. Even the "cotton snobs" socialized with one another. But slavery undermined community attachments in so many ways that contemporary observers could scarcely fail to notice. Neighbors complained about the social isolation of local planters. Slaveholders' wives were tortured by their husbands' incessant readiness to uproot their families and abandon their communities. Travelers were astonished by the high rates of turnover on plantations. And they had good reason to be. Only a small minority of planter families, as few as 20 percent, lived in the same place for more than two decades. In appearances, at least, the master class partook of the presumably American thirst for western lands.[37]

But demographic upheaval was not brought on by an infectious romantic impulse that could spread through whole nations like some cultural contagion. Migration had social roots, economic origins, historical causes. It would be a mistake to assume, for example, that the forces carrying European peasants to industrial America or the pressures pushing New England farmers into the Midwest were the same as those that dragged southern slaveholders across half a continent in less than three-quarters of a century. The reasons for the relentless migration of the slaveholding class lie in the social consequences of slavery itself.

Take away a master's land and he was still a master; take away his slaves and his entire social identity was transformed. The distinction is critical, for while land could be sold, slaves could actually be moved. And so they were—by the tens of thousands. As infamous as the internal migration of slaves across the southern United States undoubtedly was, there was nothing unusual about it. Mass migrations were perfectly emblematic of the peculiar nature of slaves as "property." By definition slavery gave the master the power not simply to dispose of the slave but to transport the slave to and fro at will. This meant that the slaveholders' power, unlike the feudal lord's, was not tied to a specific landed estate.

Slavery required relatively few ties to place and community. As a class the masters had a far greater interest in protecting their slaves than their soils—which the slaveholders in fact exhausted far more than was necessary. Thus slavery not only facilitated migration; it encouraged farming methods that actually spurred movement on. Thomas Cobb explained the process in 1858:

> In a slaveholding State, the greatest evidence of wealth in the planter is the number of his slaves. The most desirable property for a remunerative income, is slaves. The best property to leave to his children, and from which they will part with greatest reluctance, is slaves. Hence, the planter invests his surplus income in slaves. The natural result is, that lands are a secondary consideration. No surplus is left for their improvement. The homestead is valued only so long as the adjacent lands are profitable for cultivation. The planter himself, having no local attachments, his children inherit none. On the contrary, he encourages in them a disposition to seek new lands. His valuable property (his slaves) are easily removed to fresh lands; much more easily than to bring the fertilizing materials to the old. The result is that they, as a class, are never settled. Such a population is almost nomadic. It is useless to seek to excite patriotic emotions in behalf of the land of birth, when self-interest speaks so loudly.[38]

This is not to say that slaveholders were uninterested in land. Far from it. But we must distinguish the sources of their concern for landed property from their interest in chattel slavery. What made land valuable to the master class is what made slavery profitable in the New World: the capitalist demand for consumer goods. Tobacco, rice, sugar, and cotton could be produced without slaves but not without land. Thus the slaveholders' interest in land was intense, yet complex and ambiguous. Slavery tied the fortunes of the master class to land in general, but not to any piece of land in particular. The capitalist market upon which slavery flourished involved crops with certain broad requirements that conditioned the areas most amenable to staple-producing plantations. But slavery held no planter to any particular plantation. If the slaveholders had a strong attachment to land, its source was capitalism rather than slavery. Together, slavery and capitalism simultaneously created and weakened the landed interest of the master class. They made the slave economy both hungry for ever more land and wasteful of whatever land there was. They turned the masters into exuberant expansionists while limiting the areas where slave plantations could flourish.

This was how the black belts developed. They were the logical outcome of thousands of decisions by individual masters to move to areas that had what slaveownership required: access to markets, good-quality soil, decent water, and a well-timed rainy season. For most slaveowners these were not options but necessities. In the absence of canals, railroads, and turnpikes, the westward expansion of the slave economy was necessarily restricted to those areas with ready, natural access to coastal ports. Where a yeoman farmer might search for a region that easily sustained self-sufficiency, the letters of migrating masters reveal an altogether understandable preoccupation with an area's capacity to sustain organized production of cash crops. Because modern slavery had emerged precisely to supply staples to the consuming public, slaveholders needed steady and reliable access to the market.

For all its commercial orientation, however, the black-belt economy was riddled with the paradoxes common to all slave societies. On the one hand, slavery had for centuries been associated with technological and cultural "progress" as well as economic development.[39] The cotton South, for example, depended on the growth of industrial techniques for mass-producing textiles as well as a critical technological breakthrough, the cotton gin, for production of the staple crop itself. The successive ascendance and decline of the various sugar economies—Brazil, Barbados, Jamaica, Cuba—were associated with a series of technological improvements in sugar processing and refining. In a more general way, slavery's ties to the consumer market stimulated the slaveholders' interest in transportation and communications improvements. The antebellum South, for example, promoted the nation's first long-distance telegraph cable, instituted the first transatlantic packet service, and by 1860 boasted one of the most extensive railroad networks on earth.

Yet at the core of this economy was not the unparalleled dynamism of wage-labor capitalism but the distinctive social relationship of master and slave, and this put clear limits on the amount of progress that was possible. While slaves could certainly be put to work in factories, for example, it is doubtful that any slave economy could have sustained an industrial revolution within itself. The mass production of staples benefited from certain key technological improvements, but the impetus for them was the consumer demand emanating from capitalism rather than the intrinsic characteristics of slavery. By itself slavery generated relatively little consumer demand: plantations were more or less self-sufficient and the slaves received no formal compensation for their labors. Thus the slaves, unlike the industrial working class or even the yeoman farmers, provided no significant basis for the growth of a consumer society. Rather, it was slavery's ties to an external market that spurred interest in canals, railroads, and telegraphs. Above all, slavery lacked capitalism's ingenious means for encouraging the development of a work ethic among the laborers, and this, too, could only inhibit the dynamic capacities of the southern economy. It has been plausibly argued that the Old South approached the upper limit of the technological development possible in a slave society. As impressive as the South's "internal improvements" were, they were virtually unique in the history of slave economies.[40]

In the end, physical expansion was the only way the slave economy could grow enough to sustain the social reproduction of the master class. It was possible to introduce more efficient farming techniques that might enhance the productivity of the slave plantations. But given the masters' paramount interest in slaves rather than land, the advantages of reforming agriculture were never as clear to the masters as it was to their critics. Even with such techniques, the productive potential intrinsic to slave labor was probably limited anyway. The indisputable growth of the southern economy before the Civil War, in particular the rise in per capita incomes, depended almost entirely on the expansion of slavery onto new western lands.[41]

It is no surprise, then, that so many of the elements that went into the socialization of young masters were crystallized in the issue of westward expansion. Moving west and establishing a slave plantation became the means by which the sons of the master class reproduced the society of their elders. In 1849, after Phillips Fitzpatrick graduated from school and was unsure of what career to pursue, he solicited the advice of his uncle Alva. Come to Texas, his uncle told the young Alabamian. Get yourself a good piece of range land in a healthy location with plenty of timber and water. "Stick down upon it with some good woman as your wife for without a good wife it is hard to get along and raise every thing," Alva Fitzpatrick continued. "Get as many young negro women as you can. Get as many cows as you can. . . . It is the greatest country for an increase that I have ever saw in my life. I have been hear six years and I have had fifteen negro children born and last year three more young negro women commenced breeding which added seven born last year and five of them is living and doing well." Come out for a visit, he advised his nephew, and if he liked it: "then stick down and attend to the foregoing instructions and in ten or fifteen or twenty years you will do as well as any other man in this or any other country."[42]

If it was possible to synthesize slavery and liberal capitalism into a single cultural tradition, the synthesis was revealed in letters like Fitzpatrick's. The young man could not expect to inherit his father's estate intact, nor did his father have the economic power to hold his adult son at home. In the liberal South the bonds of intergenerational dependence were relatively weak. For all the benefits of a good education and a privileged upbringing, Phillips Fitzpatrick still had to re-create for himself the plantation world of his youth. To accomplish this he had to acquire slaves, but on no particular piece of land. He was therefore free to move west, and there were sound economic reasons for doing so, but he could only settle in an area that could sustain systematic production of marketable staples. As they had done for thousands of young Southerners before him, slavery and liberal capitalism together shaped Fitzpatrick's options as he contemplated his future.

* * *

DURING THE EARLIEST decades of English settlement in seventeenth-century Maryland and Virginia there were far more men than women, infants died in astonishing numbers, and not many colonists lived long or healthy lives. It was all but impossible, in such circumstances, for free men and women to establish economically viable and productive households, and this in turn made the development of stable communities of family farms unusually difficult. But slavery and indentured servitude freed settlers from reliance on the labor of their own families and the cooperation of neighbors. They made permanent colonies possible long before English settlers were able to reproduce themselves naturally, long before the number of women equaled the number of men, long before whites lived enough years to organize secure, productive families. As far back as the seventeenth century, slavery was able to survive where a yeomanry could not.

But even in the eighteenth century, long after family life had stabilized among free settlers, slaveownership remained essential to the economic security of most families. This was evident in the pattern of frontier settlement that emerged as Virginians pushed westward above the fall line and across the Piedmont plateau. Over and over again, the squatters and subsistence farmers who first settled a new area were displaced by more prosperous yeomen and small slaveholders, who together established the community's all-important ties to the market. Those ties in turn made the area attractive to large planters, whose arrival precipitated the out-migration of yeomen farmers. No doubt some of the first settlers became slaveholders; others simply moved further west. But slaveless farms fell into the minority once slavery began to flourish in a newly settled area.[43]

An important pattern was thereby established. In any staple-producing area of the South a growing proportion of slaves and slaveholders was generally an indication of rising land values. The best lands with the surest access to markets were inhabited by slaveholders who could most afford to bid up real-estate values. But high land prices, and in later years the higher taxes that often went with them, made it difficult for those without slaves to settle or remain in such areas. If the ownership of a slave virtually required production for the market, the cost of land in the black belt virtually required the use of slave labor to make farming viable.

The expansion of slavery did not eliminate all yeomen farmers from the black belt, but it radically undermined their significance. Where 50 to 90 percent of the population was enslaved, and where slaveholders owned two out of three farms, yeomen were physically outnumbered and economically overshadowed by the presence of slavery. Slaveless farmers who remained in the black belt had few options. They could purchase or hire slave labor to increase their yearly income, allowing them to meet mortgage and tax payments. Studies of those who remained in the same counties of Texas, Tennessee, and the cotton belt show that between 1850 and 1860 as many as one in four slaveless farmers became slaveholders.[44] Where the purchase price was too high, slave rental was sometimes easy enough to make the use of such labor far more common than ownership statistics indicate, indeed close to universal in parts of the black belt.[45] Without slave labor, black-belt yeomen tended to isolate themselves on the least expensive tracts, generally those areas with the most restricted access to water and transport facilities, further limiting their ability to produce for the market. Finally, and perhaps most commonly, slaveless farmers could respond to the high price of land and labor in the black belt by leaving the area altogether—and thousands, perhaps millions, of slaveless farmers did precisely that.[46]

Throughout the eighteenth and nineteenth centuries, the restless expansion of the slave economy continually undermined the communities of squatters and smallholders who opened up new territories to the west. But beginning in the 1770's, when the settlement line reached the Appalachian foothills, slavery's expansion was diverted and permanent yeoman settlement was possible for the first time. Mountainous terrain and colder climates precluded the production of marketable staples, making such areas unattractive to most slaveholding settlers. Relatively poor soils and inadequate rainfall in large parts of North Carolina and the pine barrens of southern Georgia similarly inhibited slavery's expansion into those areas during the late eighteenth century. Only then and only in those areas could yeomen farmers establish enduring communities in the South. Thus, in the fifty years centered at 1800 the southern yeomanry came into existence, and with that the distinction between "black" and "white" belts was established.

Not that this stopped slavery's expansion. On the contrary, the black belts grew conspicuously in those same decades, crossing the mountain barrier and leapfrogging halfway across America, well beyond the Mississippi River, in scarcely two generations. But before the transportation revolution that was only beginning in the early nineteenth century, the expansion of slavery bypassed large areas of the South that were too distant from the market for slave-based agriculture to be viable. The result was a demographic pattern familiar in the history of slave societies. In 1820, 70 percent of the white families in Orange County, Virginia, owned slaves. Thirty years later, 72.2 percent of the farms in the eastern cotton belt had at least one slave. Even in the states further west that had only recently been settled by small farmers, 54.3 percent of the cotton-belt farms had slaves in 1850. By contrast, fewer than one in four free farm families owned slaves in upcountry Carroll County, Georgia. Piedmont South Carolina was similarly divided. Where over 60 percent of the farms in the Laurens district of the Lower Piedmont had slaves, the proportion fell to 35 percent in Upper Piedmont Spartanburg. Across the South slaveholders and yeomen occupied different parts of the same world.[47]

Yeomen farmers were not, however, an undifferentiated mass huddled together in a single location. Clearly there were always slaveless farmers in the black belt, although in most cases they either were young men who would eventually move up into the slaveholding class, or were geographically marginalized in the least productive parts of the black belt itself. Beyond the black belt, in the pine barrens and scrub lands throughout the South, squatters and small farmers eked out a meager subsistence on the poorest soils and in conditions of more or less permanent destitution. In the most isolated mountain hollows there were also small communities of subsistence or semi-subsistence farmers who maintained hardly any regular contact with the outside world. By contrast, there were sober settlements of pious Germans who set up well-organized and relatively disciplined communities of slaveless farmers across the South, with noteworthy numbers in the Southwest.

But as a political force with a distinctive social and economic identity, the upcountry yeomen were easily the most important. They congregated in the foothills along the eastern slopes of the Appalachians from Maryland to Georgia and on the western slopes in Kentucky and Tennessee, in the hill counties of northern Alabama and Mississippi, and in scattered patches of rolling hills in central Texas, parts of Louisiana, and much of Missouri. We call these areas "upcountry" for reasons that are partly geographical and partly social. Located largely in hilly and sometimes mountainous areas, most upcountry farms had no slaves, and most of those with slaves had only a few. When planters appeared in upcountry districts, they were invariably located along the most navigable river, near the best road, closest to town. Even in the upcountry, slaveholders, small and large, tended to produce more market crops than did yeomen. But for the most part, large plantations were impractical. In the end slaveholders were unable to imprint their highly commercialized way of life on the character of yeoman society as a whole. Rather, upcountry society remained rooted in the family farm and the self-sufficient community.

Settled and resettled relatively late in southern history, the upcountry assumed much of its character from the exigencies of frontier life. Isolated by distance and terrain from the major marketing centers, yeomen organized their families and communities to ensure that subsistence needs were met first. Things were much different in the black belt. Whereas slaveholders produced first for the market and tried in addition to cultivate subsistence crops, yeomen farmers produced first for their own subsistence and tried in addition to cultivate marketable commodities. The point can be carried too far, for there were always shadings and variations that make such sharp lines seem unnecessarily rigid. For example, in 1850, when the slave economy had largely pen-

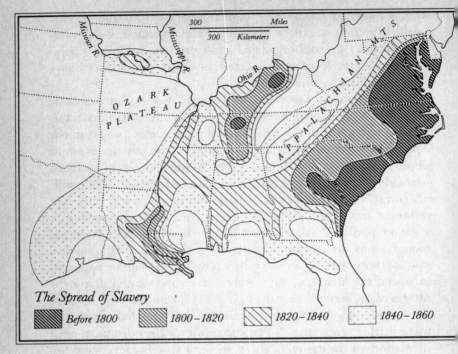

The Spread of Slavery

| Before 1800 | 1800–1820 | 1820–1840 | 1840–1860 |

etrated upcountry South Carolina, slightly more than half of the slaveless farmers in the area produced at least one bale of cotton, indicating fairly widespread if not very deep ties to the market. In the same areas many more small slaveholders—70 percent—grew cotton for sale, while approximately 90 percent of the planters did.[48] There was a reason why yeomen so often referred to their market crops as "surpluses." The word made little sense among planters in the black belt.

Many of the characteristics that repelled slaveholders from the upcountry actually attracted slaveless farmers. Heavily wooded areas may have been impractical for plantation settlements, but for yeomen farmers they provided lumber for building homes and barns, fuel for warmth, and a natural source of wildlife, which made subsistence much easier in the critical early years of settlement. Free-range animal husbandry—large droves of unfenced hogs in particular—was possible in the relatively cool, shaded woodlands of the upcountry, and it provided yeomen farmers with an inexpensive source of food and a marketable commodity that required very little expenditure of labor.[49]

For labor was the precious element in the organization of yeoman society. Yeoman households were shaped by a careful division of labor based on both gender and age. Women and children were critical to the economic well-being of the yeoman farm. Without slave labor, nearly 90 percent of yeoman women did their own household chores, whereas under 10 percent of plantation mistresses did. By sewing, tending the dairy animals, cultivating fruit trees and vegetable gardens, and a variety of other activities, yeoman women provided between one-third and one-half of the family's subsistence needs. During Isaac Griffith's boyhood his mother worked "in the house sutch as cooking carding spining and weaving and washing. Thare [were] 14 in the family," Griffith remembered several decades later, and "she did not have any servant to help her."[50] By bearing and rearing large numbers of children, women assured the stability of the yeoman family cycle, for as they grew, children added steadily to the labor pool on the farm and also ensured security for their parents in old age.

Because wives and daughters provided so many of the family's subsistence needs, husbands and sons were able to devote more time and energy to clearing the land and constructing the farm buildings during the early years of the family cycle. Without sons to assist him, any one farmer could cultivate only a limited number of acres. George Washington Lewis remembered that as a boy on his father's farm he "chopped, plowed, hoed, cradled, reaped, mowed and bound sheaves, in fact all kinds of work necessary on a farm and lots of it. Split rails, built fences, log roled and danced with the girls at the quiltings."[51] As sons matured and as more acres were cleared, the family's ability to devote more labor to the production of marketable surpluses increased.

In such circumstances self-sufficiency could assure the family's prosperity. "My farm gave me and my whole family a good living on the produce of it," explained a backwoods farmer from South Carolina in the early nineteenth century, "and left me, one year with another, one hundred and fifty silver dollars, *for I never spent more than ten dollars a year*, which was for salt, nails and the like. Nothing to wear, eat or drink was purchased, as my farm provided all. With this saving, I put money to interest, bought cattle, fatted and sold them, and made great profit."[52] "Profit" of this sort tended to peak just before children left to form households of their own. This in turn allowed the yeomen to secure land for their children, once again facilitating the social reproduction of the yeomanry itself.

It was unlikely that at any point in this life cycle the yeoman farm was truly self-sufficient. Some essentials—"salt, nails and the like"—could only be purchased at a store. While family farmers produced primarily to meet their subsistence needs, few of them were able to meet all of those needs themselves. Instead, they relied on a pattern of cooperation with neighbors that began with, and indeed was most critical in, the earliest years of a community's settlement. Daniel Hundley saw this as evidence of an instinctive gregariousness, but he inadvertently noted the practical significance of communal activities when he observed that birthdays and weddings were not the most common occasion for social gatherings. "Much more frequently it is a corn-husking, or the everlasting quilting."[53] In Beally, Tennessee, one yeoman farmer remembered some time later, the neighbors "seem to take delight in helping each other sutch as lay railings cornshucking and house raising they tried to help each other all they could and dancet all night."[54] Barn raisings, the sharing of tools and draught animals, communal grazing rights, an informal welfare system that cared for neighbors in distress: all of these eased the process of frontier settlement and at the same time set the tone of community life for years to come.

It was at the community level that yeoman self-sufficiency was most nearly achieved. In upcountry areas, especially those most recently settled, each household formed part of a local social division of labor. Artisans and craftsmen specialized in the production of goods that no one family could easily provide for itself. Farmers in turn were able to specialize in crops that could be traded, sometimes through barter but more often through the local merchant, to meet the subsistence needs of the family.[55]

Community self-sufficiency had contradictory implications for yeoman society. While it protected farmers from the insecurity of the market at a time when they were most vulnerable, it also facilitated the development of a local economy to the point where a community could enter the market on a regular and orderly basis. Store owners, merchants, bankers—such people emerged to meet local needs, but they also made it easier for farmers to produce for markets beyond the locality. Distance from or limited access to such markets could inhibit the commercialization of upcountry communities for a long time after settlement had concluded. Even the desire to produce surpluses could not, by itself, overcome the obstacles to market integration that yeomen farmers often confronted. Still, there was a potential for dynamism built into the yeoman way of life. The upcountry may have provided uniquely for the subsistence needs of the earliest settlers, but once a community was established the spartan demands of frontier life receded somewhat. As more lands were cleared and as sons reached early adulthood, the family's wealth grew along with its increased capacity to produce surpluses beyond subsistence needs. At the same time, local merchants and artisans made commercial exchanges easier.[56]

With the development of reliable transportation and communication facilities, farm families often found that store-bought merchandise was preferable to goods manufactured at home. By freeing up energies devoted to home manufacture, yeoman families were able to devote more time to the production of marketable commodities. But the same logic transformed the kinds of crops that could be produced. Once steady and reliable access to the market was established, it was often in the family's economic interest to specialize more intensively in cash crops. When the Western and Atlantic Railroad was built through the Georgia upcountry in the 1850's, yeomen farmers substantially increased the amount of cotton they grew for sale, while decreasing the amount of corn they cultivated and the number of hogs they tended.[57] Given the opportunity, Georgia yeomen quickly expanded their production for the market long before economic hardship and an exploitative credit system forced them to do so.

By increasing their production for the market, yeoman families changed forever the way they dealt with the other members of their local community. The goods and services once provided by local artisans and craftsmen, the crops once traded with neighbors, could now be purchased through a local merchant whose supplies were increasingly shipped from distant manufacturers. As children aged and the need to provide for future generations loomed larger, the family's continuity depended on its ability to purchase more land, and this pushed smallholders still further into the market. From the yeoman farmer's perspective, then, the increased wealth available through more specialized production of cash crops was not designed to undermine a traditional way of life but to preserve it.

Nevertheless, upcountry communities were substantially transformed by their gradual integration into the market. The process was the product of no single decision, no cataclysmic event. Like Frederick Jackson Turner's ever-unfolding frontier, the transformation of the yeomanry was a process that cannot be fixed with chronological specificity. Long after some communities had been thoroughly commercialized, other yeomen settlements were only being established. For some yeomen, market integration began in the earliest decades of the nineteenth century; others remained isolated for another hundred years. But the process of transformation was built into the logic of upcountry society and was fueled by the expansion of slavery and the spread of transport and communications facilities in the decades prior to the Civil War.

A way of life that demanded cooperation and an overriding concern for subsistence was, at the same time, an ideal vehicle for the primitive accumulation of wealth among the yeomanry. And wealth—the combined value of lands, buildings, livestock, and implements—turns out to be a reliable predictor of how much energy a farmer was likely to devote to cash rather than subsistence crops. In upcountry Georgia, for example, farms that reached a wealth "threshold" of $2,500 tended to shift from subsistence to market-oriented operations. Thus, once a community's ties to the market were secure and once a family's wealth reached a certain point, it was common for yeomen farmers to swing away from their traditional subsistence orientation.[58]

It is no wonder that contemporary observers and historians have offered such different characterizations of the southern yeomen. In their self-sufficiency, community orientation, and seeming aversion to the market, the yeomanry shared many of the characteristics of a traditional peasantry. But in the cycle of accumulation, the readiness to produce for the market when the opportunity arose, and the commitment to private property, the yeoman farmer had all the earmarks of a frontier capitalist. Daniel Hundley, writing in 1860, solved the problem by distinguishing the sturdy yeomen from what he called "poor white trash," whose affection for the "hilly and mountainous regions," subsistence agriculture, and limited participation in the cash economy were sufficient in his mind to justify the popular charge of "laziness." Though they owned their own land, Hundley nevertheless stressed those characteristics he least admired to make the poor whites seem different from the yeoman farmer. They had excessively large families, they were prejudiced against "the moneyed men," they were superstitious, and they voted for Democrats.[59]

But only three years earlier Hinton Rowan Helper had taken all the same evidence and, setting himself up as spokesman for the beleaguered yeomanry, turned it against the slaveholders. If the South was poor, if its small farmers lived at a lower standard than did the North's, the fault was the slaveholders'. Yeomen farmers did not want to live in ignorance and poverty, Helper insisted, they simply had no choice in the South. For slavery inhibited the South's economic development, thereby limiting the economic opportunities available to the small farmers. Yeomen "want Bibles, brooms, buckets and books, and we go to the North," he complained.

> [W]e want pens, ink, paper, wafers and envelopes, and we go to the North; we want shoes, hats, handkerchiefs, umbrellas and pocket knives, and we go to the North; we want furniture, crockery, glassware and pianos, and we go to the North; we want toys, primers, school books, fashionable apparel, machinery, medicines, tombstones, and a thousand other things, and

we go to the North for them all. Instead of keeping our money in circulation at home, by patronizing our own mechanics, manufacturers, and laborers, we send it all away to the North, and there it remains; it never falls into our hands again.[60]

In his eagerness for commercial development, Helper represented one side of yeoman culture: its readiness to participate in the anxious consumerism of capitalist expansion. In his admiration for their frugality, their "gregarious" sociability, and their fierce independence, Hundley stressed another side. Moreover, he saw no vast cultural divide that might justify the kind of class war between slaveholders and yeomen that Helper called for. For yeoman culture was no less ambiguous than yeoman society. A complex bundle of paradoxes and contradictions, yeoman culture reflected the power of tradition as well as the inroads of slavery and liberal capitalism.

Yeoman family life, for example, was both more egalitarian and more traditional than family life among the slaveholders. The father continued to define the family, and the family itself remained the basic unit of production in upcountry society. But wives continued to occupy a strategic position at the center of the family's economic productivity. Long after the demographic transition had struck the North, and even as black-belt planters reduced the size of their families, upcountry women continued to bear large numbers of children. Given his continued dependence on the labor of his sons, the typical yeoman father sought to exercise extensive control over his patrimony. By carefully regulating the disposition of the family's lands, yeoman fathers could retain control over their children, particularly their sons, until their mid-twenties. Far from rearing their children to individual autonomy, yeoman society depended heavily on the perpetuation of intergenerational dependency.

Yeoman culture was as intensely communal as it was family-centered. Indeed, the distinction between the two was meaningless in the context of upcountry society. Without community-wide cooperation the security of every family was jeopardized. When yeomen farmers moved they did so as communities rather than as individuals. When they married they intermarried within their community, further enhancing the sense of a continuum from household to locality.

Yet all of these features of yeoman culture—its traditional families, its community orientation, its sense of continuity between the generations—were matched by an equally powerful commitment to the independence of the yeoman farmer himself. No one owned the farmer who owned his own land; no one but he claimed the fruits of his labor. It was precisely this independence that in theory made the self-interest of the yeoman farmer indistinguishable from the greater interest of the commonwealth. Dependent only on his own and his family's labor, jealous of his property rights, his stake in society, the yeoman farmer was, ideally, untouched by the temptations of corruption. Here was the repository of civic virtue, the independent republican citizen in whose hands the fate of liberty rested securely. Southern yeomen thereby embraced individualism by harnessing it, just as they legitimized the pursuit of self-interest by fusing it to the community interest. What was good for the yeomen was good for the polity.

No less characteristic was the fusion of property rights and egalitarianism in upcountry political culture. The yeomanry's communal ways were always balanced by a powerful devotion to the absolute property rights of the individual farmer. But where the combination of abundant land and a limited labor supply inhibited gross concentrations of wealth, the traditional scheme of a republic of freeholders assumed unprecedented egalitarian implications. For many yeomen, therefore, property rights functioned less as a defense of concentrated wealth than as an assertion of the political equality of independent farmers. Furthermore, private property rights were a limitation on the concentrated power of the state, for they defined the homestead as a sacred preserve into which no governmental authority could intrude.

Upcountry culture preserved classical republican fears of debt, of concentrated power, of any economic or political forces that threatened the independence of the yeoman freeholder. But these fears carried no automatic antipathy to commerce itself. Even in

Jeffersonian theory, republics were commercial societies and as such were more "civilized" than pure subsistence economies. But as many republicans understood it, commerce was not the arena of an atomized *Homo economicus*. Rather, economic independence facilitated the fusion of the commercial interests of the individual and the community—hence the civilizing function of the market. Commerce "is a pacific system," Thomas Paine wrote in 1792, "operating to cordialise mankind, by rendering Nations, as well as individuals useful to each other."

Thus yeoman republicanism stood at the vortex of a great ideological transition. It was at once an embrace of and a reaction against the explosion of commercial activity that accompanied the rise of western capitalism. Republican ideology offered one of the earliest defenses of rational self-interest as a way of organizing both the polity and the economy, and in so doing immeasurably advanced the frontiers of liberal individualism. But by tying self-interest so firmly to landed interest, republicanism also preserved the more traditional doctrine of the "stake in society"—the conviction that only those who freely possessed a physical piece of the nation were suited to participation in the polity. Republicanism was at the vanguard of bourgeois ideology, but at the same time it ignited a series of ideological flares warning of the dangers posed by the spread of concentrated power in any form—railroads, banks, government, and perhaps slavery.

In culture, as in social organization, upcountry yeomen were distinct from black-belt slaveholders in significant ways. Where the slaveholders settled lands that were most immediately amenable to market production, yeomen preferred wooded hill counties that best met their basic subsistence needs. Where slavery subtly altered the roles of men, women, and children in black-belt families, slaveless yeomen maintained a more traditional division of labor grounded in gender and age. Where slavery isolated the family farm from the local community while tying it to the international economy, yeomen farmers remained dependent on the traditional resources of the community for as long as access to national and international markets remained uncertain. By concentrating the master class in the black belt and isolating the yeomanry in the upcountry, slavery facilitated the convergence of regional and social distinctions.

For all of the forces that kept yeomen and slaveholders separated, however, there were countervailing forces that pulled them together, creating an explosive attraction of mutually antagonistic societies. Part of the attraction grew out of the yeomen farmers' desire to produce surpluses for the market. But there were more powerful social pressures at work. As frontier yeoman communities developed to the point where surpluses could be produced and ties to distant markets established, those same communities rapidly became attractive to slaveholding farmers. For the slave economy was constantly pushed toward expansion onto new lands that were cheaper and more productive than older regions. Thus the expansionistic slave economy and prosperous yeoman settlements had a magnet-like attraction to one another, an attraction that eventually threatened the stability of southern politics.

Commercial interests in the upcountry often clamored for internal improvements as vociferously as did black-belt leaders. But the progress of the transportation revolution in the South was closely linked to the political power and economic fortunes of the master class. Turnpikes, canals, and railroads required at least government charters and, in the South, government funds—the bulk of which were provided by slaveholders who were interested in the expansion of the slave economy. Thus the spread of slavery into the upcountry depended upon the activity of government in behalf of commercial interests. Taxes had to be raised, corporations chartered, banks created—all of this by legislatures dominated by the slaveholding interest. The process proceeded in fits and starts, depending largely on the fortunes of the slave economy, which depended in turn on the strength of the international market. When cotton demand was strong, as in the 1830's and 1850's, state and local governments pressed forward with dozens of "internal improvements." During the protracted depression of the 1840's, however, virtually all such projects were terminated. Nevertheless, by 1860 the slave South had one of the largest and most sophisticated transportation and communication networks on earth, greatly facilitating the continued expansion of the slave economy.

This had ominous consequences for the yeomanry, if only because the slaveholders "gentrified" every neighborhood they moved into. Land prices in counties settled by slaveholders quickly rose beyond the means of most slaveless newcomers. Where taxes climbed along with land values, the slave economy further inhibited yeoman settlement. But the presence of slavery was much more than a sign that the region now had access to the roads and credit facilities that could make slave-based farming profitable. Precisely because it facilitated self-sufficiency on individual farms and isolation from the local economy, slavery also tended to break down the community of farmers, artisans, and mechanics upon which yeomen depended. Directly or indirectly, the expansion of the slave economy threatened much that was basic to the yeoman way of life: the organization of families, the social structure of local communities, substantial economic independence.

The surest way for a yeoman to survive the economic pressures of the encroaching black belt was to purchase a slave, for slave-ownership greatly enhanced a farmer's capacity to produce for the market. But by the 1850's slave prices had risen to new highs, putting ownership beyond the reach of more and more farmers. The proportion of slaveholders in the free population, which had been declining steadily for at least a generation, fell by 20 percent in the last decade before the Civil War. Thus the one means by which yeomen farmers might have been able to protect themselves against the insecurities of market integration in the South was increasingly closed off to them.

For southern yeomen this was no mere replay of the process of commercialization that spread across rural America in the nineteenth century. For the market came to the slave South without the accompanying opportunities for economic survival that allowed northern farmers to develop a prosperous relationship with the growing urban and industrial centers. There were important signs of early industrial development in the antebellum South, but the process could only go so far in a slave economy. Thus, while slavery's expansion threatened the independence of the yeoman farmer, it did not, like northern factories and cities, offer the compensation of a booming market for a variety of cash crops, many of which could be produced in huge quantities by a single farmer thanks to new developments in farm machinery. For a southern yeoman, market integration most often meant producing cotton or tobacco. In such cases cultivation was substantially unmechanized, and the slaveholders had the advantage of superior resources in land and labor. Thus slavery set in motion a process of commercialization that exposed yeomen farmers to all of the risks of cash-crop agriculture with few of its rewards. Not surprisingly, as slavery pushed its way across the southern frontier, it fueled the suspicions not only of concerned Northerners but of slaveless farmers below the Mason-Dixon Line as well.

On the eve of the Civil War many slaveless farmers could look back to a time when the market had been a less powerful force in their lives. They were more integrated than ever into the world of commerce, but they had no slaves to make market production easier and few cities and factories to generate steady consumer demand for food crops. Yeomen farmers had seen their families become more dependent on store-bought merchandise. They were growing more crops for sale than they once had. They went to the bank more often, handled cash more frequently, and were more concerned than before with the price cotton could command in New York or New Orleans. Across the South there were more wage laborers, more tenant farmers, more immigrant workers than ever before. The dual economy was breaking down, yeoman independence was being undermined, and dependent labor was becoming more common among free men and women.[61]

ITS BASIS in the traditional family, its community orientation, its suspicious stance toward concentrated economic and political power, the priority it gave to the relative safety of subsistence agriculture—all of these marked the southern yeomanry's ties to a pre-industrial world and its affinities with peasant culture. But in its embrace of individualism, of political and economic self-interest, in its equation of commerce with cultural superiority and its concern to increase its marketable surpluses, the southern yeomanry placed itself within the more modern setting of liberal capitalism. With the commercialization of the upcountry, yeomen farmers were less a peasantry than a petite bourgeoisie. And like the lower middle class throughout nineteenth-century Europe and America, the yeomanry's politics were an unstable mixture of radical populism and bourgeois individualism. Southern yeomen could be as fearful of the propertyless masses beneath them as they were disdainful of "aristocrats" of wealth—slaveholders or capitalists, they saw little difference—above them.

Marx had no patience for such ambivalence. "The proletariat alone is a really revolutionary class," he insisted. "The lower middle classes, the small manufacturers, the shopkeepers, the artisans, the peasants, all these fight against the bourgeoisie in order to save from extinction their existence as parts of the middle class . . . they are reactionary, for they try to roll back the wheel of history." Historians have been no less categorical. Faced with a yeomanry that lashed out in contradictory directions, careening wildly from radical democracy to racist paranoia, from hair-brained panaceas to trenchant critiques of concentrated economic power, scholars have habitually chosen to emphasize either the radical or the reactionary elements, but rarely both. No account of antebellum politics can be complete, however, if it ignores the fundamental ambivalence at the core of yeoman culture.

In this, at least, the yeomen were not so different from the slaveholders. The masters also lived in two distinct yet inseparable worlds, grounded in the ancient social relationship of master and slave, brought back to life by the revolutionary force of liberal capitalism. The slave economy was at once intensely commercial and resistant to technological development. The master class was drawn inescapably into the international economic order, yet lived in the rural isolation of the black belt. The slaveholders' power was grounded in a relationship that systematically undermined the slave family, individualized relations within the master's family, yet preserved the family farm as the organizing unit of economic life. Libertarian tyrants, enlightened patriarchs, frightened Whigs—the slaveholders spun out their world in a series of bewildering contradictions.

A culture with so wide an array of tangents had more than enough points at which slaveholders and nonslaveholders could intersect. The centrality of the family farm, the fear of debt, the devotion to absolute property—these were substantial elements capable of politically unifying most free Southerners. And the American Revolution demonstrated the historical significance of such shared convictions. Consider, for example, meritocracy. It was, for all its contradictory implications, a profoundly significant point of agreement among free men in the South. It located masters and yeomen alike in a liberal world that began from the simple but all-important conviction that a social hierarchy grounded in hereditary legal privilege was fundamentally illegitimate.

By the late eighteenth century meritocracy was something all but the most hardened reactionaries in the South took for granted. "To talk of a man's being born a Gentleman is as inconsistent as to say he was born a fiddler, and with a fiddle in his arms," the *Virginia Gazette* declared in 1769; "no man deserves the appellation *a gentleman* until he has done something to merit it."[62] With a clear sense of a contrasting English and European world, southern writers distinguished their own vision of the social order. "Monarchies and aristocracies, being founded in the principle of distributing wealth by law, can only subsist by frauds and deceptions . . . ," John Taylor wrote in 1818, "but in genuine republics, founded on the principle of leaving wealth to be distributed by merit and industry, these treacheries of government are treasons against nations."[63]

A later generation carried the rhetoric of meritocracy deep into the mainstream of southern political culture. But by the time Jacksonian Democrats squared off against the southern Whigs, the unity of their assumptions was overshadowed by the intrinsic ambiguity of meritocracy itself. To the Democrats, it was an egalitarian ideal. The only privileges recognized at birth were male gender and a white skin, but among white men no laws recognized an artificial social hierarchy. The only legitimate distinctions were those of talent and merit. All white men were, after all, created equal. Like Jefferson before them, Jacksonians agreed that this made some degree of inequality among white males unavoidable. "Distinctions in society will always exist under every just government," Andrew Jackson admitted. "Equality of talents, of education, or of wealth can not be produced by human institutions." Nevertheless, Jackson preferred to put his emphasis elsewhere. "In the full enjoyment of the gifts of Heaven and the fruits of superior industry, economy, and virtue," he declared, "every man is equally entitled to protection by law." Like-minded politicians across the South stressed the same thing. "Place all your citizens upon a footing of perfect equality as to their political rights," Louisiana's attorney general declared, so as to "promote the well-being and happiness of all."[64]

This emphasis on the egalitarian implications of meritocracy separated the Jacksonian Democrats from the Whigs—and even from Thomas Jefferson—in several ways. Pass a law granting a corporate charter or setting up a tariff and somewhere a Jacksonian was bound to smell an artificial preference, a legal privilege, an aristocracy in the making. Reserve public office as a reward for the most successful men, and the Democrats cried élitism. Instead, Andrew Johnson hoped that "the offices of this nation . . . from the President down to the lowest in the gift of the people, will be filled with the farmers and mechanics of the country."[65]

The Whigs saw the world differently. For them it was precisely the meritocratic ideal that justified the social hierarchy—what Jefferson's generation called the "aristocracy of talent." Where the Democrats set their sights on the commonality of free men, the Whigs put the talented and successful individual at the center of their vision. Let all men start out on an equal footing, the Whigs conceded, but always let the best men win. To the talented belonged the spoils—the wealth, the success, the public recognition, the political offices. In a meritocracy, the Whigs believed, the differences among men were not the artificial impositions of an overactive state; they were the products of nature itself. From here it took little effort to reverse the causal flow of meritocratic logic: differences of talent did not produce distinctions in society, but rather social distinctions implicitly proved that there must be differences in native talent. So where Jacksonians culled from the meritocratic ideal its most egalitarian implications, the Whigs emphasized its more élitist undertones.

Relatively undisturbed by the existence of social inequality, southern Whigs were similarly sanguine about the role of the state in fostering such distinctions. For them the ideal public policy was not one that avoided the odor of inequity, but one that enhanced every individual's opportunity to use his talents to the fullest, to rise up the proverbial social ladder. To that end the southern Whigs advocated government activism in behalf of economic development, "sound" banking policies to ensure fiscal stability, and social programs that might bring to perfection the myriad native talents of each individual.

Even within the shared assumptions of a liberal political culture, then, there was plenty of room for significant ideological disagreement over the most basic issues of equality, economic development, and the power of the state. And indeed, unity was the last thing contemporaries would have noticed about antebellum society. Foreign observers, northern visitors, and southern travelers were agreed in their impression that profound differences separated free Southerners from one another, and they were nearly unanimous in the conviction that the divisions more or less followed the lines separating upcountry yeomen from black-belt slaveholders.

The tensions between slaveholders and yeomen burst into full-scale political warfare in the early 1830's. Having given nearly unanimous support to Andrew Jackson, the slaveholders quickly and almost as unanimously repudiated his efforts to break the ties between the federal government and the banking and transportation industries. As soon as the Whigs organized themselves as the anti-Jackson party, black-belt voters in most southern states began to cast their ballots for the Whigs in overwhelming numbers. Upcountry districts, with a few noteworthy exceptions, remained loyal to the Jacksonian Democrats. For a generation the battle between Whigs and Democrats raged with ferocious intensity across most of the South. More than anywhere else in ante-bellum America, class differences virtually defined southern political culture.

To be sure, the political split between slaveholders and non-slaveholders was rarely neat and never absolute. Class divisions were frequently obscured by shared convictions, conflicting impulses, changes over time, and always, exceptions to the rule. Nevertheless, what remains unusual, almost unique, about politics in the Old South is not its predictable obscurities and inconsistencies but its unusual clarity. With the slaves politically silenced and with a relatively homogeneous white population, racial, ethnic, and religious tensions were unlikely to mask fundamental class divisions. Thus slavery generated regional divisions that were uniquely exposed by the representative system of government embedded in the liberal state. It was as if the very ambiguity of the relationship between slaveholders and yeomen farmers had actually intensified their political animosities.

But slavery itself became the major dividing line in southern politics only indirectly, in much the same way that it became the chief source of division in national politics. In both cases it surfaced less as a moral conflict between supporters and opponents of slavery as such than as a political conflict over slavery's most visible consequences. At the national level the slavery issue erupted in fights over the power of the Supreme Court, the distribution of western lands, and the rights of states to guarantee due process to fugitive slaves. In the South, slavery provoked major battles over the disproportionate power of the old plantation districts, property qualifications for voting and officeholding, internal improvements, and the growing power of banks, railroads, and the state. And in most southern states these issues revealed a clear pattern of sectionalism, dividing black-belt districts dominated by slaveholding farms from heavily white counties where slaveless yeomen were in the majority.

While slavery and the liberal state obscured the social basis of the slaveholders' political power, it could not mask the reality of their power. The slaveholders' disproportionate influence seemed most insidiously maintained through the unelected offices, malapportioned legislatures, and franchise restrictions retained in many southern state constitutions dating from the late eighteenth century. But the strength slaveholders garnered from the preservation of undemocratic political structures merely added insult to the injury they inflicted as the advocates of active government in behalf of entrenched economic interests. Democratic government and economic development, the two great issues of politics in the Jacksonian South, were in fact one issue: the distribution of power among free men.

That these were issues fought out throughout the United States in the first half of the nineteenth century suggests once again the inescapable influence of the larger political context upon the South. But as always slavery altered the meaning and significance of every conflict that fell within the scope of southern society. Only in the South did democratic reform pit slaveholders against nonslaveholders; only in the South did economic development divide the black belt from the upcountry. Only in the South did every major issue of antebellum politics become, at some point, a test of slavery's strength. In most of the debates over democratic reform, economic development, or state power, sooner or later the issue of slavery showed up.

It appeared, for example, in the struggles for democratization in the most conservative southern states along the eastern seaboard. In Virginia, where the revolutionary constitution preserved the legislative domination of the tidewater planters, western reformers were periodically treated to lectures on the danger democracy posed to the slaveholding interest in the east. Abel Upshur's conservative pronouncements at the 1829–30 constitutional convention reveal the paradoxical dilemma of a slaveholding class dependent for its strength on the kinds of protection afforded by the liberal constitution. Paper guarantees alone were an inadequate protection of the slaveholders' *"peculiar* property," Upshur argued. The interests of the slaveholding minority in the east demanded that the state constitution give as much weight to *"property"* as it does to "persons." Thus Upshur fitted his resistance to democracy into the ideological framework made familiar by the Federalists a generation earlier. The function of the liberal state was to protect the property rights of the individual against the tyranny of the majority, and that included property rights in slaves.[66]

Inevitably, democratic reformers turned Upshur's logic against itself, claiming that slavery's security was in fact threatened by the tidewater's élitism. "Let it once be openly avowed and adopted as a principle of your Constitution," Chapman Johnson warned, "that the price . . . the Western people must pay for the protection of your slaves, is the surrender of their power in the Government, and you render that property hateful to them in the extreme, and hold out to them the strongest of all possible temptations to make constant war upon it."[67] Upcountry politicians were incensed by black-belt resistance to the elimination of property requirements for voting and officeholding or to reapportionment of the state legislatures. "I deny that this inequality, in the number of slaves East and West, constitutes any sound reason for giving to the east the preponderance of power in the legislature," Zachariah Jacob declared at Virginia's "Reform Convention" of 1850. "I ask if slave property is entitled to any other consideration in this particular, than any other property is. . . . Stript of its verbiage and reduced to its practical bearing," he continued, "what does this argument that you must have control of the government, because of your slaves, come to? Is it not this, and this only, that we of the West must agree to make ourselves slaves, that you may defend yours?"[68] Thus, while democratic reforms entered southern politics at the same time they did in the North (and with many of the same rhetorical themes attached), slavery shaped the structure of the debate and raised the stakes involved.

The slaveholders had placed themselves in a political bind. They understood that slavery's legality rested on positive laws enacted by legislatures, and that as such slavery was vulnerable to democratic assault. But the more they tied their opposition to democratic reform to the defense of slavery the more they subjected slavery to the very assaults they feared would undermine it. "It is repugnant to the true principles of democracy," a Louisiana politician insisted, "to say that a farmer without slaves, working on his own farm, should have less weight in the government than the rich proprietor adjoining his little farm, who had a hundred negroes."[69] Talk that way often enough and at least some slaveholders were bound to start worrying.

If the slaveholders eventually accommodated themselves to political democracy, the pill was made easier to swallow by the democratic reformers' own accommodation to slavery. Out of conflict an ideological consensus was born. Gradually, then repeatedly, the theme of democracy and slavery was elaborated and extended until it became a staple of proslavery ideology in the Old South. Slavery and democracy were not merely compatible, reformers argued—they were complementary. Indeed, they reinforced each other. A Louisiana reformer invoked this line of reasoning in an argument for the elimination of suffrage restrictions. "Elevate every freeman in the state to an equal participation in its government," he argued, and this would establish "the broad political distinction between him and the slave . . . you will raise a wall of fire kindled from the united souls of freemen, around our state and its institutions, against the diabolical machinations of abolitionism."[70]

Trumpeting such themes, the slaveholders bowed to the pressures for democratic reform and hoped for the best. Slave states admitted to the union after 1800 had few of the offending restrictions on who could vote and hold office and how legislative seats were to be apportioned. Alabama, Tennessee, Kentucky, and Texas all included universal white manhood suffrage and proportional representation in their earliest constitutions. Over time the legislatures were regularly reapportioned on the basis of free or voting population, depriving the black belt of any advantages to be gained by counting slaves. By the 1840's the Whig party abandoned its overt hostility to democratic reform in most parts of the South. This was only common sense, for, as one planter's son pointed out many years later, "The slave holders could not get their desires on election days and public gatherings without the aid of the non slave holders."[71]

Democratic reform remained an issue separating upcountry districts from the black belts only on the eastern seaboard. And even there the conservatives suffered significant losses as class tensions heightened in the 1850's. In Virginia, the 1850 convention substantially reapportioned the legislature and eliminated most of the franchise restrictions that had long angered the yeoman-dominated counties in the west. In North Carolina, years of struggle between the western upcountry and the slave counties of the east finally produced an equal-suffrage amendment in 1855. In South Carolina and Georgia, secession itself brought the final transition from appointive to elective offices and the elimination of the notorious three-fifths clause that had long preserved the domination of the black belts.

But democratic reform was hardly the only issue that stoked the fires of social division in southern politics. On the contrary, as the commercialization of the upcountry proceeded apace, debate raged over the role of the state in promoting economic development. But while the sectional lines separating upcountry and black belt were less evident in this debate than they were in the struggles for democratization, the intensity of the battle over internal improvements was, if anything, more ferocious. As with democratic reform, what seems at first to be a southern gloss on a national debate takes on new meaning in the context of a slave society. Thus any issues that divided free Southerners became ominous portents of disunity in the face of a rising antislavery threat. Debates over banks, internal improvements, and economic development in general were drawn into an emerging defense of slavery itself. The pattern was already evident in the early 1820's, when an aging John Randolph argued against Congress's power to fund internal improvements by raising the specter of legislative interference in slavery. "If Congress possess the power to do what is proposed by this bill," Randolph warned, "they may not only enact a sedition law,—for there is precedent, but they may emancipate every slave in the United States."[72]

If Randolph's views were well on their way toward anachronism, his tactics were not. Across the South the black belts were becoming the centers of support for government activity on behalf of commercial development, putting the slaveholders in rough opposition to an upcountry that remained consistently uncertain about the political and social consequences of internal improvements. But even ambivalence was enough to raise again the prospect of yeoman disloyalty to slavery in debates that seemingly had nothing to do with it. Thus Whitmell P. Tunstall, a prominent planter from southside Virginia and a strong advocate of southern industrialization, formulated an 1837 petition for government support of a railroad in terms that were at once nationally familiar and yet sensible only in a slave society. Tunstall included the unification of the conflicting sections within Virginia among the "unspeakable and transcendent benefits" of a rail line to Danville. Then, perhaps glancing backward to the Nat Turner slave insurrection of a few years earlier, he argued that the industrialization of Virginia would be useful

> Should the time in the progress of events arrive when it may be wise and politic to engage more extensively in the manufacture of arms. . . . And if in the progress of time it may be a consideration of great magnitude that the ancient and renowned commonwealth should possess within herself the means which may enable her to maintain her rights, her dignity, and her peculiar institution. . . .[73]

In the Old South, everything eventually turned on the security of slavery. Every issue—from democratic reform to banks, from public schools to railroads—became a test of competing visions of the world, the one centered in the black belt and the other in the upcountry. If this was true in the 1820's and 1830's, it was truer still in the 1840's and 1850's, when nonslaveholders in the North raised their voices against the "peculiar institution" at the same time that slaveless yeomen in the South grew ever more hostile to the power of the swiftly encroaching black belt.

It is within this context that the racism of proslavery ideology in the Old South played one of its most crucial roles. The speeches, editorials, pamphlets, and books in defense of slavery served many purposes, but they were aimed primarily at building political support for the slaveholders among free men who did not own slaves. The arguments masters eventually latched onto most often were those that struck the most responsive chords among the nonslaveholders. Masters could hardly question the legitimacy of the American political system. That would have alienated precisely those groups they were trying to convince. Proslavery ideology had to make sense of slavery as the masters themselves understood it while simultaneously making sense of the world as the nonslaveholders saw it.

To fill so tall an order, property rights alone were inadequate. To these the slaveholders and nonslaveholders were equally committed anyway. Nor could the rights of property alone settle the question of who should be defined as human property and why. For this the slaveholders relied most heavily on racism—the ideological proposition that black-skinned Africans and their descendants constituted a distinct "race" that was inherently inferior to the "race" of white-skinned Anglo-Saxons and their descendants. Racism shared many of its precepts with traditional cultural prejudices about the superiority of western civilization and with enduring social stereotypes about the lower classes in general. But in the end racism differed in its assertion that inferiority and superiority were grounded in biology rather than culture or class.

For New World slaveholders, racism was a logical expression of the intrinsic nature of the master-slave relationship. Above all, it recast the traditional dichotomy between insider and outsider in the starkest terms of white and black. If slaves everywhere were outsiders, racism made them naturally so. Racism effectively denied the slaves a national identity, confirming their traditional status as noncitizens.[74] It declared that blacks were biologically unsuited to a demanding life of freedom and that only the totality of the master-slave relationship assured their survival in a world of racial superiors. Emotionally simple and intellectually underdeveloped, black slaves were deemed inherently more responsive than whites to the motivating force of physical coercion and relatively undisturbed by the tragic consequences of their legal kinlessness. Through such logic the masters could interpret their world in a way that seemed continually justified by most of the important characteristics of their day-to-day relationship with the slaves.

But racism also appealed to the characteristically petit bourgeois prejudices of slaveless farmers across America. Like the lower middle class elsewhere in the nineteenth century, yeoman farmers were as likely to focus their anger on the dependent classes beneath them as on the wealthy and powerful above them. In France, Parisian shopkeepers joined a radical critique of commercial relations to violent spasms of anti-Semitism. In the antebellum North, artisan radicalism periodically swerved off into virulent attacks on black workers. In the Midwest, small farmers grounded their antislavery sentiments in a combination of class hatred for wealthy slaveholders and racist assaults on blacks. In each case the intrinsic insecurity of life at the center of the class structure bred a profoundly schizophrenic politics.[75]

Southern yeomen were not very different. They assailed the power and pretensions of the slaveholders to great effect, but because they feared the turbulence of the propertyless classes as much as the prospect of their own dependency, their radicalism almost never included a sympathetic view of the slaves' plight. On the contrary, they indulged in the increasingly violent rhetoric of racist denunciation, arguing over and over that the equality of all free men was imminently threatened by the prospect of abolition. Thus, while property rights remained the philosophical basis of most proslavery arguments, racism draped them in populist garb. The southern yeomanry thereby gave *Herrenvolk* democracy its mass appeal.[76]

Racism thus had the one advantage that all dominant ideologies must have to be effective: it meant such different things to different people that it could bring together those for whom no other terms of agreement were available. Say that slavery was justified because black people were inferior, and two very different visions of society have been made compatible. What, after all, did it mean to say that black people were a distinct and inferior "race" of human beings? For some it meant that all white men were equal, for others it proved the gross error of egalitarianism. In the world of free men, where every political issue became a test of slavery's strength, where class differences were forever threatening the structure of southern society, and where slavery separated North and South into increasingly hostile camps, racism was the quintessential language of consensus.

As social divisions within the white South intensified along with sectional divisions in the country, the slaveholders sought to broaden their appeal by infusing racism into the core of every argument raised in slavery's defense. Was slavery natural to all human societies? George Fitzhugh asked. Yes, he answered, and how fortunate the South was to have an inherently inferior black population to fill a universal social need. Did every society have its "mudsills," as James Henry Hammond argued? The only positive answer that made sense to most men was that blacks alone were the mudsills of the South. Did God ordain the inequality of mankind? Racism answered that He did. Was the equality of all white men a self-evident truth? Racism showed that it was. For élitists and populists alike, there was no better evidence of divine will than the inherent inferiority of black people. Racism was an argument for equality and an argument for hierarchy, a justification of slavery and a justification of democracy, evidence of consensus and of the driving need for it. In the end, only racism could accommodate itself to the ambiguous instincts of the nonslaveholders, the ideological needs of the master class, and the intrinsic constraints of a liberal political culture.

Racial slavery as a unifying force of free society—this was one of the recurring themes of proslavery writers throughout the South. "The mass of laborers not being recognized among citizens, every citizen feels that he belongs to an elevated class. It matters not that he is no slaveholder," T. R. R. Cobb explained,

> he is not of the inferior race; he is a freeborn citizen; he engages in no menial occupation. The poorest meets the richest as an equal; sits at his table with him; salutes him as neighbor; meets him in every public assembly, and stands on the same social platform. Hence, there is no war of classes. There is truthfully republican equality in the ruling class.[77]

Ideas have implications beyond their immediate rationale, and the conviction that black people were naturally suited to slavery generated problems of its own. Having justified slavery by resorting to racist ideology, for example, free Southerners were naturally troubled by the presence of blacks who were not slaves. Rather than adjust their ideology to conform to the reality of several hundred thousand free blacks, the slaveholders brought reality itself more into line with their stated convictions. They hardened the already restrictive laws limiting manumission and increased the legal handicaps on blacks who were already free. Excluded from political participation and from the full enjoyment of basic civil rights, free blacks in the late antebellum South were slapped with further restrictions on freedom of movement, property rights, educational opportunities, and economic options. The process reached fever pitch in the 1850's. Under pressure from white artisans and wage laborers, some slaveholders proposed the reenslavement of free blacks, and in at least one southern city—Charleston—the free black community was thrown into turmoil as officials actually began to enforce laws that would have sent hundreds, if not thousands, of blacks back into slavery.[78]

Nationally, the slaveholders carried their racist logic to unprecedented lengths in the *Dred Scott* decision of 1857. When Chief Justice Roger Taney wrote his opinion, he invoked a distinction between citizens and outsiders that had appeared in slave societies since the time of Aristotle. "The question is simply this," Taney declared: "Can a negro, whose ancestors were imported into this country, and sold as slaves, become a member of the political community formed and brought into existence by the Constitution of the United States?" But where slaveholders in other societies had no trouble granting citizenship to the emancipated slave, the logic of racial determinism precluded that possibility. If blacks were slaves by nature, the very idea of a "free" black was an anomaly. The logic of proslavery racism therefore dictated Taney's conclusion that the rights of national citizenship could not be extended to black people. The Founders had never intended that they should be counted as "citizens," he argued:

> On the contrary, they were at that time considered as a subordinate and inferior class of beings, who had been subjugated by

the dominant race, and whether emancipated or not, yet remained subject to their authority, and had no rights or privileges
but such as those who held the power and the government might
choose to grant them.

With the *Dred Scott* decision, Taney carried proslavery principles
to the height of their influence in United States history.[79]

But the storm of protest that greeted Taney's decision showed
the limits of the slaveholders' power. Driven by the evidence of
dwindling political support to ever more extreme pronouncements of proslavery racism, the slaveholders discovered that once
the logical extreme had been reached it only undermined their authority further. But then double edges were nothing new to the
history of racism. It had always been a language of consensus,
whose very intensity implied deep social division. All of racism's
power to unify free men could not erase the source of social unrest:
slavery.

For centuries the slave economy had been expanding aggressively across the American frontier, spilling over state, sectional,
and international boundaries. It had threatened the integrity of
yeoman society, displaced Native American cultures, and broken
up tens of thousands of black families. "Diffusion," Jefferson and
his contemporaries had labeled the hopeful notion that the harsh-
ness of slavery might somehow be ameliorated by its expansion
westward. But by the late antebellum era such hopes were rarely
voiced, and whatever line may have existed between expansionism and imperialism had clearly been crossed. The needs of the
slave economy and the rights of the slaveholders were invoked to
justify the war with Mexico, imperial escapades in the Caribbean,
and "border ruffianism" in Kansas and Nebraska.

This, finally, is what set slaveholders and nonslaveholders
against each other, within the nation as well as within the South.
Over the years "free soil" had become central to the political justification for economic development in the North. To Republican
party spokesmen, a western "safety valve" protected eastern labor
from the degradation popularly associated with European workers—and southern slaves. By the 1850's slavery was far more than

a negative frame of reference among free-labor ideologues. It was an imminent threat. Decades of political and social tension between slaveholders and yeomen had demonstrated that no free-soil utopia of independent farmers could survive where the slave economy flourished. Centuries of western history had also demonstrated slavery's insatiable urge to expand. And just as the yeoman and slave economies were drawn together despite their intrinsic incompatibility, so were the North and South linked by strong commercial bonds and yet unable to avoid increasingly hostile encounters. For slavery threatened the imagined safety valve of free soil, and with it the legitimacy of wage labor in the North. By 1860, to protect wage labor was to restrict the slaveholders. Capitalism and slavery, after coexisting for centuries, now came to arms.

Thwarted on their own continent, the slaveholders chose secession over territorial limitation. Throughout the winter of 1860–61, most slaveholders made it clear that they were no more prepared to accept restrictions on their right to migrate than were the victorious Republicans prepared to accept slavery's continued expansion. Who would dare defy what the delegates to the Mississippi secession convention called "the greatest material interest in the world"? With good reason, therefore, many contemporaries came to view the sectional conflict as irrepressible.

But King Cotton misjudged his own strength. The proslavery ideologues had failed in the North and were only partially successful within the South. As the secession crisis spread in the wake of Abraham Lincoln's election, the yeomen responded with the same ambivalence that had for so long defined their politics. They were neither hearty Unionists nor fire-eating secessionists. Independent to the end, they provided little substance to the confident predictions of either northern Republicans or southern slaveholders. Instead, the yeomen sat firmly on the fence, casting their votes for a variety of "conditional unionists" and "cooperationists." Given its intrinsic ambivalence, this position can be read as implicitly supportive of the Confederacy or as a firm rejection of the slaveholders' revolution. But it is better understood as characteristically uncertain. So too with the yeomanry's war record.

They fought for the Confederacy bravely and fiercely for the first two years of the war, but they were the first to desert (and in swelling numbers) as the South's fortunes dwindled. It was a fitting coda to a tumultuous history racked by the anxieties and insecurities of life at the middle.

At the bottom, things were not so ambiguous.

Dobly is killed instead of accepting chastisement

Dobby face it ~~death to~~ by

the slavish work includes chastisement of self

CHAPTER 4

Slaves and Masters

> Only the Slave can transform the World that forms him and fixes him in slavery and create a World that he has formed in which he will be free. And the slave achieves this only through forced and terrified work carried out in the Master's service. To be sure, this work by itself does not free him. But in transforming the World by his work, the Slave transforms himself, too, and thus creates the new objective conditions that permit him to take up once more the liberating Fight for recognition that he refused in the beginning for fear of death. And thus in the long run, all slavish work realizes not the Master's will, but the will—at first unconscious—of the Slave, who—finally—succeeds where the Master—necessarily—fails.
>
> —Alexandre Kojève
> *Introduction to the Reading of Hegel*

WE CANNOT SAY why Lydia, the slave John Mann had hired for the year, refused to accept her master's punishment. She comes to us from records that give her no last name, much less assign her motives. Perhaps she had been abused too often before; perhaps she had one of those "saucy" dispositions of which so many slaveowners complained. But whatever her reasons, sometime in the late 1820's, Lydia did something for which Mann sought to "chastise her" and "in the act of doing so the slave ran off." Mann then "called upon [the slave] to stop, which being refused, he shot at and wounded her." Mann was indicted for committing a battery upon the slave and the case went all the way to the North Carolina Supreme Court.[1]

A few years later another North Carolina slave whose last name we do not know also turned and walked away rather than accept chastisement, and was also shot in the back. But this time the slave, Will, kept walking, and the overseer who had shot him pursued him for several minutes. When he caught up with Will, the

Rowling attempts a revision
in the law of slavery
SLAVERY AND FREEDOM

slave physically resisted and finally pulled a knife, stabbing the overseer, Richard Baxter, in three different places. That evening Baxter bled to death. Will was subsequently indicted for murder, convicted, and sentenced to die. He, too, appealed his conviction to the state supreme court.[2]

Both cases began when a slave refused to accept the most basic precept of human bondage: total subordination to the master. The refusal need not have grown out of any seething resentments or from any well-formulated conviction that slavery itself had to be challenged. Lydia and Will did what slaves across the South did all the time—they got angry and refused to accept punishment. Theirs were among the thousands of acts of refusal so commonplace in slavery that historians refer to them as "day-to-day" resistance.

Whether in Athens, Brazil, the Caribbean, or the American South, the prevalence of day-to-day resistance is no longer in dispute. Slaves engaged in a variety of acts designed to ease their burdens and frustrate their masters' wills. They broke tools, feigned illness, deliberately procrastinated, "stole" food, and manipulated the tensions between master and overseer. When pressed, the slaves took up more active forms of resistance: they became "saucy," ran away, struck the overseer or even the master. And throughout the slave community a tradition of solidarity sustained and justified individual and collective forms of resistance.[3]

This is the tradition within which Lydia's and Will's acts of refusal must be understood, although the consequences of their behavior were anything but ordinary. Having made their way to the North Carolina Supreme Court, their cases produced two of the most intriguing decisions in the history of southern slave law. State v. Mann and State v. Will were classic instances of the ordinary becoming extraordinary. Lydia and Will, in their simple acts of resistance to a master's authority, had forced the courts to confront the intrinsic nature of slavery and its place in a liberal political system. In so doing the slaves helped provoke a significant revision of the law of slavery, one that threatened to redefine the balance of power in the master-slave relationship. Add up all the similar cases, accumulate the relevant precedents, and the history of slavery in the Old South comes steadily into view.

How could this happen? How could a system that demanded the total subordination of the slave, that was virtually defined by the slave's exclusion from politics, become so sensitive to the political consequences of seemingly trivial and isolated acts of slave resistance? As we shall see, part of the answer lies in the intrinsically ambiguous relationship between slavery and the polity. The explosive combination of anarchy and absolutism—there were as many laws as there were masters, yet the law remained fundamentally totalitarian—created problems wherever slavery existed. But in the South those problems were unusually heightened by the nature of the liberal polity. In the face of an overbearing colonial authority, the slaveholders had helped create the liberal institutions within which they exercised their power; in the face of an independent yeomanry, the slaveholders reinforced rather than weakened their commitment to liberal government; in the face of an increasingly hostile North the slaveholders relied ever more insistently on the protections afforded them by the liberal state. And yet liberalism, in the end, provided the slaves with the crack into which their acts of resistance drove the decisive wedge.

SLAVES RESISTED for many reasons, but most often they were provoked by the masters' various efforts to reproduce, protect, and increase their wealth. The slaveholders' prosperity rested on the market value of their chattels as much as on the value of the cash crops the slaves produced, and both were related to the value of the land and farms on which the slaves worked. To "improve" each of these sources of wealth was the goal of most owners. This was the broad meaning of a "good crop" among those who thought most carefully about plantation management. "A good crop," one master explained, "means one that is good, taking into consideration everything, slaves, land, horses, stock, fences, ditches and farming utensils; all of which must be kept up and improved in value." P. C. Weston, a rice planter from South Carolina, was more specific. Among the criteria by which he judged his overseers he listed the number and condition of the slaves, the condition of the fields, livestock, tools, and fences, and "the amount and quality of the rice and provision crops."[4]

In all such efforts to improve productivity, the organization of labor took precedence. The unparalleled level of consumer demand for slave-produced goods emanating from the capitalist world—what distinguished the southern slave economy from the economies of antiquity—sustained a competitive environment in which masters had little choice but to impose some rationalized system of labor management on the slaves, however ineffective or informal. Seventy-five percent of the slave population was concentrated on farms with ten or more slaves, and for most of them systematic management of some sort was all but impossible to avoid. "System and order [are] important in everything," one planter explained as he recited the rules he established to govern the slaves' workday.[5] "My creed, as an agriculturist," another owner wrote, "is to make the greatest possible product, from the least possible labor."[6] Some masters claimed bold success in increasing their slaves' productivity by careful management techniques. "By paying particular attention to the slaves," a Louisiana planter wrote, "the amount of work done, beyond what they used to do some years past under different management, has increased surprisingly."[7] An "Alabama Planter," after outlining his particular system, claimed that he knew "of no man who realizes more to the hand than I:"[8] With millions of slaves, hundreds of thousands of masters, and commodity prices that guaranteed few quick fortunes, the most successful farms were those that sustained the best levels of productivity over the long haul.

Nevertheless, slavery actually provided little room for significant improvements in productivity. As laborers, the slaves had little incentive to care very much or to work very hard. They had nothing like the serf's powerful claim to rights on the land. Slaves also lacked the incentives built into a wage-labor economy: the sheer need to go to work to survive, the promise of more pay for more work, and the added enticement of upward mobility in the

long run. They had nothing to gain fror
crops that added nothing to their basic s
hierarchy within the slave community o
of social advancement. Slave parents co
own nor their children's eventual indep
alized promise of future freedom provi
to work hard. So, while countless slav
their skills as nurses, managers, cooks, or
jority of slave laborers, the field hands, had no good reason
care much about the success of the master's efforts to produce a
"good crop."

Thus, southern masters tried to rationalize the labor of slaves
who had every reason to resent such efforts, and this proved a major source of tension within the master-slave relationship. Work
is what the slaves did all day, and so work is what provoked many
of the conflicts between master and slave. The rules of the workplace set the daily, seasonal, and yearly rhythms of life on farms
throughout the black belt. Yet the very effort to impose a "system" that would increase worker output appeared to slaves as a
direct reminder of the master's arbitrary power.[9]

Plantation reformers often complained that masters placed too
much emphasis on the productivity of slave labor. Because the
slaves themselves were valuable property, reformers argued,
treatment of slaves took precedence over the exploitation of their
labor. Critics disputed the presumably common opinion that humane treatment reduced the revenue generated by the slave's
work. "In our exclusive attention to the growth of cotton," John
Savage warned, "we have been led astray by visionary expectations, and have wandered far from the path of our true interest."[10]
Another planter acknowledged the risk of smaller crops, but insisted that the overall gains justified the gamble. With "a judicious
division of our skill, time, and care, between the soil, and the negroes," he argued, "the produce of the first will be little, if at all
less; and that of the latter much greater, than heretofore."[11]

Many owners thus distinguished the management of slaves
from the rational organization of their labor, and they often insisted that slaves were at least as important as what they pro-

servation and experience" taught one slaveholder that
cess of the planter depends as much upon the judicious
gement of his slaves as upon the proper cultivation of the
."[12] On a profitably managed plantation, the "first thing that
resents itself to [the owner's] serious consideration is the management of his negroes."[13] The reason was simple. "The blacks
constitute, either absolutely or instrumentally, the wealth of our
southern states," one writer pointed out.[14]

The masters' concern for the laborer as a valuable commodity
was a distinguishing feature of slavery. No comparable interest in
serf "management" appears in the manorial documents that survive from medieval Europe, nor should slave management be
equated with the problem of labor control in capitalist enterprises.
To be sure, the systematic organization of slave labor was in certain ways analogous to the problem of labor management in industrial factories or, for that matter, medieval manors. "Every
man accustomed to manage labour," one master wrote, "whether
black or white, in the field or the factory, knows that the presence
of a superintendent is indispensable."[15] But when masters contemplated the "management of slaves" they were reflecting on the
appropriate exercise of powers that extended far beyond those of
a factory owner or feudal lord.

Because slaves were a source of wealth separate from the crops
they produced, their care and feeding, and ultimately their sexual
reproduction, were as important to masters as the productive cultivation of crops and soil. Hence the humane treatment of slaves,
it was said over and over again, was in the best interests of the
slaveholding class. "Of all the motives which influence the intercourse between men, *interest* is certainly the strongest," a local agricultural society in Georgia reported in 1846. Thus "with the
owner of the slave, as the slave is his property, and he is bound
for his support under all circumstances, we can readily conceive
[the] strong . . . motive of the master in taking good care of the
slave, and thus extending the time of his usefulness."[16] Fully
aware of the value of slaves as such, masters constantly emphasized the utilitarianism of decent treatment. "It is clearly and un-
questionably to *your advantage* to provide comfortable lodgings for

your servants. . . . Whatever tends to preserve the health and promote the general well-being of the slave," one master observed, "is an advantage to the owner, and, therefore, well worthy of his attention."[17] Assuming that humanity and interest did indeed coincide, some masters reversed the usual emphasis on utility without sacrificing the basic precept. "It is not alone, their mere personal value, nor the pecuniary profits arising from their labor, nor the more distant and prospective advantages of their increase," John Savage explained, "but above and beyond these, are those high and paramount claims of humanity and kindness."[18] Still, it was far more common to argue, as J. A. Ruff did, that because "the health of the slave is directly connected with the interest of the planter," good slave management was sure to "promote the pecuniary welfare" of all owners.[19]

Just as masters boasted of their success in improving the productivity of slave labor, so did they emphasize the material rewards of maintaining a healthy slave population. Thanks to his concern with the diet and cleanliness of his slaves, one planter explained, "My little negroes are consequently very healthy; and from pursuing the plan I have laid down, I am confident that I raise more of them, than where a different system is followed."[20] Another master spoke of the "many privileges" he reserved for "the breeding women" on his plantation, "no inconsiderable part of a farmer's profits being in the little negroes he succeeds in raising."[21] Only in a slave system could "the raising [of] little negroes" be proposed as "an employment, distinct from tilling the ground." Successful "negro raising," a letter to the *Southern Agriculturist* explained, "must be conducted as a business separate from and unconnected with the market crop."[22]

But few masters openly exalted the most significant consequence of their "interest" in the slaves as property—the internal slave trade. In fact, all of the words used to explore the utilitarian basis of humane treatment—value, advantage, worth, quality— were meaningless outside the existence of a market in slaves. In the end, only the price a slave commanded on the auction block could validate the claim that it was in the owner's pecuniary interest to keep his slave assets in prime condition. Slavery itself can scarcely be imagined without the master's right to move a slave from place to place, to dispose of slave property at will, or to purchase a chattel on the open market. The interstate slave trade in the Old South was thus inseparable from the master's interest. Between 1790 and 1860 perhaps a million slaves were bought and sold within the South, their prices rising steadily until, on the eve of the Civil War, a healthy young man might cost as much as $2,000.

If the vibrancy of the internal slave trade shows that there was more to the masters' interest than they were willing to acknowledge, the very detail with which they explored the subject of slave treatment inadvertently reveals that the essence of slavery was not treatment at all but, rather, the master's power over the intimate details of slave life. The masters cared about the treatment of slaves not simply because they had an "interest" in them but because they had the power to control the slaves' private lives. Masters could decide for themselves whether slaves could get married, where they would live, what they would eat, when they woke up and went to bed, and how they would dress. What the masters exposed in their detailed examinations of slave treatment was not that they were uniquely humane but that they were extraordinarily powerful.

They exposed more than that. Nowhere did the force of capitalism appear more strongly in the slave South than in the masters' efforts to extend their rationalizing impulse beyond the workplace and into the private lives of the slaves. Owners addressed the "treatment" question by trading suggestions about how best to arrange the most mundane aspects of slave life, things free men and women simply assumed were private matters. It seemed perfectly ordinary for one master to require that slaves not overcook their vegetables, for another to insist that slave women "have a change of *drawers* for the winter," and for still others to set rules determining what time and in which manner the slaves could eat their suppers. This was not the language of uninhibited greed but of rational calculation.

Nevertheless, it was a rationalism that exposed the distinctive character of slavery. The distinctiveness derived in large part from the fact that the slave family subsisted within the master's "household." The family remained a procreative unit, but the economic functions of the household were under the control of the master, giving him power to make many of the domestic decisions denied to the slave family.[23] Every time the masters extended their control over another aspect of the slave's daily life they demonstrated in precise and highly personal terms what it meant to be unfree. For slaves there was no such thing as a right of privacy. To be a slave could mean filing past the master to be examined for cleanliness, for torn clothing, or for receipt of weekly rations. Slave cabins were not simply built to the masters' specifications, they were open to periodic inspections. One owner required his overseer to "visit every negro house at daylight" to see that the slaves were out and "once a week or more . . . after horn blow at night, to see that all are in." An overseer boasted that "once or twice in the month, I made it my business to visit each negro house: I examined everything therein; saw that the negroes permitted no dirt or filth."[24]

If "total subordination" meant that masters could demand much more than hard work and obedience from their slaves, the denial of rights had similarly practical consequences for the day-to-day treatment of slaves. Masters took it for granted that they had every right to choose which ministers the slaves would hear, when slaves could attend church services, and which sermons were appropriate. Slaveholders enforced the laws restricting the slaves' freedom of movement by prohibiting bondsmen from "strolling about" or leaving the plantation without permission. Others denied slaves permission to trade commodities they cultivated on their own. Some were so intent on restricting trade that they did not allow slaves to plant their own gardens.

The slaveowner's power was nowhere more evident than in slave families. Masters often reserved the right to veto a proposed marriage. On large units they sometimes prevented slaves from marrying anyone off the plantation. Masters set the rules about how much work pregnant women could perform, when nursing mothers should return to the fields, how small children were to be cared for while the parents were at work, and the age at which slave children should begin labor. Even the personal relations of husband and wife were subject to the owner's arbitration. W. W. Hazzard claimed to have forbidden wife-beating among his slaves and a great deal more besides. "If the wife teases and provokes [the slave husband] by her nightly clatter, or crabbed deportment," Hazzard wrote, "and he complains and establishes the fact; she is punished." And masters never abandoned their power to break up a marriage.

Hence the fatal paradox: nowhere did capitalism penetrate slavery more deeply than in the masters' attempts to rationalize the private lives of slaves, yet nowhere did the conflict between slavery and capitalism take on such concrete form as in the slaves' resistance to those same rationalizing impulses. What masters defined as issues of "treatment," as problems of management, appeared to slaves as extreme assertions of the master's power. The most trivial rules—making sure slaves got to bed on time, for instance—were among the most palpable symbols of unfreedom. For, unlike the periodic shock of family breakup or the brutal beating of a particularly unruly field hand, the day-to-day treatment of slaves was a relentless and perpetual reminder of how far the master's power extended and how completely the freedom of slaves was denied. This was, with labor control, the second of the two great sources of conflict between masters and slaves.

Indeed, the pervasiveness of the conflict stands as a warning. The rules owners set down for the treatment of slaves and the management of their labor are not necessarily a reflection of life as it was actually lived. In many cases the rules were themselves the product of conflict. They were provoked into existence by slaves who did not go to bed when they were told, attended their own religious services, listened to their preachers, found ways to get more food than masters allotted, insisted on marrying off the plantation, and rebelled when masters interfered in their private affairs. Rules were promulgated by masters who sought to counteract the slaves' frustrating lack of motivation in the workplace —their deliberately slow pace, their disregard for tools, and the countless evasive maneuvers that reduced the slaves' workload in small but consistently aggravating ways.

Even where there seemed to be little overt conflict, the appearance of harmony could be misleading. As Eugene Genovese has demonstrated, the fact that so many masters learned not to interfere too deeply in the private lives of slaves is testimony to the implicit compromise that masters and slaves had to respect if the system was to function at all.[25] Rules governing the treatment and behavior of slaves are best viewed from a similar perspective. They were the issues over which master and slave most often came to odds, the moments when the negotiations between master and slave began. Patterns of accommodation between masters and slaves can, therefore, have the ironic effect of exposing what they were designed to conceal—those points at which the master's exercise of power was likely to provoke the sharpest reactions among the slaves.

It is no surprise that most of these tensions—even those that erupted in the workplace—eventually involved the slave family. Here the conflict between rational and emotional impulses was all but inescapable. Consequently, it was often the strength of family ties that determined the strength of a slave's militancy. Pushed too hard by an overseer, whipped once too often by the master, a field hand's decision to strike back or not was most often made in consultation with family members and in consideration of family attachments. In more direct ways resistance was commonly tied to family life. Slaves ran away to protect their children, to prevent their families from being broken up, or to find relatives from whom they had been separated. Acts of resistance were often provoked by the master's abuse of a slave's spouse or child, or by a particularly galling intrusion into the slaves' personal affairs.

Thus slave resistance repeatedly exposed a contradiction perhaps distinctive to slavery in the Old South: the same families that had no recognition under the law had nonetheless become essential to slavery's survival. The "peculiar institution" could not reproduce itself without slave families. As early as 1750 southern slavery was becoming uniquely dependent upon the physical reproduction of the slave population, and with the withdrawal from the Atlantic trade in 1808 the masters no longer had a dependable alternative source of slaves. The system could only survive with slave families. And yet these families lacked all legal standing; they were neither the primary units of economic productivity nor the chief mechanism for the distribution and redistribution of property in society. As one recent scholar put it, the slaves could form families, but not households, of their own.

Without the civil recognition that distributes legal and property rights among husbands, wives, and children, the slave family was neither patriarchal nor matriarchal—for neither spouse had the formal powers that normally justify the use of such terms. If all slaves had no rights, husbands could have no more of them than wives. If slaves could own no property, the family could not be the vehicle for the transmission of estates. If slavery was perpetual, slaves could not rear their children for the eventual assumption of power or independence. The family structure that emerged from such conditions was unique in American social history.

Gender distinctions that prevailed in free families, for example, were undermined by the slave-labor system. The work each slave was expected to perform was limited primarily by sheer physical capacity, and women could do most of the jobs men could do. From early childhood all slaves—boys and girls, men and women—mostly did the same kinds of tasks. The majority of slave women spent their days in the fields alongside slave men, hoeing, plowing, and in some cases digging ditches and hauling wood. To be sure, there were gender differences, even in the type of field work men and women performed. But there was no sense that the labor of slave women was primarily domestic, and that their work should be confined to meeting the subsistence needs of their families.[26]

Nevertheless, many of the distinctions associated with family life did emerge within the slave community. Masters assigned communal cooking and child-rearing tasks to women, while traditional artisanal crafts were reserved for male slaves. Domestic service in the master's house was largely restricted to females. Above all, as bearers of children, as nursing mothers, slave women assumed roles and obligations different from those of slave men. This made slave women uniquely vulnerable to their masters' interest in sexual reproduction, but it also gave them a kind of leverage unavailable to slave men. In the master's very dependence upon her fertility the slave woman found and exercised a degree of influence—a bargaining chip—in her dealings not only with her master but with her own family. Slave women thereby assumed a degree of influence within their families that helped to counteract the formal powerlessness of both husbands and wives.[27]

With the modicum of influence they recovered from their reproductive capacities, slave women protected the integrity and emotional life of their families as best they could, and with surprising success. The slave family was notoriously subject to the disruptive intrusions of the master and at the same time profoundly important to the cultural stability of the slave community. Above all, the slave family was a creative adaptation to the anarchic realities of slavery. As a legal nonentity the slave family's existence was tolerated by a master who could respect it or destroy it as his interests and inclinations determined. But as a cultural anchor within the slave community, the family developed in ways that compensated for its intrinsic vulnerability. Here the survival of African traditions often proved decisive.

Kinship, for example, radiated outward from the slave family, embracing cousins and nieces, nephews and in-laws, as close rather than distant relatives. Fictive kin—"aunts" and "uncles" with no blood ties—further extended the lines of family outward until they blended smoothly and indistinguishably into the slave community as a whole. In a world where nuclear families were intrinsically vulnerable to the master's power to break them apart, the extended relations of the slave community—a manifestation of the continuing strength of African patterns—preserved a sense of family stability in the wake of otherwise wrenching dislocations. And where the family provided an anchor for the larger community of slaves, the slave community in turn nourished a sense of self-worth and solidarity that helped sustain each member of the family.[28]

As if to compensate for the family's intrinsic insecurity in slavery, Afro-American culture placed extraordinary emphasis on ancestral ties. The ring shout—"movement in a ring during ceremonies honoring the ancestors"—took myriad forms among the peoples of central and western Africa, yet it survived as a generically "African" folk custom in the United States. By collapsing the western dichotomy between the natural and the supernatural, and by maintaining a sense of the interconnection between the living and the dead, the distant and the close, the ring shout symbolically sustained a distinctively African conception of family relations in the face of the overt disruptions of slavery. The ring shout has been seen as the single most important cultural tradition in Afro-American history. Generalized from its multiple ethnic origins, the ritualized music and dancing of the ring shout helped make a unified sense of African nationhood possible in America precisely because slavery broke down the local loyalties that continued to inhibit the growth of nationalism in twentieth-century Africa.[29]

All the distinctive features of slave culture—the folktales, the theology, the music and dance—not only were unified around the slaves' conceptions of familial and ancestral ties but were surprisingly uniform across the South by the nineteenth century. The slaves' emerging sense of "national" identity, in combination with liberal revolutionary ideology and messianic Christianity, substantially heightened the possibilities of militancy within the slave community. It was this dual appeal to African nationalism and western rhetorical traditions that made the lessons of the Old South's leading slave rebels—Gabriel Prosser, Denmark Vesey, and Nat Turner—so difficult for the master class to forget. For the culture they represented had implications that could not be discounted simply because their insurrectionary plans failed.

Yet slave culture also gave masters potent weapons in the perpetual struggle with their slaves. Owners clearly recognized, for example, that the strength of slavery rested in large measure on the strength of the slave family. The stronger the family attachments, the less likely was a slave to run away. Thus most escapees were young men, grown beyond the protective umbrella of their childhood families and not yet established in new families of their own. A wife and child were powerful restraints on a slave who yearned to escape but who could not face the prospect of leaving his family behind. The slaves had taken full advantage of the contradictions of the system to create a family life, a community, and a culture that could generate, support, and justify the acts of resistance that the master's demands provoked. But the more successfully the slaves protected their families, the more fully they realized their community life, the more effectively their culture explained their circumstances—the more bearable, and peaceful, slavery became.[30]

On the other hand, it was a precarious peace that rested on the security of the slave community and the vibrancy of Afro-American culture. The slaveholders saw the advantages of family stability, but there was no way for the master class to maintain itself without disrupting and destroying slave families on a massive scale. To "manage negroes" was to interfere inevitably in the personal lives of slave families and thereby to provoke hostility. To "discipline" a slave was to anger and horrify that slave's husband, wife, parent, or child. To own slaves was to enjoy the right to break up a family, but to exercise that right was to rekindle within the slave community a passionate hatred of bondage. Family life made slavery bearable, it held slaves to their plantations, it gave slaves something whose integrity was not worth risking. But children gave parents a powerful incentive to struggle for freedom, while the family in general gave all slaves something worth protecting. In the end, the legal kinlessness of the slaves made slavery itself the inveterate enemy of the very families it created. And so the slaves resisted.

The question, then, is not whether the slaves resisted but what difference it made, whether resistance was effectively contained, whether slavery functioned, survived, and even flourished in spite of resistance, or whether it disturbed the balance of power between master and slave enough to weaken slavery itself. The masters would have been a foolish and unusually stubborn ruling class if they had not at least tried to compromise with their slaves for the sake of the system's preservation. And the slaves would have been unusually ascetic, not to say heroic, if they spurned all negotiations and concessions offered by their masters. Compromise and negotiation are commonplace in the history of relations between the powerful and the powerless. Yet social conflict and political upheaval are not brought to an end by such compromises. The political significance of slave resistance remains to be demonstrated.

ANCIENT HISTORIANS used to speculate at length about why the slaves of Greece and Rome rebelled so infrequently, and Gilberto Freyre raised the same question about the slaves in Brazil. In recent years American historians have gone to great lengths in an effort to explain why southern slaves did not rebel more often. In fact, slaves hardly ever rebelled. "What is most characteristic, most striking in the history of slavery," one scholar has recently pointed out, "is not revolt but the absence of revolt."[31] M. I. Finley believed that in all of human history there were only four full-scale rebellions in which slaves engaged in organized warfare against the armies of their masters. And of those four—three in ancient Sicily and Italy and one in Saint-Domingue (now Haiti) —only the latter succeeded. To be sure, there were differences from one slave society to the next. There were more slave uprisings in Brazil and Jamaica than in the American South, while the South had more slave revolts than did Barbados. But a single successful slave rebellion in all of human history surely suggests the overwhelming odds all rebels faced, notwithstanding the variations from place to place.

The military might of the slaveholders was almost always enough to suppress a revolt, but the power to crush an uprising does not adequately explain why there were so few of them to begin with. The most important obstacles to rebellion were intrinsic to slavery itself. As outsiders, slaves had no firm base in any legally recognized community. Unlike peasants, for example, slaves could not launch a rebellion from the relative security of a formally established social organization, nor could slaves justify rebellion as a defensive maneuver to protect their traditional place in society. When peasants rebelled, they could do so as established communities determined to resist threats to their traditional

The above is revolt

rights. But this "restorationist" theme made no sense to slaves who had no rights to restore and no place in society to preserve.

New World slave rebellions usually reflected the African tribal loyalties that survived within the slave community, and in this more restricted sense many revolts were restorationist. In Brazil, for example, revolts were usually led by African-born slaves whose shared ethnic origins enabled them to sustain a sense of communal solidarity. In most cases, as in the relatively numerous Bahian revolts in the early nineteenth century, clearly delineated ethnic and religious subcultures united the Brazilian rebels far more effectively than could any formal or informal ties binding them to one another as slaves. Throughout Latin America and the Caribbean, maroon societies—organized communities of runaway slaves—drew their greatest numbers from those born in Africa. Like other rebels, maroons often sought to "restore" African society in the New World. But to do so the slaves needed to withdraw from the slaveholders' world as far as was possible. Thus maroon communities remained an attraction to escaping slaves in large part because runaways could not claim rights and privileges within the slave society, the way peasants did when they sought to restore a traditional balance of power by appealing over the heads of their landlords to the king or the czar.

The cohesive force of African ethnic or religious loyalties was also its own limitation. Given its Islamic overtones, the 1807 plot by Brazilian slaves of Hausa origin had trouble appealing to those sent to America from other parts of Africa. Similar ethnic identities both unified and confined the bulk of New World revolts, a situation that persisted largely because so heavy a proportion of slaves were African-born. But given their intrinsic limitations, such uprisings were always quickly repressed.

With slaves born in the Americas—creoles—the ethnic identities that sustained organized revolt diminished. Thus the creolization of slaves in the southern United States is probably the most significant reason for the difference between patterns of rebellion in the South and other New World slave societies. Even when the slave trade reached its height in the mid-eighteenth century, southern slaves only occasionally lived in clusters of homogeneous African subcultures. By the nineteenth century the bulk of southern slaves were native-born and their sense of community was not limited to identifiable ethnic groups within a restricted locale. While African culture retained much of its salience in the South, it was no longer grounded in the ethnic origins that inspired restorationist dreams among slaves born and raised in Africa.

Nevertheless, long after the slave population was overwhelmingly native-born, English-speaking, and Christian, insurrection panics continued to sweep across the South. For by the antebellum decades the absence of significant ethnic divisions among the slaves had removed not only the most important spur to revolt but its most significant limitation as well. Slavery and racism, having denied southern slaves a place in the American nation, allowed Afro-Americans to "imagine" instead a separate community—a nation within a nation—peopled by the descendants of Africa rather than Europe. By the nineteenth century a surprisingly unified Afro-American culture had synthesized otherwise diverse local traditions with important features of the Anglo-American heritage.

This is what made the prospect of slave rebellion so frightening in the Age of Revolution: its universal appeal to a slave culture and a liberal ideology that together transcended ethnic and local loyalties. Most of the major plots and insurrections fused traditional African conceptions of spirituality with Christian millennialism. In addition, the "Gabriel" plot in 1800 followed closely in the wake of the Haitian revolution, which was itself inspired by the French Revolution. Two decades later Haiti's influence surfaced again in Charleston, South Carolina, where Denmark Vesey— who had been to Saint-Domingue in the 1790's—was discovered plotting another slave insurrection. And southern patriots were scandalized when Nat Turner confessed in 1831: "It was intended by us to have begun the work of death on the 4th of July last." In such circumstances it was small comfort to the masters that their slaves rebelled less often than did those of Brazil.

For the slaveholders had every reason to fear that the influence of liberal ideology extended well beyond a few unsuccessful slave rebellions. In particular, the Age of Revolution had also transformed the political significance of the more common forms of slave resistance.[32] Masters knew that the slaves could not influence American politics with their votes, petitions, speeches, and editorials. But as the decades passed it was becoming apparent that slaves could affect the political system by intruding themselves into it as runaways, criminals, victims, or even witnesses. Any action that forced the legal system to recognize the slave as in any way independent of the master represented an implicit threat to the principle of total subordination. Grounded in the presumption of universal, inviolable rights, the American political system at once defined the slaves as rightless and yet risked undermining slavery every time it recognized the legal personality of the slave.

The American political system also limited the master's capacity to contain the consequences of slave resistance. As a legal entity, the master-slave relationship was defined by slave codes passed in representative legislatures, protected by state constitutions, and interpreted by local and national judiciaries. Yet not one of those political structures was determined by or dependent upon slavery. Quite the reverse: the slaveholders' legal survival depended on political institutions that slavery did not create, and in the end this put the master class at a fatal disadvantage. For the slaveholders' domination of liberal political institutions had the paradoxical effect of legitimizing the same government structures that would ultimately be used to destroy slavery.

Slavery's dependence on the state exposed still another paradox, one that was common to all slave systems but whose significance was transformed in a liberal political culture: the fact that slaves were "totally" subordinate to the masters did not mean that the master's power over the slave was absolute. On the contrary, the state formally (and the community informally) regulated the master's power in a variety of ways—even in the United States where the law gave masters unusually wide leeway. For this reason, John Codman Hurd defined slavery "as that condition of a natural person, in which, by the operation of law, the application of his physical and mental powers depends, as far as possible, upon the will of another *who is himself subject to the supreme power of the state.*"[33]

How much power did the state have? Beyond simply calling slavery into existence, the government's role in regulating and maintaining the master-slave relationship was essential, nowhere more so than in the determination of who could be legally enslaved. Here the state's power was nothing less than overwhelming, for if it could say who was or was not rightfully enslaved, it could theoretically enslave everyone or abolish slavery in effect even when constitutionally prohibited from doing so. For example, in some parts of the world the children of slaves were freed almost automatically, particularly when the father was free. Southern law invoked the more common rule that the slave's status followed that of the mother. Yet there was nothing intrinsic to slavery, nor to the United States Constitution, that required the southern states to lay down this injunction. Indeed, the slave codes were filled with elaborations of the rule, often including special provisions for the offspring of white women and black slaves.

The slaveholders never seriously questioned the state's right to say who was a slave, and the reason for their silence was undoubtedly the consensus southern legislatures operated within when they addressed this issue: slaves should be Negroes and Negroes should be slaves. Thomas Cobb summarized the logic in his treatise on the law of slavery: "White persons may not be enslaved. . . . The presumption of freedom arises from the color." Since "all the negroes introduced into America were brought as slaves," Cobb explained, "the black color of the race raises the presumption of slavery."[34] This was the universal supposition by the eighteenth century, and it served to mask the awesome implications of the authority the state exercised when it codified that presumption.

Yet over and over again the southern legislatures went further than this. They had to. What, after all, was a "Negro"? All the pseudo-scientific flimflam produced by men like Samuel Cartwright and Josiah Nott could not alter the fact that "race" was a cultural construction rather than a biological reality.[35] Consider *this relates to the argument among wizards on who was a beast*

the problems raised by miscegenation, the fact that whites and blacks could together produce children whose "race" was instantly problematical.[36] Genetics inevitably failed the racial theorists, though it took a century for it to do so. In the meantime, the law stepped in to provide official sanction as well as clarification for a powerful cultural proposition. "Every person who has one-fourth, or other larger part, of negro blood, shall be deemed a mulatto," the Kentucky legislature decreed in 1852, "and the word negro, when used in any statute, shall be construed to me_ mulatto as well as negro."[37] In these and many other area_ state exercised its prerogative to determine who was legiti_ a slave.

The government also decided whether and under v_ stances a master could free a slave. It specified hov_ _ _to be distributed among contending heirs wheneve_ _ _ _died intestate. The state even reserved the right to take _ _es away from masters for a variety of reasons. It could expropriate a slave if the master did not pay his taxes, if he was convicted of a criminal offense, or if it was determined that he was simply too cruel. The state of Louisiana reserved the right to free any slave it chose. After piously declaring that "no master of slaves shall be compelled, either directly or indirectly, to enfranchise" his slaves, the legislature went on to make a huge exception "in cases where the enfranchisement shall be made for services rendered to the State, by virtue of an act of the Legislature."[38]

this made the slave an rule for the humor cell

Finally, the state required that the masters observe minimum standards of humane treatment. Premeditated and unprovoked murder of a slave was illegal in the South by the end of the eighteenth century. Some states—Alabama, for instance—charged every master to "treat his slave with humanity, and . . . not inflict upon him any cruel punishment; he must provide him with a sufficiency of healthy food and necessary clothing; cause him to be properly attended during sickness, and provide for his necessary wants in old age." As of 1830 Kentucky law provided that "slaves, if inhumanely treated, shall be taken from their masters and sold to others."[39] The fact that such laws were common to slave societies throughout history suggests that they were vague enough to

→ *this rule was ignored according to F. Douglass*

encompass sadistic beatings and near-starvation at least as often as they ensured genuine kindness and concern.

The law, of course, is not a reliable guide to everyday practice. And it is worth remembering that restricting the power of the masters, even to the point that slaves could be taken from them for mistreatment, had no liberating implications for those who were unfree. Once again, the fact that the master's power was less than absolute did not imply that the slave's subordination was less than total. The Kentucky law, like most of its kind, provided only that expropriated slaves be sold to other, presumably more humane, masters.

Still, the law restrained the slaveholders in important ways. Masters could not enslave anybody they wanted, they could not free a slave under any circumstances, and their slaves could be expropriated for a variety of reasons, including gross mistreatment. Yet the slaveholders were the last to acknowledge that the state had such tremendous powers. After all, the discipline imposed on masters by the law of slavery was, at least in part, self-discipline. Slaveholders wrote these laws and almost always held clear majorities in the legislatures that enacted them. Hence the powers granted to the state in the southern slave codes must be taken as in some manner an expression of the slaveholders' assumptions. The prosecution of a sadistic master, for example, could actually serve the larger interests of the slaveholding class by demonstrating the masters' willingness to abide by the standards of decency upheld in the rule of law. Thus state power posed no threat when governmental authorities were called upon to distinguish the commonplace brutality of the system from the wanton murder of a helpless slave.

But the power of the state, once legitimized, was not easily controlled. It was the arbitration of difficult cases, those in which the boundaries of acceptable behavior were put to the test, that raised the power of the state from a theoretical to a practical concern. Those boundaries were usually at issue in the most important judicial cases concerning slavery in the Old South. In some ways it was an ordinary legal problem: where do you draw the line? In this case, where did the state's power end and the individual master's begin? But the intrinsic ambiguity of slave law—the total subordination of the slave to a master who himself owed allegiance to the state—transformed a simple problem into a profound dilemma. For it was all but impossible for a liberal political culture to place limits on the masters' power without implicitly granting rights to slaves.

This made the jurisprudence of slavery intrinsically subversive. Thomas Cobb sought to evade the problem by declaring that the rights accorded slaves were not really "rights" at all, but merely procedural guarantees granted by the state for pragmatic reasons. For some, this was a critical point: the guarantee of certain legal procedures for accused slaves was not the same as the vesting of rights in slaves. But for others, the distinction was far too delicate since it was difficult, perhaps impossible, to separate the legal (and social) consequences of procedural guarantees from inherent rights. How else can rights be implemented in the real world, critics wondered, except as procedural guarantees? As Hurd pointed out, "every recognition of rights in the slave, independent of the will of the owner or master, which is made by the state to which he is subject, diminishes in some degree the essence of that slavery by changing it into a relation between legal persons."⁴⁰

Slave law, therefore, had to maintain a delicate balance. The state's right to regulate slavery was implicit in the very nature of the master-slave relationship. Slavery could not survive without some legal recognition of its existence, some legal determination of who was and was not a slave, some rudimentary definition of slavery itself. At the same time, extensive regulation that restricted the master's power over the slave necessarily "diminished" the essence of slavery.

This posed a dangerous dilemma in the best of circumstances. But in the South the dangers were multiplied by the fact that the laws and decisions regulating slavery were formulated within a liberal state that was not the historical creature of the slaveholding class. Not only was the slaveholders' political system inherited from an Anglo-Saxon tradition largely unrelated to slavery, not only did the Constitution establish the sovereignty of a federal government that could deny as well as secure the slaveholders' power, but even within the South the slaveholders' political influence depended increasingly on the votes and support of a nonslaveholding majority whose loyalty to the master class was anything but certain. This situation inevitably altered the significance of every act of slave resistance that ended up in the legal and political system.

Hence the tone of desperation that hovered over the case law of slavery in the Old South. Every instance in which the courts were called upon to draw a new line, to set new limits on the master's power, tended "to diminish the essence" of slavery. It was an issue that divided the most powerful legal minds in the antebellum South. When Lydia, refusing to be "chastised," was shot by John Mann, she could not have known that her case would inspire Judge Thomas Ruffin to issue one of the South's most forceful judicial defenses of the master's power over the slave. Nor could Will have known, when he stabbed his overseer to death, that his action would end in Judge William Gaston's conclusive repudiation of Ruffin's principles. The difference between Ruffin and Gaston, both distinguished North Carolina jurists, was at bottom a difference over where the state's authority stopped and where the master's became unassailable.

For Ruffin, the owners' right to "full dominion" over the slaves was "essential to their value as property." Ruffin concluded in *State* v. *Mann* that "the power of the master must be absolute to render the submission of the slave perfect." Though the judge acknowledged the right of "the whole community" to interfere in the master's authority by legislation, he nevertheless argued that such interference undermined the master's "absolute" authority. As extreme as Ruffin acknowledged his formulation to be, "in the actual condition of things it must be so," he insisted. "There is no remedy. This discipline belongs to the state of slavery." Thus Ruffin had scarcely conceded the hypothetical possibility of state interference in the master-slave relationship before hastening his retreat from such dangerous speculations. "We cannot allow the right of the master to be brought into discussion in the courts of justice. The slave, to remain a slave, must be made sensible that there is no appeal from his master; that his power is in no instance usurped."[41]

But Ruffin's logic was too extreme even for the North Carolina Supreme Court on which he sat. Within five years his own colleagues repudiated the philosophy expounded in the Mann decision and retreated to the more familiar effort "to draw the line . . . between the lawful and unlawful exercise of the master's power." The issue in *State* v. *Will* was not whether the slave was guilty of a crime but whether the crime was murder or the lesser offense of felonious homicide. By deciding the latter the court upheld the principle that there were not only limits to the master's authority but that the slave had a right to resist the master who stepped beyond those limits.[42]

It took some doing to evade the *Mann* precedent. Nevertheless, in Ruffin's seemingly unequivocal rhetoric, B. F. Moore, arguing in Will's behalf, discovered an exquisite loophole: Ruffin's words, he said, "were never intended to cover the entire relation between master and slave." And with that Moore felt free to renounce everything Ruffin had clearly asserted. Absolute power "is irresponsible power," he declared, "circumscribed by no limits save its own imbecility." He emphasized the distinction between the total subordination of the slave and the absolute power of the master. About the need for "the *perfect* submission of the slave" there was no doubt. "But whether it will more certainly result from the *absolute* power of the owner, than from a *large* but *limited* authority, is questionable indeed."[43]

Judge Gaston's decision was less forthright in its rejection of Ruffin's logic. But writing for the court he nevertheless drew the line in favor of limiting rather than strengthening the master's power. "Unconditional submission is the *general* duty of the slave; unlimited power is, in general, the *legal* right of the master," Gaston admitted. Nevertheless, "it is certain that the master has not the right to slay his slave, and I hold it to be equally certain that the slave has a right to defend himself against the unlawful attempt of his master to deprive him of life." For the next generation the court continued to expand the limitations it placed on the master's power over the slave, while Judge Ruffin sat in frustration issuing futile dissents.[44]

Not even Ruffin, however, was able to escape the rhetorical conventions of liberal political culture. He understood as well as did Gaston that the issue in these cases was the balance of power within the master-slave relationship. Yet he glided unconsciously from the reality of power to the language of rights, defining the master's authority in recognizably "liberal" terms. "We cannot allow the *right* of the master to be brought into discussion in the courts of justice . . . his *power* must in no way be usurped." Nor could Gaston escape those same ideological conventions. He, too, defined the slave's subordination as the "legal right" of the master. And notwithstanding Cobb's distinction between the inherent rights of freemen and the pragmatic privileges granted to slaves, Gaston held that the slave "has a *right* to defend himself" against a master's murderous assault.

It is pointless to ask whether Ruffin or Gaston correctly captured the true essence of slavery. The *Mann* and *Will* cases are of interest because they reveal the divergent trajectories intrinsic to the law of slavery—the one flowing from the total subordination of the slave to the master, the other from the master's subordination to the state. Ruffin acknowledged the legislature's theoretical capacity to inhibit a master's right to commit a battery on the slave. But he denied that the legislature could do this without undermining slavery itself. He thereby equated the slave's total subordination with the master's "absolute power," something no slave society had ever done. Cobb noted some years later that while "pure" slavery put the bondsman "under the absolute and uncontrolled dominion of his master . . . no such state of slavery exists in these States."[45] By carrying the degree of the master's power to its logical extreme, Ruffin sought to resolve the dilemma by denying it out of existence.

But Gaston carried the logic of the state's authority over the master in another, perhaps more subversive direction. For once the slave's right to resist a murderous assault was legally acknowledged, it was not easy to stem the flow of residual rights. Gaston correctly understood that no slave society could countenance truly absolute power in the master—a law that acknowledged in the slave no human passions whatsoever. "I cannot believe," he wrote, "that this is the law of a civilized people and of a Christian land." But Ruffin's overheated prose grew out of his recognition, no less correct than Gaston's, that a law that progressively interfered in the master-slave relationship was a law that diminished the essence of slavery.

Every new law regulating slave behavior was therefore a status report on the balance of power between masters and slaves in the Old South. What did the slaves do that they were not supposed to, and do with sufficient regularity to require legislation? They burned barns enough to stir Virginia's lawmakers into action in 1807. They poisoned their owners enough to provoke the Kentucky legislature in 1810. They learned how to read and got their hands on "incendiary" abolitionist literature often enough to raise fears across the South in the 1830's and 1840's. Far more often slaves left their plantations without passes, forged passes, or simply ran away. Once gone, they committed a variety of petty and not so petty crimes that state and local governments made it their business to prosecute. Slaves were tried for theft and robbery, assault, rape, and murder—all of which raised special problems precisely because the persons involved were not supposed to have "legal personalities" to begin with.

Reading the slave codes in this light is a shorthand way to evaluate the political significance of slave resistance. For every crime a slave was accused of having committed, the law had to make special provision for the rights of due process. The legal structure thus invested every slave crime with potentially significant political implications. The codes were, in effect, a litany of actions taken by slaves often enough to provoke state recognition of their legal personalities, a recognition both Thomas Cobb and John Hurd, the two greatest chroniclers of slave law in antebellum America, saw as incompatible with the nature of slavery.

The statutes begin to suggest the larger dimensions of the problem. They demonstrate that despite the totality of the master-slave relationship, some slaves would always engage in acts of resistance that were beyond the master's control, and often beyond the master's purview. When that happened—when slaves as outsiders disturbed the lives of free insiders—slaves found themselves in a political universe whose assumptions were antithetical to those of slavery. By definition a slave was rightless. By its very nature slavery reversed the great premise of Anglo-American law: that certain basic rights were universal and inalienable. So whenever an act of resistance moved a slave from one world to another, the fundamental status of the slave was thrown open to debate. This was how slave resistance began to influence American politics.

The groundwork for this influence was laid down in the late eighteenth century, when liberal and evangelical individualism combined to inspire a wave of humanitarian reforms throughout the Anglo-American world. The movement to abolish slavery was perhaps its most visible manifestation, but humanitarianism's most pervasive influence was felt in the amelioration of the criminal law. Bourgeois sentiments, both secular and religious, recoiled from the overt use of physical cruelty as a weapon of social discipline. Whipping, ear cropping, branding, and other forms of corporal punishment were substantially eliminated from the law. The number of capital offenses was reduced, and public executions were gradually abolished between the late eighteenth and early nineteenth centuries.[46] In the South, the slave codes were revised to eliminate the most extreme punishments—notably castration and other forms of physical mutilation—for slaves convicted of crimes.

Most significantly, the slave's right to "personal security" was increasingly recognized in a series of laws and court decisions restricting the master's power to brutalize the slave. The process began when the murder of an unresisting slave was outlawed. But this was only the beginning, for the enforcement of such laws inevitably raised excruciating questions: Who would determine whether a slave was or was not resisting? If slaves were the only witnesses, as was often the case, could they testify against their masters or any other white men? If murder was illegal, did slaves have any rights of self-defense? And how were such questions to be decided when a free man other than the master was one of the parties to a dispute? Slave law alone had no answers to these questions. Whenever they arose, southern lawmakers had no choice but to borrow from the principles and rules of procedure governing the criminal law of free society, principles incompatible with the very nature of slavery: the right to a jury trial, the right of self-defense, the right to swear an oath, to bear witness, to face one's accusers.

These procedural guarantees were not simply granted to slaves in a generous spirit of liberal humanitarianism. Quite the contrary: they were grudgingly conceded by men who were fully aware of the dangerous implications of their actions but who could find no alternative given their political circumstances. In fact, nearly every major court decision elaborating a slave's rights was provoked by some act of resistance on the part of the slave. In *State* v. *Hoover*, for example, the master was held criminally liable for an "immoderate and unreasonable" punishment that led to the slave's death. The case grew out of a sadistic beating he administered to the slave on the grounds that "she stole his turnips and sold them to the worthless people in the neighborhood, and . . . she had attempted to burn his barn, and was disobedient and impudent to her mistress." So brutal was the murder that even Judge Ruffin sided with the majority on the North Carolina Supreme Court, declaring that "the master's authority is not altogether unlimited. He must not kill. There is, at the least, this restriction upon his power."[47]

But Ruffin dissented ten years later when the same court held, in *State* v. *Caesar*, that a slave who killed a white man in a fit of passion could be tried not for murder but for the lesser crime of manslaughter. Having clubbed to death a man who had physically attacked a fellow slave, Caesar raised yet again the problem of how far the common-law rights of free persons could be extended to slaves. To Ruffin, the "dissimilarity in the condition of slaves from anything known in the common law cannot be denied." But deny it is precisely what the majority on the court did. "If you say, the prisoner is not entitled to the rule of the common law, which knows no difference of caste," the court held, "then you not only strip him of a defence, which the common law secured to him, but you establish another rule, that a slave shall, in no case, strike a white man for an assault and battery upon another slave."[48] Ruffin was infuriated.

And so it went, one court extending the legal protection of slaves on the grounds that the master's authority was limited by law, another resisting such extensions on the ground that "slave rights" was a contradiction in terms.[49] It never went very far; even in 1860 the slaves had scarcely any of the rights free men and women took for granted. If southern courts and legislatures extended somewhat the slave's right to life, they did little or nothing to ensure, much less recognize, the slave's right to liberty or property. Yet over time the tendency was clearly toward extending rather than limiting slave rights, a tendency that was fraught with subversive implications. As he laid out the process by which southern law backed into an increasing recognition of slave rights, Thomas Cobb's footnotes to his *Inquiry into the Law of Slavery* revealed the explosive controversy the process touched off. "I cannot agree with the Court, in South Carolina," Cobb announced,

> that "every attempt to extend to the slave positive rights, is an attempt to reconcile inherent contradictions. . . ." Nor that "in the very nature of things, he is subject to despotism . . . ." There is no inconsistency in speaking of the rights of a slave, where those rights are well defined by law, nor is there any inherent difficulty in enforcing those rights by law, even against his own master. Every statute passed to protect the life or limb of the slave, gives to him a right to the protection provided. And if the law omitted, the Court should provide a remedy. The slaves of other countries have positive rights, and yet are not relieved from slavery.[50]

The conflicts between Lydia and John Mann, between Richard Baxter and Will, and finally between Ruffin and Gaston, were not isolated outbreaks of conflicting principles but emblematic demonstrations of the problem of slave resistance in a liberal society. The smallest incidents of refusal could exacerbate the fundamental tension between the master's authority and the power of the state.

* * *

IF THE EXTENSION of "rights" to slaves could touch off such powerful conflicts within the South, where the consequences of slave resistance could be most effectively contained, the issue became even more explosive when it transcended sectional boundaries. It is not surprising, then, that slaveholders became unusually sensitive to the potential power of the federal government. Decades of agitation over the extension of slavery—from the Missouri crisis in 1820 through the debate over the disposition of lands acquired during the Mexican War in the late 1840's—put slaveholders on their guard. To the general hostility toward centralized government that was widespread throughout America, slavery added a tone of severity that slipped further and further into desperation with the passage of time.

This became clear as early as 1828 when the state of South Carolina reacted with unusual fervor against new federal tariff schedules. The tariff was no abstract issue over which the South Carolinians chose to make a stand for the principle of states' rights. On the contrary, it exposed a growing fear that the federal government was using its powers to favor the interests of the nascent manufacturing economy in the Northeast to the disadvantage of the southern slave economy. Coming at the end of a decade of depressed cotton prices, the tariff of 1828 so disturbed the legislature of South Carolina that it commissioned John C. Calhoun to write an *Exposition and Protest*. Published anonymously, Calhoun's pamphlet raised to a new level of theoretical sophistication an idea that had in fact been voiced much earlier and fairly often in American politics: that states had the right to "nullify" or "interpose" federal legislation that violated their interests. In this instance, however, South Carolina's position provoked a full-scale debate in the United States Senate and, subsequently, a major constitutional crisis. In 1832, when Congress "reformed" the tariff hardly at all, South Carolina formally declared the law null and void as far as "this State, its officers or citizens" were concerned.[51]

The nullification crisis was resolved when Congress passed a compromise tariff the following year, but the episode revealed the degree to which leading spokesmen for the South were becoming increasingly disturbed by the potential power of the federal government. The event was yet another turning point in the developing conflict between North and South. For it was out of this debate that northern leaders fashioned the first argument for the perpetuity of the Union.[52] Calhoun, meanwhile, continued to move in the opposite direction. By the 1840's the fear of the central government's power not only to favor the manufacturing interests of the North but to interfere with the slaveholding interest of the South had pushed Calhoun into an extraordinary philosophical rejection of some of liberalism's basic tenets. His *Disquisition on Government* revealed how the ambiguous relation between slavery and American political culture could provoke a reaction against liberalism as easily as a defense of it.

To be sure, Calhoun was not alone in his repudiation of the "social compact" and the principle of "natural rights." By the middle of the nineteenth century the revolt against the Enlightenment and the reactionary rejection of the Age of Revolution were in full swing throughout the western world. The most conservative end of the proslavery ideological spectrum partook heavily of this antiliberal trend. Calhoun, for example, replaced the centerpiece of liberal ideology—the primacy of rights—with the doctrine of the "concurrent majority." Precisely because liberalism made the rights of the individual primary, it could not propose any ideal of community that consistently outweighed individual rights. But Calhoun's philosophy began with a vision of the social forms distinctive to each section and held that their preservation took precedence over all else. "By giving to each interest, or portion, the power of self-protection, all strife and struggle between them for ascendancy is prevented," Calhoun explained. The fear of government's power to tamper with southern slavery had steadily pushed Calhoun outside the liberal consensus. It remained to be seen how many Southerners would follow his lead.[53]

Certainly the fear of the central government would only grow with time. By the 1850's the expansion of slavery once again raised the ever-present specter of the federal government's power to legislate on the South's "peculiar" institution. The Compromise of

1850 had scarcely settled the question of how the spoils of the war with Mexico were to be divided when the struggle over Kansas and Nebraska once again brought slavery expansion into the heart of national politics. By then, however, a second issue—slave resistance—had burst its sectional confines, seriously undermining the slaveholders' capacity to control its political consequences.

The problem for slaveholders was that they themselves had always relied on the federal government to sustain their power. In 1787 they had fought hard and with great success for constitutional provisions recognizing and protecting slavery in a variety of different ways. Since three out of five slaves were counted for purposes of representation, free Southerners held extra seats in Congress, which they repeatedly used to protect the slaveholders' interests. For seventy-five years slaveholders dominated the Presidency. Holding the fugitive-slave clause paramount, the Supreme Court consistently upheld the masters' interests by striking down the personal-liberty laws of one northern state after another. From the American Revolution through the outbreak of the Civil War, the slaveholders successfully pressed their case in the legislative, executive, and judicial branches of the federal government.

But in their reliance on the power of the federal government the slaveholders laid the groundwork for their eventual destruction. As the legal and political consequences of slave resistance extended beyond the borders of the southern states, the slaveholders found themselves in a political universe whose assumptions were antithetical to their own. If slave resistance created excruciating problems within the South, in Washington, D.C., the master class eventually lost all control of its subversive consequences.

Consider the problem of fugitive slaves. As resistance went, running away was a modest but consequential act. Its political significance could be direct—as in the fugitive-slave crisis of the 1850's—or indirect, as when abolitionists used escapes for propaganda purposes. And in some contexts, as we shall see, the political significance of running away could reach revolutionary proportions. In each of these ways, running away contributed to the crisis that divided the United States by forcing the federal government to take up an issue that the slaveholders wanted left out of national politics altogether. Whatever it was that frightened southern jurists about the state's recognition of the slave's legal personality paled by comparison with the potential consequences of the federal government's increasing involvement in the slavery issue. To the extent that runaway slaves compelled such involvement, slave resistance helped destroy the political power of the master class.

At the heart of the fugitive-slave controversy rested a "conflict of laws" that could have political significance only if slaves actually ran away. Northern law presumed that black people, however "inferior" and however much discriminated against, possessed the basic rights of life, liberty, and property. Southern law presumed the opposite. To protect free blacks from kidnapping by fugitive-slave catchers, northern states established legal procedures for determining whether or not a slaveholder's claim of ownership was valid. These "personal-liberty laws" necessarily extended the presumption of freedom to fugitive slaves, flatly contradicting southern law. They thereby created a potential for sectional conflict every time a slave set foot on northern soil. Nor could such conflicts be confined to relations between individual states, for the United States Constitution and the Fugitive Slave Act of 1793 together guaranteed slaveholders the right of "recaption."[54]

So long as no slave ever set foot in a free state, this conflict of laws was a matter of mere theoretical interest. The personal-liberty laws posed no direct threat to slavery, for while they may have discouraged some masters from claiming their runaways, the laws never prevented a single fugitive slave from being returned to the South once a master's claim was validated. By the 1850's runaways had become a major source of sectional antagonism solely because of the political conflict they both exposed and provoked. Far more directly than abolitionist propaganda, fugitive slaves forced both the North and South into ever-hardening defenses of their conflicting social structures.[55]

The North's extension of the Somerset principle posed a more direct threat to slavery than did the legal protection of fugitives.

the laws of England do not translate in HP's world

As originally enunciated in England by Lord Mansfield in 1772, the Somerset principle extended to slaves certain protections against arbitrary seizure by masters. As interpreted by many contemporaries, the Somerset principle held that in the absence of positive laws establishing slavery, all persons standing on English—and perhaps American—soil were presumed to be free. Massachusetts jurists invoked this interpretation of the principle a few years after it was declared, and it was subsequently adopted by other northern states as sectional tensions increased. The Somerset principle held out the prospect of freedom to anyone who set foot in the North, including slaves who were merely in transit with their owners. By contrast, the personal-liberty laws simply established procedures regulating the capture of fugitive slaves, but they could do little more than delay the eventual return of runaways. Like the personal-liberty laws, however, the Somerset principle was more significant for its political consequences than for the number of slaves it could possibly free. When Dred and Harriet Scott rested their famed lawsuit on the claim that they had once resided on free soil with their master, the political threat proved far more consequential than the prospect of two slaves being emancipated.[56]

Dred Scott's case was only one of a climactic series of incidents that politicized the issue of slavery to the point where sectional animosities gave way to civil war. In many of those cases the precipitating action was taken by slaves who claimed their freedom, often without militant intentions. Margaret Morgan simply assumed her freedom to move from Maryland to York County, Pennsylvania. This put her putative owners in a precarious legal position after they recaptured the slave and returned her to the South. For in so doing they violated Pennsylvania laws against kidnapping and found themselves tied up in a lawsuit that went all the way to the Supreme Court. And while the captors won their case in *Prigg* v. *Pennsylvania*, the precedent they established subsequently proved as useful to abolitionists as to slaveholders. For although Chief Justice Joseph Story's "opinion of the court" recognized Congress's right to legislate on the subject of slavery in free states, it also exempted states from having to enforce the

Fugitive Slave Law of 1793. Thanks to Margaret Morgan's successful lawsuit, a half-dozen northern legislatures passed statutes prohibiting state officials from enforcing the fugitive slave clause of the U.S. Constitution. By contrast, George Latimer ran away claiming a former master had promised him freedom, but with full knowledge that his claim was in dispute. Regardless of his motives, however, the controversy generated by Latimer's escape led directly to the passage of the Massachusetts personal-liberty law of 1843.[57]

The abolitionists were quick to use these and other acts of slave resistance to build their case against slavery. Theodore Dwight Weld's famous antislavery tract *American Slavery as It Is* could hardly have been written had the slaves been a compliant and tractable work force. Weld's polemical effect was achieved by his documentary style: a deceptively straightforward litany of fugitive-slave advertisements, many of them gruesome in their details of physical abuse and mutilation. Since slaveholders were not a peculiarly barbaric people, it is safe to assume that the brutality Weld exposed was less a function of sadistic masters than of resisting slaves. Nor was Weld's rhetorical strategy diminished by arguments that his evidence was selective. The point is that he could never have made his selections had there been no fugitive slaves with their identifying scars.[58]

Propagandists used slave resistance in more direct ways to make their political points. One need not have been an abolitionist to sympathize with Harriet Beecher Stowe's Eliza as she crossed the perilously icy waters of the Ohio River in a desperate effort to keep her child from being sold away. Yet how many readers who held their breath until Eliza's escape was secure could temper their sympathies with the knowledge that in crossing that river Eliza was committing a crime for which she could legally be killed, or that those who assisted the slave mother in her effort to save her child were liable to federal prosecution under the terms of the Fugitive Slave Act of 1850? Stowe's genius lay precisely in her ability to evoke a sympathetic response to criminal acts of resistance.[59]

Stowe's point was made all the more effective by the fact that

Eliza was clearly not a habitually rebellious slave, that she was motivated by no overpowering desire for freedom nor by any festering hatred of her master. What Stowe demonstrated, instead, was that the master-slave relationship inescapably pitted Eliza against her owner in spite of the warm feelings each had for the other. Eliza's motives did not change the fact that her behavior directly thwarted her master's will, violated state and federal law, and still won the sympathies of hundreds of thousands of northern readers. Abraham Lincoln is said to have greeted Stowe as "the little lady who made this big war," but he might just as easily have blamed the Civil War on the author's sympathetic character, the fugitive slave Eliza.

In such subtle but powerful ways, slave resistance redefined the ideological battle lines in the sectional crisis. The racism of white Northerners and their widespread animosity toward abolitionists are well established. But slaves who ran away or sued for freedom did not compel Northerners to repudiate their racism, to support abolition, or even to interfere in the southern slave system. Such cases did require Northerners to decide whether they were willing to jeopardize their own liberties by reenslaving those who claimed their freedom without observing the minimal rights of due process. Many citizens who were perfectly prepared to defend the masters' right to own slaves were increasingly unprepared to let the slaveholders exercise their privileges as masters at the expense of northern liberties and safeguards.

Runaways themselves contributed immeasurably to the propaganda war throughout the decades that preceded secession. Fugitive-slave narratives are well known—and sometimes criticized—for their formulaic quality: the slave too often seethes under the weight of his or her oppression. Gradually, the slave's determination to be free becomes all-consuming. There are unsuccessful escapes, but recapture only strengthens the slave's determination. And finally, often unexpectedly, an opportunity arises, and the dramatic climax is reached. The slave escapes and, once secure, works tirelessly to advance the cause of freedom for all slaves—beginning with a published autobiography. Such narratives were indeed formulaic, which is precisely why they were so effective. By pressing the issue in the most categorical terms of slavery and freedom, runaways helped transform the simple act of running away into a politically explosive fugitive-slave controversy.[60]

Slave resistance thus contributed to the ideological war that was forcing the slaveholders into ever more explicit defenses of their social order. The long period of "agitation" over the slavery issue, a New Orleans newspaper noted in late 1860, "has evolved the true principles on which the institution of slavery is based. It has convinced all Southern men of the moral right, the civil, social and political benefit of slavery." In their final form proslavery principles reflected the influence within the South of the wider intellectual universe of the nineteenth century. Reactionaries invoked the themes of romantic anti-modernism. Theologians ran the gamut from anti-rationalist conservatism to evangelical individualism. Radical democrats transformed eighteenth-century republicanism into proslavery racism. Whiggish advocates of commercial development joined slavery to the language of nineteenth-century boosterism, whereas the most conservative proslavery ideologues reiterated the critiques of urban industrial society pouring forth from disgruntled artisans, reform-minded novelists, parliamentary committees, and revolutionary socialists. In each case, cultural traditions that had little to do with slavery were drafted into the service of southern slave society and in the process were dramatically transformed into a complex and highly developed body of proslavery thought.[61]

If proslavery ideology reflected the increasingly powerful revolt against liberalism, it is worth remembering that the revolt matured even as liberalism reached its greatest achievements and widest influence. It is no surprise, therefore, that in the liberal-capitalist world the southern masters inhabited, proslavery thought focused most often on the primacy of rights—with particular fidelity to the right of property. The political structure of the liberal state placed an added burden on the slaveholders as they formulated their defense of human bondage. For in the context of the protracted tensions between upcountry yeomen and black-belt planters, the voting power of the South's slaveless farmers compelled the master class to emphasize still other features of their distinctive social order: the political equality of all white men and the absence of aristocratic barriers to slaveownership.

Each of these influences was at work as the slaveholders turned to the North in answer to the rising chorus of denunciation against them. Each and all were readily visible in the works of leading proslavery intellectuals—and still more so in the final defense of slavery put forward by the advocates of secession. Slavery's apologists were pushed to the limits of liberal ideology, and in some of the most interesting cases beyond those limits. As most of them searched for a justification of a social order that systematically inverted liberalism's fundamental precepts, they found themselves trapped, by cultural inheritance and political circumstances, within the language of liberalism itself. Nevertheless, the debate over slavery in the nineteenth century provoked sharp, categorical analyses of the relative merits of an agricultural society grounded in the labor of slaves and an urbanizing, industrializing society grounded on wage labor.

In his influential analysis of the debate over slavery in the Virginia legislature during 1831–1832, for example, Thomas R. Dew came close to suggesting that the very nature of the master-slave relationship contradicted the rancorous competition endemic to liberalism. "We do not find among [the slaveholders] that cold, contracted, calculating *selfishness*, which withers and repels everything around it," Dew argued, "and lessens or destroys all the multiplied enjoyments of social intercourse." Nevertheless, Dew's argument against the gradual emancipation and colonization of Virginia's slaves rested on the force of economic self-interest, the very thing he later claimed slavery diminished. Citing bourgeois economists from Adam Smith to Thomas Malthus, Dew slammed repeatedly at the economic impracticality of emancipation schemes, bemoaning "the intrusion, in this matter, of those who have no interest at stake." As proof against all claims that slave labor was inferior to free, he pointed to the high price a slave commanded on the open market. This, he claimed, was "an evidence of his value with every one acquainted with the elements of political economy."[62]

At the core of Dew's argument rested the simplest of all liberal assumptions: the right of property. "We take it for granted that the right of the owner to his slave is to be respected," he wrote. For the "great object of government is the protection of property." Beginning from this premise, Dew launched a Madisonian attack on the tyranny of the majority in language that anticipated Calhoun's theory of the "concurrent majority," yet did not forsake the liberal presumption of fundamental rights. "The fact is, it is always a most delicate and dangerous task for one set of people to legislate for another, without any community of interests," Dew explained. "It is sure to destroy the great principle of responsibility, and in the end to lay the weaker at the mercy of the stronger. It subverts the very end for which all governments are established, and becomes intolerable, and consequently against the fundamental rights of man."[63]

A few short years later, William Harper fared little better than Dew in his effort to reject the philosophical presuppositions of those who had by then perfected the radical abolitionist critique of slavery. In his *Memoir on Slavery*, published in 1838, Harper made much of his rejection of the revolutionary doctrine of natural rights, though by then most Northerners were coming to exactly the same conclusion anyway. For Harper, the conviction that "rights" were socially created—while common to mid-nineteenth-century Americans—became the centerpiece of his defense of slavery as a "civilizing" force in society. Without the social inequality that inevitably arose when some men commanded the labor of others, he argued, there could be no sense of higher aspiration and achievement and hence no "civilization."[64] Yet Harper, like Dew, could not break completely from prevailing liberal assumptions, for it was quite clear that the primacy of individual rights and the sanctity of property were perfectly compatible with the various forms of inequality that Harper considered essential to the preservation of civilized society.

Harper went beyond Dew in some respects, but usually in ways that exposed still further his reliance on the commonplace tenets of American political culture. In particular, he fell into the republican habit of dividing the world into only two forms of labor: dependent and independent. By defining independent labor as "free" and everything else as "slavery" he effectively collapsed the critical distinctions between slavery, serfdom, and wage work. Harper's dichotomy had a long tradition in America, one that had become particularly important at the moment he wrote his *Memoir*. Northern labor radicals, disturbed by the growth of the industrial economy, had launched a vocal campaign against the "slavery" of the wage system—comparing it unfavorably to the chattel slavery of the South. By the 1840's leading radical laborites in the North looked to none other than John C. Calhoun as their preferred presidential candidate. Their shared republicanism left both proslavery ideologues and northern radicals with a strong conviction that the central government was using its power to prop up a rising industrial aristocracy in the North.[65]

Harper's attacks on industrial society thus partook of a powerful republican tradition that stretched back into eighteenth-century America. Because republican ideology ranked personal independence as the highest form of virtue, it had a pronounced tendency to look upon cities and wage-earners with a mixture of suspicion and contempt. "Sores on the body politic," Jefferson had called them. And as English and northern abolitionists stepped up their critique of slavery, Jefferson's legacy was put on active duty as a proslavery counterattack against the foundations of industrial society. In the late 1850's Edmund Ruffin attacked England's wage-labor economy as a "widespread, miserable and life-destroying hunger slavery and pauper slavery." He painted an even more lurid picture of the consequences of the recent economic depression in the North: the "free hired laborers were thrown out of employment, or employed only at much reduced wages. Hence all such persons were greatly damaged or distressed, and thousands of the most destitute were ready to starve. Hence hunger mobs were menacing the city of New York with pillage, and the last evils of a vicious and unbridled and starving populace, excited to insurrection and defiance of legal authority."[66] In such conditions free laborers were only nominally free, George Fitzhugh declared, while in practice they "are already slaves without masters."[67]

By repeatedly comparing the condition of southern slaves to the misery of the most impoverished wage-earning classes of England and the North, proslavery ideologues upheld shockingly low standards for their own society. Long before the Republican party in the North had set itself the task of distinguishing wage labor from slavery, and defending the former by invidious comparison with the latter, the defense of slavery had become fixated on demonstrations of the superior health, the preferable diet, and the ample clothing and shelter offered to the slaves. The benevolence of the master, his sheer kindness and goodwill, were put forward as a justification for the complete denial of freedom. We may leave to one side the question of how accurate were the masters' claims that they treated the slaves kindly—although there is more than enough evidence to suggest that the slaves saw things somewhat differently. At issue here is the question of why the defense of slavery seemed to move further from the issue of freedom and power as the attack on slavery grew ever more pronounced.

The increasingly inflated claims about the physical well-being and creature comforts of the slave quarters exposed yet again the depths of the slaveholders' immersion in the culture of liberal capitalism. If the ethic of consumption was beginning to transform the way Americans talked about freedom, it could not help but transform the way they talked about slavery. Critics of slavery held that the superiority of capitalism was proved by the unprecedented levels of wealth it generated and by the widespread opportunities it offered men and women to partake of that wealth. Masters answered not by rejecting the standards to which they were being held but by claiming that those standards were more fully satisfied in the South than anywhere else—that the South was wealthier than the North and that the slaves benefited from that wealth even more than the wage earners of industrial society.

The more insistently the slaveholders defended their "treatment" of the slaves, however, the more clearly they revealed the totality of their power over the lives of others. At issue in the master-slave relationship was not whether slaveholders exercised their power responsibly but the intrinsic injustice of their power to begin with, not whether the slaves were overworked but the terms under which they were compelled to work, not whether slave families existed but whether they were secure against the masters' power to destroy them. With every new detail the slaveholders added to the argument that they treated their slaves kindly, they succeeded only in exposing the extremity of their power—the very thing the slaves so deeply resented and so consistently resisted.

Not all of slavery's defenders followed this train of logic. As we have seen, John C. Calhoun was developing a powerful alternative to the doctrine of individual rights. By the 1850's it was possible for the slaveholders to go still further by transforming the critique of wage labor into a fundamental rejection of liberalism. They could begin, as George Fitzhugh did, with a vision of an ideal society grounded on the labor of slaves rather than on the primacy of rights. Far more explicitly than had William Harper, Fitzhugh equated slavery with feudalism. He littered his analysis of master-slave relations with references to reciprocity and organicism, language more reminiscent of the Middle Ages than the nineteenth century. He had nothing to say about the social death of the slaves, about their kinlessness, or about the way they were systematically dishonored—all the things that made slavery a distinct form of subordination. Nor did he acknowledge any of capitalism's influence on the way slave labor was driven in the South. Instead, Fitzhugh rather innocently supposed that it was capitalism whose vitality depended on slavery rather than the other way around.

But if Fitzhugh's characterization of the workings of slave society was considerably more romanticized than Calhoun's had been, his critique of liberalism was far more trenchant. The most thoroughly reactionary of all proslavery ideologues, Fitzhugh zeroed in on the core of liberal ideology and explicitly repudiated it. He pronounced "Locke's theory of the social contract" a catastrophic "heresy . . . pregnant with mischief." But where many others had merely rejected the doctrine that rights were "natural," Fitzhugh went on to dispute the great liberal postulate that rights, whether grounded in nature or secured by mankind, should take precedence over the interests of society. Man "has no rights whatever, as opposed to the interests of society; and that society may very properly make any use of him that will redound to the public good. Whatever rights he has are subordinate to the good of the whole," Fitzhugh concluded, "and he has never ceded rights to it, for he was born its slave, and had no rights to cede."[68] From these premises the conclusion followed almost automatically that slavery, not freedom, was the "natural" form of social organization.

Yet both Fitzhugh and Calhoun faced a similar dilemma. Their impulse to defend slavery had pushed them outside the confines of liberalism, forcing them to blaze a trail that few of their fellow Southerners saw fit to follow. For by the 1850's it was also possible for the slaveholders to take from American political culture its fear of centralized government, its racism, its republican disdain for dependency, and its consumerism—and to fashion from these another defense of slavery grounded not in the vision of an alternative society but on the sanctity of private property.

The historical circumstances within which the masters developed their defense of slavery all but assured that they would choose the latter path. The great issues that had nationalized the debate over slavery—its expansionism and the intractable problem of runaways—tended to lead the slaveholders into an ever more resolute defense of the rights of property. The forums in which they presented their arguments (the Supreme Court and the United States Congress, for example) could hardly accommodate a proslavery ideology that repudiated the philosophical premises upon which those political institutions operated. And the yeomen farmers who finally had to be convinced that secession was the only way to protect southern slavery were hardly receptive to assaults on the very idea of free society.

So, forced by the expansion of slavery and the resistance of slaves to engage in a debate they would have preferred to avoid, the slaveholders overwhelmingly fell back on the rhetoric of constitutional rights and the security of private property. Citing the North's "Personal Liberty Bills and such legal 'aid and comfort,' " a Kentucky editor predicted that runaways would slowly drain the state of its slaves unless it joined the Confederacy. In "the present Union" there were "no *efficient* provisions for the protection of Southern rights and property," he warned in December 1860. "That Congress has no power to interfere with slavery in the States is admitted," another editor explained earlier in the year.

> The fugitive slave law providing for the rendition of slaves escaped into other States, perfects the remedial protection to the institution as it exists in the States. In the Territories slave property is equally well guarded against invasion. It is now decided that neither the Federal nor Territorial government has the power to interpose between the slave holder and his property, either to wrest it from him or impair his rights.—More than this, it is decided to be the duty of both these governments to secure every species of property, including slaves, all needful protection. And here arises the only political issue which now divides parties.[69]

Constitutional rights. Property rights. States' rights. Southern rights. The language of liberalism permeated the rhetoric of secessionists. Even as slave resistance hurled southern jurists into an excruciating controversy over the anomaly of "slave rights," the slaveholders asserted more firmly than ever their commitment to the primacy of rights. On the eve of a bloody war between the North and the South, southern slave society remained trapped within the ideological conventions of American political culture.

POLITICAL CONTROVERSY gave heightened significance to slave resistance, but such resistance often generated political controversy to begin with. The lines of influence ran in two directions. There may be no way to tell whether the insurrection panics of the 1850's were based on a rising level of slave resistance or a rising tide of paranoia among free Southerners. But we can say with certainty that as the conflict between North and South intensified, acts of slave resistance had increasingly disruptive effects. This was equally true of the regional tensions within the South, where class conflict between slaveholders and nonslaveholders was always subtly but powerfully influenced by the pervasive fear of insurrection. On more than a few occasions, democratic reformers explicitly invoked the specter of slave rebellion to press their cause. When class tensions reached new heights in the 1850's, so did talk of insurrection. And when political tensions gave way to armed conflict, as they had during the War for Independence and as they would in the Civil War, there were very real upsurges of slave resistance. This pattern of slaves taking advantage of disunity among whites constitutes one of the most important themes in the history of slave resistance.

This is not to say that acts of resistance were the precipitating cause of every major controversy in the sectional crisis. But slave resistance did play a powerful role in shaping the general climate in which such controversies took place. As that climate was continually shaped and reshaped, so did slave resistance take on ever greater significance. Over the long run the political consequences were cumulative, and they were never greater than during the Civil War itself.

The myriad implications of slave resistance in the antebellum years were confirmed by the wartime experience. Once again, acts of resistance mattered more than individual motives. The significance of those acts was derived in large measure from the intensity of the divisions in white society, and those divisions were in turn intensified by the acts themselves. More clearly than ever, the most significant political consequence of slave resistance was that it shifted the terms of the debate in a way that ultimately served the interests of the slaves over their masters.

And yet the situation after 1860 was without precedent. White society in the South was only tenuously united in defense of the Confederacy, while northern and southern whites had literally come to arms. Wars of this sort make for strange bedfellows, and a significant number of slaves appear to have understood this situation from the start. With so many hostile groups vying for supremacy, a tacit coalition formed between the Union Army, the Lincoln administration, and the slaves. No one ever signed a treaty or announced a pact. But within months of Lincoln's inauguration, almost as soon as the fighting began, slave resistance was forcing the North to establish a policy to deal with the "problem" of fugitive slaves. As that policy developed, always pushed along by further evidence of the slaves' willingness to resist, the Lincoln administration backed into a pro-emancipation stance.

"I have no purpose, directly or indirectly, to interfere with slavery in the states where it exists," Lincoln insisted in his inaugural address in March of 1861. "I believe I have no lawful right to do so, and I have no inclination to do so." Yet within two years he issued his famous Emancipation Proclamation, and at the time of his death two years after that he was lobbying for the Thirteenth Amendment abolishing slavery. It is important to understand that Abraham Lincoln was prepared to back into this position: his roots in the Republican party and his oft-stated conviction that slavery was a political, economic, and moral evil made him more responsive than most Democrats and conservative Republicans to the pressure to adopt a pro-emancipation policy. Nonetheless, he was quite sincere in his inaugural address; all the evidence suggests that when he assumed the Presidency Lincoln really had no intention of advocating emancipation. What caused him to change his mind?[70]

Clearly there were pressures emanating from within the North, particularly from the abolitionists, whose moral stock rose to record-high levels after the South seceded. And there was concern about which way Europe would go if the North could produce no better justification for its crusade than the sanctity of the Union. But the most direct and irresistible pressure came from the slaves, who behaved pretty much as they always had: they ran away. Only now the circumstances were different and so the consequences were different also. If running away had significant political consequences before the Civil War, it would not be exaggerating to say that during the war escapes took on revolutionary significance. The slaves did not organize guerrilla bands or slink into the homes of their former masters and slit their throats. They formed no Sons of Liberty, no revolutionary cells. But if slave resistance contributed in important ways to emancipation—as the evidence suggests it did—and if emancipation was a revolutionary transformation—as it clearly was—then under the conditions of Civil War, it had not only political but revolutionary significance.

Not every slave struck out for freedom. Some actually protected their masters in wartime. But such behavior is common to revolutionary situations. Neither the Loyalists in the War for Independence, the White Russians during the Bolshevik Revolution, nor the Nationalists of the Chinese Revolution diminish the reality of those revolutions any more than faithful slaves diminished the consequences of resistance. When the war was over the faithful slaves were free along with all the others. Clearly, enough slaves had acted so that by 1865 a war that Confederates fought to save slavery and that the North entered to preserve the Union nevertheless ended with emancipation.

This was the logical outcome of day-to-day resistance, for it was accomplished in large part by thousands of small acts of defiance whose cumulative consequences were immense. From the moment the secession crisis erupted, slaves across the South began to "talk" of their freedom and showed extraordinary interest in the course of the war. House servants listened in on white conversations and reported what they heard to field hands in the slave quarters. Slaves hid under beds listening to whites read newspapers aloud; they climbed trees to overhear dinner-party conversations. One illiterate slave memorized the letters her master spelled out in her presence, hoping she would not understand, but she later had the letters translated in the quarters. Every neighborhood had one or two literate slaves who got hold of newspapers to spread reports of the war effort along what slaves called the "grapevine telegraph."[71]

Early on, free Southerners learned that the approach of the Union Army meant more than occupation or physical devastation. As Union troops moved through the South, tens of thousands of slaves left their farms and plantations—long before there was any official emancipation policy. Runaways were rarely organized and were therefore difficult to control. Slaves often knew the swamps and forests better than their owners, and so defections were both unpredictable and often impossible to stop.[72]

As early as May of 1861, within weeks of Lincoln's inauguration, the problem of runaway slaves was already occupying the attention of Union commanders. From eastern Virginia, General Benjamin Butler wrote his superiors on May 27 that "the question in regard to slave property is becoming one of very serious magnitude." Slaves were running to Butler's encampments from Confederate lines, and they were arriving in whole families. Since the Confederates were using slaves to fortify their own positions, Butler obviously could not send the fugitives back. "As a military question it would seem to be a measure of necessity" to deprive "their master of their services," Butler explained. Would it not be better to put willing slaves to work for the Union Army? But this posed another dilemma. "As a political question and a question of humanity, can I receive the services of a father and a mother and not take the children?" Thus, within weeks of the war's outbreak slaves running to Union lines had presented the military with an unprecedented choice: either send able-bodied men and women back to the enemy, or make a conscious decision to harbor fugitive slaves. What would have been unconstitutional six months earlier had already become what Butler labeled a "measure of necessity."[73]

By midsummer of the first year of war, when the problem of fugitives was already overwhelming, the United States Congress responded to the Confederacy's use of slave labor by enacting the first Confiscation Act. In it, the Congress declared that any master who allowed the use of his slave property to support the Confederacy would forfeit the right to that property. By itself, however, the Confiscation Act had a paradoxical quality that would later provoke criticism of the Emancipation Proclamation: since the Act applied only to those areas under Confederate control, the Union was in no position to enforce it.[74]

Nevertheless, the law's opponents saw nothing but revolutionary implications. "Are we in a condition now," Congressman John J. Crittenden asked, "to hazard this momentous, irritating, agitating, revolutionary question?" What gave the Confiscation Act its "revolutionary" character was the fact that, implicitly but inescapably, it depended for its effect on the actions of the slaves themselves. Most of the slaves actually freed by its provisions were those who ran away.[75]

This had become clear only a few days before Congress passed the law. By late July, thousands of slaves had fled to Union lines, and Butler—who had declared in May that fugitives should be held as "contraband" of war—was now compelled to apply his decision to huge numbers of runaways. But drawing the line at fugitives who had worked on Confederate defenses was impractical, Butler pointed out. That would not solve the problem of what to do about women and children. Moreover, all fugitives by definition had deprived the masters of at least some of the subsistence necessary to sustain their rebellion. Butler would therefore draw a wider net: "In a loyal state I would put down a servile insurrection," he said. "In a state of rebellion I would confiscate that which was used to oppose my arms." With those words Butler made it clear why men such as Crittenden saw the Confiscation Act as intrinsically revolutionary. For a policy of "confiscation" was close to what Butler implied it was: the refusal to suppress a servile insurrection.[76]

This far the Lincoln administration was still unwilling to go. The property rights of loyal masters had to be protected, wrote Secretary of War Simon Cameron. But because it was logistically impossible and militarily undesirable to return any fugitives, Cameron instructed Butler to keep a careful record so that "[a]fter tranquility shall have been restored," Congress could provide "a just compensation to loyal masters." Lincoln's own qualms surfaced a few weeks later. On August 30, 1861, General John C. Frémont declared martial law in the area around St. Louis, Missouri, and included in his order a provision that the slaves of rebel masters "are hereby declared free men." Lincoln insisted that this provision went well beyond the language and intent of the Confiscation Act, and he required the general to modify his order accordingly. Lincoln subsequently fired Cameron for, among other things, circulating in December 1861 a proposal to emancipate and arm the slaves. The following May another Union commander, in low-country South Carolina, General David Hunter, began issuing certificates of freedom to the thousands of fugitive slaves who were fleeing into Union-held territories. Once again Lincoln countermanded the order.[77]

Determined to press further than the President, Congress again took the initiative in early 1862. After a bitter debate the legislators passed a law abolishing slavery in the District of Columbia. Lincoln made no secret of his misgivings about the law, and only after intense pressure from northern blacks did he finally sign it. The slaves in surrounding Maryland had far fewer qualms; they immediately abandoned their owners in huge numbers, flocking into Washington, D.C., to gain their freedom.[78]

Responding to the willingness of thousands of slaves to run for freedom if given the opportunity, and to Lincoln's repeated frustration of the actions of Union officers, Congress enacted a second Confiscation Act in July 1862. In effect, the statute resolved the fugitive-slave problem along the lines established by General Frémont and Hunter by promising freedom to all slaves held by rebel masters.[79]

Thus, well before the preliminary Emancipation Proclamation was issued, runaway slaves had created political crises for whites in both the North and South. Once behind Union lines the slaves' mere presence edged the Union closer toward an emancipation policy. The fact that so many fugitives were already separated from their masters and under the purview of the Union Army meant that Northerners had to decide not whether to free the southern slaves but what to do with those who had already escaped. The choice was no longer emancipation or not, but reenslavement or not. For Northerners, these were two very different issues, reminiscent of the situation in the 1850's when whites who were unprepared to interfere with slavery were nevertheless unwilling to allow slave catchers to interfere with northern civil rights laws. Ten years later slave runaways pushed the North toward an emancipationist policy by once again changing the terms of the debate. If most whites were unprepared to accept a general emancipation, neither were they prepared to reenslave fugitives, especially those who labored for Union victory. Thus a bill passed by Congress on the same day as the second Confiscation Act promised freedom to slaves who served in the militia, as well as to their wives and children. By actively pursuing their own free-dom, slaves made it easier for northern whites to support such policies.

Lincoln acknowledged all of this in strikingly explicit language. Having signed the second Confiscation Act, he returned it to Con-gress along with reservations he had put in writing before the bill's passage. He argued that while Congress had no legal right to emancipate slaves, it did have the right to transfer ownership of the slaves to the federal government. At that point, Lincoln noted, "the question for Congress in regard to them is, 'shall they be made free or sold to new masters?' " But having forced that ques-tion onto Congress, the "forfeited slaves" also limited the answers available to the government. Would it ever be possible for federal officials to sell off runaway slaves that had been "transferred" to the government's ownership? Lincoln knew the answer as well as anyone did. "I do not believe it will be physically possible for the General Government to return persons so circumstanced to actual slavery," he wrote. "I believe there would be physical resistance to it, which could neither be turned aside by argument nor driven away by force."[80]

Southern whites were certainly aware of the problems created by runaway slaves. The mobilization of a huge proportion of whites in the military was possible only because black slaves were doing the work at home. Thus runaways clearly threatened the Confederate war effort. To halt the flight of slaves, the Confed-erate government exempted from the draft one able-bodied male on every plantation with twenty slaves or more, so long as he hired a replacement draftee. But the cure proved worse than the disease. While it did little or nothing to halt the flood of fugitives and ref-ugees, it provoked enormous resentment among southern whites, many of whom saw the planters' exemption as class bias pure and simple. Thus the problem of slave resistance further weakened the Confederacy by reinforcing the resentment of slaveless whites.[81]

Lincoln finally accepted the military necessity of emancipation once he recognized that tens of thousands of fugitives could si-multaneously strengthen the northern war effort and weaken the

Confederacy internally. Yet even Lincoln's final Emancipation Proclamation of January 1, 1863, depended on the slaves for its full effect. The proclamation has been criticized by historians, as it was by contemporaries, for freeing only those slaves who were beyond the control of the Union Army. Because it applied only to those parts of the South still "in rebellion," Lincoln was attacked for tacitly rewarding loyal masters in Union-controlled areas by allowing them to keep their slaves.

But this criticism hardly diminishes the proclamation's importance. At the point it was issued it must have been clear to everyone that fugitives would give the proclamation real meaning by running to Union lines, or that slaves would enthusiastically accept their freedom as the Union Army advanced through the South. When the British had made a similar offer to slaves in the South during the American Revolution, King George III had been roundly assailed—even by Thomas Jefferson in the Declaration of Independence—for having "excited domestic insurrections against us." While no one in the Lincoln administration was prepared to say as much, the Emancipation Proclamation did almost exactly the same thing.[82]

Frederick Douglass's memoirs suggest that Lincoln fully understood that the force of the Emancipation Proclamation rested on its ability to encourage the massive desertion of slaves. In a meeting with Douglass shortly after the proclamation was issued, Lincoln inquired "as to the means most desirable to be employed outside the army to induce the slaves in the rebel states to come within the federal lines." The spectacle of an American President encouraging domestic insurrection is sufficiently rare to justify extended quotation from Douglass's account of the event:

> The increasing opposition to the war, in the North, and the mad cry against it, because it was being made an abolition war, alarmed Mr. Lincoln, and made him apprehensive that a peace might be forced upon him which would leave still in slavery all who had not come within our lines. What he wanted was to make his proclamation as effective as possible in the event of such a peace. He said, in a regretful tone, "The slaves are not

coming so rapidly and so numerously to us as I had hoped." I replied that the slaveholders knew how to keep such things from their slaves, and probably very few knew of his proclamation. "Well," he said, "I want you to set about devising some means of making them acquainted with it, and for bringing them into our lines."[83]

Eventually, large numbers of slaves did learn of the proclamation and did use it as a pretext for claiming their freedom, regardless of its geographic limitations. Even in areas exempted by the document, slaves took advantage of the presence of the Union Army and simply assumed their freedom on the day the proclamation was issued. Despite the fact that Norfolk, Virginia, was under Union control and therefore exempted, four thousand slaves celebrated their freedom with a parade and a festival when the proclamation was issued. Much the same thing happened in New Orleans, which was also under Union control and as such technically untouched by the proclamation. In low-country South Carolina thousands of contrabands had lived as if free ever since General Hunter had acted two years earlier, despite Lincoln's revocation of the general's order. With the proclamation, they celebrated what they interpreted as official recognition of their status as free people.[84]

In countless areas outside Union control slaves got word of the proclamation and assumed their freedom as soon as it was safe to do so. More and more slaves ran to Union lines whenever the army approached. Slaveholders reported widespread insolence and intransigence among their slaves. As historian Bell Wiley concluded, "disorder and unfaithfulness on the part of the Negroes were far more common than post-war commentators have usually admitted."[85]

To be sure, the Emancipation Proclamation was a document with many origins and many consequences; its history is too complicated to have depended on slave resistance alone. The point is not that Lincoln issued the proclamation as a direct result of slave resistance, or that its importance stems entirely from the President's willingness to foment widespread desertion. But the problem of runaways did help shape the atmosphere within which the proclamation was formulated and, once it was issued, its meaning was forever transformed by the slaves' interpretation of it. In the final analysis, the "meaning" of the Emancipation Proclamation does not inhere in its words and sentences, nor does it reside solely in the motives and expectations Abraham Lincoln brought to it. Its meaning rests also in the actions the slaves took to facilitate its issuance and to breathe their quest for freedom into its otherwise lifeless prose. Like so many aspects of the Civil War, the Emancipation Proclamation was a revolutionary banner disguised as a conservative treatise.

Consider what it unleashed. From disorder and running away, slave resistance escalated into organized and disciplined attacks on the Confederacy under the auspices of the Union Army. Northerners initially resisted the idea of black troops, and white Southerners were positively horrified by it. But many blacks were clearly anxious to fight and pressured for the right to do so. Northern acquiescence required no diminution of white racism. On the contrary, blacks who wanted to fight actually benefited from the argument that black soldiers might as well replace white ones. And the miserable conditions fugitives often experienced in contraband camps only enhanced the determination of many refugees to join the Union Army. And join they did, for while the Emancipation Proclamation finally allowed blacks to enlist, they were never drafted. Within a year 50,000 blacks had served and by war's end 179,000 had enlisted, nearly three-fourths of them from the South. They made up 9 percent of the Union Army. Nine thousand more blacks enlisted in the Union Navy.[86]

With the enlistment of freed slaves into the Union Army the line between resistance and revolution all but faded into irrelevance. We may never know how many slaveholders died, directly or indirectly, because of the 135,000 southern blacks who put on blue uniforms and joined the war against their former masters. If black troops were too often relegated to garrison duty, how many white troops were thereby freed for battle service? One thing is clear: the combined effects of fugitive slaves and black troops proved devastating to the slaveholders' cause. Numbers alone suggest the dimensions of the upheaval. Rough estimates put the proportion of slaves liberated by the war—either by running away or by assuming their freedom with the arrival of the Union Army—at 20 percent, or between 800,000 and 900,000 blacks. Yet when historians compare the relative strengths and weaknesses of the Union and the Confederacy, they rarely consider this internal collapse of the southern social structure. The most intense resistance to the war effort in the North did not begin to match the social revolution that was destroying the Confederacy from within: yeomen deserted in increasing numbers as the war dragged on; the slaveholders themselves resisted the sacrifices demanded by their wartime governments; and when "the moment of truth" arrived the slaves reduced to bitter ashes every prewar declaration of their unswerving loyalty.

But sheer numbers do not establish the significance of slave resistance, nor do they account for the slaves' success. No law of history required the North to assume the pro-emancipationist stance it finally adopted. In other times and places governments responded very differently to the mass desertion of slaves during wartime. When Roman bondsmen took advantage of civil war during the last years of the Republic, Augustus suppressed the rebellion by crucifying six thousand slaves and putting twenty thousand more to work in his navy. In addition, as he later boasted, "I captured about 30,000 slaves who had escaped from their masters and taken up arms against the republic, and I handed them over to their masters for punishment."[87] Clearly it matters that the Republican party would not do the same thing after 1861, just as it matters that the Lincoln administration acted as it did in response to the problem of fugitive slaves.

The critical difference extended beyond Lincoln and his party into the larger political context within which masters and slaves operated. The Old South was unlike Ancient Rome but not unlike nineteenth-century Africa, where European colonization had set up an alternative government structure into which massive numbers of slaves escaped, undermining slavery despite the absence of an explicit colonial policy of emancipation.[88] So too in the South did the existence of an overarching sovereignty—whether it was London in the 1750's or Washington, D.C. in the

1850's—deny the slaveholders the kind of political control that was indispensable to the containment of slavery's inner contradictions. In the end, divided sovereignty established the opening wedge for the eventual destruction of slavery. For in such circumstances every act of human resistance that brought a slave before the law exposed the paradox of freedom and slavery. Repeated exposure, even in small doses, weakened the system until legal contradiction gave way to military conflict.

With civil war, slavery's fate was sealed. The alliance between the Union forces and the slaves may have been tacit and the circumstances unique, but the pattern was by no means historically anomalous. The American revolutionaries had once taken advantage of essential French support, and the Bolsheviks would later take advantage of the immense disruption of the Great War. Between 1861 and 1865 Americans went to war over slavery—over its expansion across the land and into the law, over its effects on the yeomanry and on the civil rights of free men. But the slaves knew that it was actually a war about them. They had helped provoke it, they took full advantage of it when it finally came, and in so doing they gave the Civil War a meaning that few free Americans had ever intended it to have.

The slaves showed that a war about slavery could not be anything but a moral struggle over the basic principles of human freedom. Most Northerners emphatically denied that in prosecuting the war they were engaged in a high-minded crusade to free black people in America. Secessionists were no less insistent that their motives were self-interested—that the central principle justifying their action was the right to protect their property in slaves. But the war was a moral crusade nevertheless—a powerful struggle over the very meaning of freedom and unfreedom in America, a struggle that did not end when slavery was finally destroyed.

IN 1865 it was clear that the Civil War had ended slavery. It was not clear what freedom meant. Along the spectrum from slavery to freedom there had developed a host of statuses into which the American political system traditionally deposited those who fell outside the privileged circle reserved for grown men with white skin fortunate enough to have been born in the United States. For immigrants, women, children, Native Americans, and African-Americans, nineteenth-century liberalism tempered its promise of universal freedom by distributing its social and political rights with a fine selectivity. After slavery ended in the United States, everyone was entitled to the basic rights of life, liberty, and property, and in that sense everyone was free. But some people were freer than others. A four-year war over slavery thereby gave way to a struggle for equality that has now continued for more than a century. And it became an ideological struggle as well as a social and political one. For it was in the turmoil of the late-nineteenth- and twentieth-century South that the meaning of the Civil War was discovered and rediscovered with each succeeding generation.

The Meaning
of the Civil War

*B*URIED IN the sixteenth chapter of Ulrich B. Phillips's monumental study *American Negro Slavery* (1918) is an extraordinary footnote. To document his rhapsodic account of "plantation life" in the antebellum South, Phillips cited his "own observations in postbellum times in which, despite the shifting of industrial arrangements and the decrease of wealth, these phases have remained apparent." He bolstered his case with two additional postwar memoirs, a traveler's account and the journal of an eighteenth-century plantation tutor. Yet in his preface only a few hundred pages earlier Phillips told his readers that throughout the book "Reminiscences are . . . disregarded, for the reason that the lapse of decades has impaired inevitably the memories of men." Instead the author would rely on the "contemporary records of slaves, masters, and witnesses." With one stroke he disregarded his own good advice in three different ways: first by relying on memoirs, second by citing his own recollections of plantation life, and finally by failing to cite even a single "contemporary" source from an antebellum master or slave.[1]

There is more involved here than mere inconsistency. What Phillips "observed" in the late nineteenth century was a radically transformed social hierarchy topped by a landlord-merchant class that was anything but a reincarnation of the antebellum planter élite. Yet his interpretation assured readers that the postwar landlords were continuous with their antebellum counterparts. Phillips was not the only historian of his generation to emphasize the continuity of southern history. But it is not enough to point out that he observed his region's past from a perspective common to the Progressive Era. For southern progressivism was itself the culmination of a profound social and political upheaval, set in motion by emancipation, and accompanied by a startling reinterpretation of the meaning of the Civil War. To appreciate the connections between what Phillips and his contemporaries wrote and the world they observed at close range we must return briefly to the social and political history of the South from the moment the slaves won their freedom.

Emancipation did not settle the meaning of the Civil War. Revolutions do not define themselves so readily. Not only are they chaotic and unpredictable by their very nature, they are often followed by counterrevolutions whose leaders inevitably attempt to redefine the revolution in their own terms. The American South was no exception. Formal freedom was followed by several years of tension and suspicion between the ex-slaves and the former masters. No one could be sure what it all meant, because no one could predict how it would finally turn out.

Imagine how volatile the years after 1865 must have been. With the freed people in possession of their own labor and their old masters still in control of the land, the stage was set for a substantial reorganization of labor relations. Within a few years landowners and the freed people began to reach an arrangement that had no precedent in the history of southern society. It was called sharecropping, a system in which a farmer agreed to work someone else's land for a full year in return for a "share" of the final crop. This arrangement gave most of the freed people far more autonomy than had slavery. Sharecroppers usually worked their own plots in family-sized units rather than in large gangs. As free laborers, they had the right to move about in search of whatever opportunities were available. By one estimate as many as one in three sharecropping families changed employers each year.[2]

Yet after several generations of freedom, most sharecroppers remained dependent for their livelihoods on those who owned the land.[3] Emancipation had destroyed the master class, but it had not significantly altered landownership patterns. The planters therefore retained substantial control of a thoroughly reorganized labor force as well. And there were few alternatives to sharecropping for the former slaves in the postwar South. In mill towns and cities they were locked out of the best jobs; in the countryside freed men and women found it all but impossible to purchase their own homesteads. The majority remained in agriculture, and they had no choice but to continue working for those who owned the land.

The postwar social order was no mere restoration of slave society, however. This was graphically illustrated by the dramatic increase in the number of merchants. Many landlords, devastated by the war, were in no position to provide credit and supplies to the ex-slaves. Local merchants quickly filled the void, taking their business directly onto the plantations and thereby competing with landlords for authority over sharecroppers. Croppers contracted with local merchants who loaned them food and other necessities over the course of the year. After the harvest the merchants claimed payment from the freedmen's "share" of the crop. Because both planters and merchants claimed a lien on the products of the sharecroppers' labor, this arrangement was fraught with potential conflicts. By the 1880's, landlords and merchants reached a *modus vivendi*, in part because planters won the right to the prior lien on the sharecroppers' harvest. In practice, the two classes effectively merged into one as merchants became landlords and landlords became merchants. Thus it was that by the end of the nineteenth century a consolidated landlord-merchant class dominated the rural economy of the plantation South.[4]

In the same decades an entirely new landlord-merchant class emerged and expanded its influence among yeoman farmers in many parts of the South. The legal conflict with the landowners in the plantation districts sent many merchants searching for opportunities in the upcountry. With the spread of transportation, credit, and marketing facilities into those areas, an increasing number of yeomen lost their land to merchant-creditors and eventually fell into tenancy. This gave the landlord-merchants more direct economic influence over white farmers than the slaveholders had ever enjoyed. Market integration, therefore, involved a significant loss of independence for many southern yeomen. In fact, tenancy rates are merely the statistical manifestation of a profound and disruptive transformation of the social relations that had long shaped the history of the upcountry South. Local arti-

sans could no longer compete with the flood of cheaper manufactured goods that flowed into their communities as they were
absorbed into the national market. And with the breakdown of a
local economy of farmers and artisans, traditional patterns of exchange could no longer be sustained. Independent farmers became steadily more dependent on the encroaching cotton
economy, with its crushing cycle of debt and poverty.[5]

Locked into the market by a largely irreversible process of economic development, the average yeoman farm shrank in size dramatically, while the number of farmers who lost their land
altogether rose steadily. The social character of tenancy changed
from a temporary stage in a life-cycle to a permanent condition.
By 1900 a tenant farmer was as likely to fall into wage labor as he
was to rise into landed independence. This was a dramatic departure from antebellum conditions. Until 1850 as many as 70
percent of slaveless farmers owned their own land. To be sure,
the slave economy had restricted the areas in which yeomen farmers could thrive, and in the late antebellum decades slavery's expansion threatened the economic independence of the upcountry.
But it was not until the late nineteenth century, especially after
1880, that the proportion of family-owned farms dropped precip-
itously. By 1910 nearly half of the South's white farmers no longer
owned all of the land they worked. By the turn of the century,
the new landlord-merchant class that emerged after the Civil War
had come to exercise significant and unprecedented social and economic influence among those who remained in the agricultural
economy.

Clearly the social structure that Phillips observed in the rural
South of the late nineteenth century bore only a superficial resem-
blance to its prewar antecedent. There is no discounting the poverty and oppression that still marked African-American life after
emancipation. But it was not slavery. No landlord in the late nineteenth century enjoyed the legal right to break up a family, to buy
and sell a human being, or to extract labor by sheer physical force.
Sharecroppers worked not in slave gangs but on family farms in
a free-labor system with its own structure of incentives, its own

relations of production and exchange, and its own economic consequences. The prewar planters whose papers Phillips so diligently uncovered were not the landlord-merchants he had observed in his youth. The power and wealth of the antebellum masters had rested on their ownership of slaves. The power of the postwar planters rested squarely on their ownership of the land, and this tied them to their plantations in a way that slavery never had. Only then did the land take on the legendary significance it had lacked in the years before 1860.[6] Nor were yeomen farmers untouched by this transformation. Enticed into the staple economy by the spread of transport and credit facilities, smallholders steadily lost their economic independence to a landlord-merchant class that had scarcely existed in the antebellum years. The planter class and the plantation system that Phillips saw in the late 1800's were not the remnants of the prewar South but the products of a fundamental restructuring of the social order.

Like the antebellum slaveholders, however, the postwar planters were defined more by their power than their wealth. In many cases postwar landlords were poorer than antebellum masters, and they could scarcely claim the kind of authority over their employees that owners had once exercised over their slaves. Yet as the decades passed and the legal nature of sharecropping was settled in southern courts and legislatures, it was clear that while the slaveholding class was destroyed by emancipation the postwar planters had succeeded in winning considerable legal authority. And legal authority implied political influence. At every point in its rise to power, the postwar planter class had to translate its economic interests into legal doctrines, making the social transformation a political as much as an economic process.[7] Who controlled the legislatures, how judges were appointed, and who had the right to vote would all determine how effectively the planter class could consolidate its power. Who would write the lien laws that established whether sharecroppers, tenants, merchants, or landlords could make a legal claim on the crops? Who would write the fence laws that could protect or destroy the security of small farmers? Who sat in the appellate courts that arbitrated the disputes between tenants and landlords, sharecroppers and plant-ers?[8] Clearly the political power of the landlord-merchants was a critical part of what defined them as a class.

It is in this context that the struggle over political rights for the freed slaves takes on its historic significance. In the United States, as in no other modern slave society, the former slaves had won the right to vote and hold public office. Only in the American South could the freed people participate extensively in the lawmaking process that was so critical to the shape of post-emancipation society.[9] Certainly the planters appreciated the threat to their interests represented by the voting power of blacks. At the critical moment in the 1880's, when the economic supremacy of the land-lords was being legally secured in southern courts, black-belt planters inaugurated a concerted and ultimately successful attack on the democratic franchise. When the process was complete, for example, the votes of only 5 or 6 percent of Virginia's adults were enough to win election to the governorship. A paltry electorate and grossly malapportioned legislatures preserved the domination of the black belt. Landlord-merchants and a shrunken class of independent farmers formed a tacit alliance against the majority of landless Southerners, urban and rural, black and white. In those states that granted suffrage to the descendants of Civil War veterans, the right to vote became, in effect, a hereditary privilege.[10]

The means by which the planter class achieved such power were many and varied, but all depended on the failed efforts to build a biracial alliance among white and black farmers. Having won the right to vote, the freed people quickly discovered that this was in many ways a Pyrrhic victory. To begin with, the black vote profoundly disrupted the class relations that had long shaped southern politics. Slavery's "dual economy" had physically separated most yeomen from most slaveholders, making geographical and class divisions coincide. Before the war, therefore, when the yeomen pushed for democratic reform, they generally aimed at taking power from the black belt. The success of antebellum democratic reform can be measured in the steady elimination of property requirements for voting and officeholding and by the repeated reapportionment of the state legislatures. Once blacks secured formal admission to the polity, however, the same reforms had radically different consequences. Indeed, they implied a wholesale realignment of political power, for universal male suffrage in the postwar South gave heavily populated black-belt counties unprecedented influence. For many white yeomen, the enfranchisement of the freedmen meant not black power but planter power.[11]

The political rise of the planter class, therefore, began with the reapportionment of the state legislatures under the terms laid down in the Reconstruction constitutions. The more democratic the prewar political structure, the more dramatic were the effects on the postwar legislatures. Mississippians, for example, had apportioned their prewar legislatures on the basis of white population, leaving the wealthiest plantation district along the Mississippi River with surprisingly few seats in the state legislature. The Natchez region was overwhelmingly black; three out of four residents of Adams County were slaves who counted for nothing in the apportionment of legislative seats before the Civil War. But the Reconstruction constitution of 1868 defined the state's adult black males as "qualified electors," instantaneously doubling the size of the voting population. Accordingly, Mississippi's black belt reaped the political harvest from this deceptively simple constitutional readjustment.[12]

The effects were visible in the actual distribution of legislative seats in Mississippi. Today every district elects a single representative, and district boundaries are periodically redrawn to assure that each representative has roughly the same number of constituents. But in the nineteenth century the most common method of apportionment was to give heavily populated counties more seats in the legislature than sparsely settled counties. Mississippi's Reconstruction constitution gave three or more seats to only thirteen of the state's sixty counties. Every one of the thirteen most favored counties had a black majority in 1860, and seven of those thirteen could not have qualified for so many seats under prewar rules. Tishomingo County is a classic example. With 879 adult white males in 1860, it had only one legislator in the state's House of Representatives. But after the war, when its 4,300 adult black males were added to the ranks of the county's "qualified electors," Tishomingo automatically earned the right to a second representative. Other heavily black counties—Adams, Lowndes, and Warren, for example—increased their representation in the lower house of Mississippi's General Assembly in 1868, reversing a process that had prevailed for decades.[13]

Opposition to the black vote thus became one of the few rallying cries around which the majority of southern whites seemed capable of uniting. Black-belt planters resented black voting power, upcountry yeomen resented the power of the black belt, and both groups nurtured a powerful animosity toward the Reconstruction governments. For nearly two decades this hostility persisted, its effects extending far beyond the dissolution of black voting power. Where fraud, terror, and manipulation reduced the political significance of the black vote, the collapse of competitive party politics effectively narrowed the political options open to white voters.

Until the crisis of the 1850's, two-party politics had provided an important mechanism for expressing the political differences that separated yeomen from slaveholders. After the war, however, the Republican party became the virtually exclusive voice of the freedmen, while the Democratic party could organize itself around no principle greater than white supremacy. Sustained political competition within the white South declined substantially, even as the potential for class conflict swelled. Some whites continued to vote Republican; others enlisted in Independent or Greenback movements. But by the 1880's radicalized Southerners began to step outside the confines of the major parties altogether. Across much of the South, whites and blacks joined Farmers' Alliances and the Knights of Labor, and both organizations soon translated economic needs into political demands.[14]

Nervous reformers reacted by promoting a structural change even more significant than the domination of state legislatures by the plantation districts: the systematic disfranchisement of blacks. Some advocates of disfranchisement argued that suffrage restrictions were necessary in order to restore healthy political competition to the white South. In the words of one Alabama disfranchiser, the "grant of unrestricted suffrage to the negroes . . . has prevented any division of our people on economic or political questions." In the face of radical third-party threats from blacks and whites, constitutional reformers asserted that the revival of stable party politics among whites hinged on the elimination of the black voter. This was no easy task, however. Given the Fifteenth Amendment's ban on explicit racial discrimination, electoral reformers developed an ingenious variety of devices to weed out black voters. Among their more effective accomplishments were the white primary, in which the omnipotent Democratic party declared itself a private club closed to blacks; grandfather clauses, which exempted the descendants of Confederate veterans from obnoxious registration restrictions; and the ubiquitous literacy test, which even the most educated blacks seemed unable to pass.[15]

Although aimed primarily at the disfranchisement of blacks, the constitutional reform movement of the late nineteenth century often solidified the political power of the planter class. In some states constitutional changes combined legal disfranchisement of blacks with legislative reapportionment. But this did not necessarily return power to heavily white counties. In states like Alabama, where legislative apportionment was based on total population, the disfranchisement of blacks simply enhanced the power of black-belt whites. And although its effects varied from state to state, certain forms of disfranchisement—especially poll taxes—successfully reduced the voting power of the poorest whites along with that of most blacks. Blacks loudly protested these constitutional "reforms." But even among whites there were objections from those who understood that disfranchisement threatened the voting power of the growing body of propertyless whites. In the end, electoral reform gave tiny white minorities in the black belt political power equal to that of overwhelming white majorities elsewhere in the South.[16]

By the late nineteenth century, when Ulrich B. Phillips looked about his native Georgia and began to formulate his interpretation of the Old South, he was bound to be misled by what he witnessed. The political power of the plantation owners was evident for all to see. Nevertheless, postwar politics were as different from prewar politics as slavery was different from sharecropping. In the Old South the formal exclusion of blacks from the polity and the growing threat to slavery at the national level had compelled slaveholders to seek the support of white yeomen by acceding to their demands for democratic reform. In sharp contrast, postbellum planters had every incentive to undermine all political opposition, black and white. By playing on pervasive racial prejudices, the postwar élite successfully defended the enhanced power of the black belt and at the same time prevented fundamental issues from arising within the omnipotent Democratic party. For all the superficial resemblances to slavery days, the South of 1900 was a very different place.

That difference notwithstanding, turn-of-the-century reformers sought repeatedly to justify their political programs by locating them deep within the South's past. By defining slavery not as a labor system, which had clearly been destroyed, but as one of "race control," which was now being restored, leading Southerners argued that the social order of their own age was largely continuous with its antebellum counterpart. They carried the argument for continuity still further by equating the inequitable distribution of rights in the postwar South with the complete denial of rights to antebellum slaves. Finally, they defined the Civil War as an independence movement whose termination required only that the seceded states be reincorporated into the Union. By this reasoning, the central theme of Reconstruction was not the transition from slavery to freedom but the unwarranted interference of the Radical Republicans in the government of the defeated states. Reconstruction should have ended with the simple restoration of the *status quo ante bellum*.

By the end of the century this argument was commonplace among leading white Southerners. It was clearly discernible in the rhetoric of southern Progressivism, beginning with the disfranchisement conventions that swept through the region between

1890 and 1910. Because electoral reform required constitutional amendment, Progressive historical revisionism began with a wholehearted repudiation of the Reconstruction constitutions. The delegates to the disfranchisement conventions made repeated reference to the "dark and perilous days of the Reconstruction period," when a " 'Congressional Aristocracy' . . . in its imperious, disdainful and revengeful legislation, absorbed all executive and legislative powers." At Louisiana's 1898 constitutional convention, Dr. J. L. M. Curry tied disfranchisement directly to the repudiation of the Reconstruction Acts. "These acts annulled the State government," Curry told the assembled delegates, "enfranchised the Negro and disfranchised the largest and best portion of the white people."[17]

A year before Curry spoke, as the disfranchisement movement in the South reached its peak, William Archibald Dunning at Columbia University gave his scholarly imprimatur to the Progressive interpretation of Reconstruction history. Dunning defined the Reconstruction years almost exclusively in political terms, stressed the "revolutionary" nature of the black franchise, and assured his readers that the protracted experiment of Radical dominion—"seven unwholesome years"—was doomed to fail on racial grounds alone. If whites were destined to rule, blacks were destined to lose the vote. And if the black vote was the chief legacy of Radical Reconstruction, it followed that disfranchisement was the final phase in what Dunning called "The Undoing of Reconstruction."[18]

That was Dunning's urgent message in his influential *Essays on the Civil War and Reconstruction*. Fully aware of the immediate significance of his writings, Dunning interjected arguments countering those who saw that disfranchisement would eliminate poor, uneducated white voters along with blacks. As reformers in several southern states prepared to launch their campaign for disfranchisement, Dunning reinforced their sense of historical purpose. "With the enactment of these constitutional amendments by the various states," he wrote in 1897, "the political equality of the negro is becoming as extinct in law as it has long been in fact, and the undoing of reconstruction is nearing completion."[19] Only then could the status quo of the prewar years be fully restored.

The theme of restoration implied a vision of the Old South that was compatible with the realities of the New South. Accordingly, the movement to disfranchise blacks was necessarily tied to a specific understanding and defense of the prewar social structure. Here, too, the relentless emphasis on white supremacy became a rhetorical device for discounting the centrality of slavery in antebellum society. By focusing on the attitudes that persisted rather than on the social structure that had been transformed, turn-of-the-century Southerners backed into a revisionist interpretation of the entire sectional crisis. "The ultimate root of the trouble in the South had been, not the institution of slavery, but the coexistence in one society of two races so distinct in characteristics as to render coalescence impossible," Dunning wrote. Slavery had merely been a "*modus vivendi* through which social life was possible," he concluded, and "after its disappearance, its place must be taken by some set of conditions which, if more humane and beneficent in accidents, must in essence express the same fact of racial inequality."[20]

The same set of assumptions infused the rhetoric of educational reformers in the late-nineteenth and early-twentieth-century South, for their goals were inseparable from those of the disfranchisers. "Ignorance at the ballot box" was the ostensible enemy of good government, and so literacy tests and better schools sprang from the same reforming impulse. Not surprisingly, educational experts were conspicuous at many of the disfranchisement conventions. They reassured delegates that a good education was the best guarantee of the right to vote wherever literacy was the standard. But it was a guarantee offered only to white children. Taking their cue from recent Supreme Court decisions that legalized segregation, reformers set out to build an educational system suitable for whites, secure in the conviction that what was best for black children was best determined by white planters. Their logic was simple, and like so much of progressive ideology it rested on a particular vision of southern history. The same themes of restoration and continuity were evident in the words of a distinguished educational reformer at the turn of the century:

> I find in the State men who think that the negro has gone backward rather than forward and that education is injurious to him. Have these men forgotten that the negro was well educated before the War? Do they not recall that he was trained in those things essential for his life work? He has been less educated since the War than before. It is true that he has been sent to school, but his contact with the old planter and with the accomplished and elegant wife of that planter has been broken. This contact was in itself a better education than he can receive from the public schools, but shall we, for this reason, say that he is incapable of training. Ought we not, on the contrary, to study the conditions and realize that the training which he needs has not been given to him since the war?[21]

It was left to Dunning's most prominent student, Ulrich B. Phillips, to complete the circle of logic embedded in this view of history. More than anyone else, Phillips provided his contemporaries with an interpretation of the Old South that progressive-minded Southerners would find comfortably familiar and strikingly useful. In language that closely paralleled the words of educational reformers, Phillips explained how in the antebellum South "the plantation was a school." He went so far as to compare the plantation schools with the settlement houses established by urban reformers in the early twentieth century. "The white household taught perhaps less by precept than by example," Phillips explained. "It had much the effect of a 'social settlement' in a modern city slum, furnishing models of speech and conduct along with advice on occasions, which the vicinage is invited to accept."[22]

Phillips wrote those words in 1928, just as the social and economic system of the postbellum South was entering its death throes. Already weakened by the boll weevil, which had spread across the cotton states in the early twentieth century, and further disrupted by the great migration of both blacks and whites out of the South during World War I, the southern rural economy limped through the 1920's only to confront the devastating effects of the Great Depression. With World War II, a second and even greater wave of migration sucked tenants and sharecroppers out of the cotton economy into northern factories and southern cities at the threshold of the Sunbelt. Progressive politics—grounded in the power of the landlord-merchant class—were rendered hollow and brittle by these changes. The final blow was dealt by the steady force of legal and political challenges that reached their climax in the massive civil rights movement that erupted in the 1950's.

For all its majesty and scope, Phillips's scholarly legacy could not withstand, much less explain, the events that were once again transforming the South in fundamental ways. As the earliest leaders of the NAACP pursued their cause beyond the notice of most white Americans, so did pioneer black historians set about to overthrow Phillips's interpretation of southern history. And just as the civil rights movement burst into public consciousness in the 1950's, so did the debate over slavery at last assume a central place in the reinterpretation of American history.

Phillips's vision was overthrown, of course, but through the 1950's and 1960's it remained unclear what image of slavery would take its place. As had always been true, the political divisions of the age were reflected in the modern debate over slavery. A northern liberal interpretation, sometimes labeled "neo-abolitionist," marched forward to reclaim the field once Phillips's forces had been vanquished. But neo-abolitionism was quickly confronted by the challenge of black nationalism, as students of slave culture uncovered the vibrancy of the African heritage within the black community and with it a new perspective on the history of slavery. As the struggles against overt forms of racial bias passed and the militancy of the civil rights movement waned, the tenacious realities of class domination took center stage in the debate over slavery as well.

Yet Phillips's great intellectual shadow still hovers over all discussions of the subject. He wrote as a member of the generation that sought to remove the most distressing social problems from the realm of politics. Disfranchisement of blacks and poor whites was only the most extreme manifestation of a more general demobilization of the electorate in the United States (a tendency that would eventually produce one of the lowest rates of voter turnout among the western democracies). It was no accident that Phillips wrote about slavery as though it had no political content, as though it were somehow lifted from any political setting. Nor is it surprising that when Phillips wrote about antebellum southern politics—which he did with characteristic acumen—he made almost no mention of slavery. He separated slavery from southern politics in much the same way that his generation sought to strip black sharecroppers of their ballots, defining disfranchisement as a restoration of the prewar order.

The separation of politics from society persists in the scholarship of our own day. It is the source of some of the greatest contention among students of slavery. To be sure, southern history would not be what it is without civil wars forever raging among its most accomplished chroniclers. But there is perhaps no greater dividing line than the one separating those who study slavery as social and cultural history from those who take southern politics as their point of departure. Historians who emphasize southern distinctiveness are usually concerned with society and culture, while those who see the South as fundamentally "American" are most often political historians. Where the former usually turned away from the history of southern politics, the latter generally failed to appreciate the historic distinctiveness of slavery.

There are signs, however, that this conceptual barrier is finally breaking down. The social turmoil at the heart of Reconstruction politics has become more fully understood in recent years. Political historians have made concerted efforts to show how thoroughly the slavery issue entered into antebellum politics in subtle and indirect ways. Underlying these developments is a growing recognition that societies and economies, however natural and immutable they appear to their participants, are in fact the handiwork of ordinary human beings engaged in ordinary politics.

The political underpinnings of the relations that define our place in society—as working people or as family members—are increasingly appreciated. The "revisionist" historians who once cursed the sectional crisis as a needless conflict missed this when they argued that the Civil War was the deformed offspring of a relentlessly partisan politics. We have learned in the last generation that the war was, inescapably, a fight about slavery. We are only beginning to understand why it was therefore a political struggle over the meaning of freedom. Once this last lesson is learned, our generation will have reached its own understanding of the Civil War.

Notes

INTRODUCTION

1. Among M. I. Finley's more important statements are: *The World of Odysseus*, 2d rev. ed. (Middlesex, 1978), 51–73; "Slavery," in David L. Sills, ed., *International Encyclopedia of the Social Sciences* (New York, 1968), 14:307–313; *The Ancient Economy* (Berkeley, 1973), 62–94; *Ancient Slavery and Modern Ideology* (Middlesex, 1980); *Economy and Society in Ancient Greece*, ed. and intro. Brent D. Shaw and Richard P. Saller (Middlesex, 1981), esp. 97–195.

2. For examples of Finley's influence, see Frederick Cooper, *Plantation Slavery on the East Coast of Africa* (New Haven, 1977); Richard Hellie, *Slavery in Russia, 1450–1725* (Chicago, 1982); Paul Lovejoy, *Transformations in Slavery* (Cambridge, 1983); William D. Phillips, Jr., *Slavery from Roman Times to the Early Transatlantic Trade* (Minneapolis, 1985); Robin Blackburn, "Defining Slavery—Its Special Features and Social Role," in Léonie J. Archer, ed., *Slavery and Other Forms of Unfree Labor* (London, 1988), 262–279.

3. Keith Hopkins, *Conquerors and Slaves: Sociological Studies in Roman History*, v. I (Cambridge, 1978); Orlando Patterson, *Slavery and Social Death: A Comparative Study* (Cambridge, Mass., 1982).

4. Marc Bloch, *Slavery and Serfdom in the Middle Ages*, trans. William R. Beer (Berkeley, 1975), 1–31; Perry Anderson, *Passages from Antiquity to Feudalism* (London, 1974), esp. 15–142; Finley, "The Decline of Ancient Slavery," *Ancient Slavery and Modern Ideology*, 123–149; Chris Wickham, "The Other Transition: From the Ancient World to Medieval Feudalism," *Past & Present*, 103 (May, 1984), 3–36; Pierre Bonnassie, "Survie et extinction du régime esclavagiste dans l'Occident du haut moyen age (IVe–XIe siècles)," *Cahiers de Civilisation Médiévale*, 112 (1985). For a more controversial account, see Pierre Dockes, *Medieval Slavery and Liberation*, trans. Arthur Goldhammer (London, 1982).

5. Davis, *The Problem of Slavery in Western Culture* (Ithaca, N.Y., 1966), esp. pp. 29–61. See also Davis, *Slavery and Human Progress* (New York, 1984), 8–22.

6. Daniel J. Boorstin, *The Americans: The Democratic Experience* (New York, 1973), 89.

7. Frances Anne Kemble, *Journal of a Residence on a Georgia Plantation in 1838–1839*, ed. John A. Scott (New York, 1863; New York, 1961), 3.

8. Karin D. Knorr-Cetina, "Introduction: The Micro-sociological Challenge of Macro-sociology: Towards a Reconstruction of Social Theory and Methodology," in K. Knorr-Cetina and A. V. Cicourel, eds., *Advances in Social Theory and Methodology: Toward an Integration of Micro- and Macro-sociologies* (Boston, 1981), 1–47.

9. Among the most important attempts by political historians to connect politics and slavery, see William W. Freehling, *Prelude to Civil War: The Nullification Controversy in South Carolina, 1816–1836* (New York, 1966); William L. Barney, *The Secessionist Impulse: Alabama and Mississippi in 1860* (Princeton, 1974); William J. Cooper, *The South and the Politics of Slavery, 1828–1856* (Baton Rouge, La., 1978); J. Mills Thornton III, *Politics and Power in a Slave Society: Alabama, 1800–1860* (Baton Rouge, La., 1978); Alison Goodyear Freehling, *Drift Toward Dissolution: The Virginia Slavery Debate of 1831–1832* (Baton Rouge, La., 1982); Frederick F. Siegel, *The Roots of Southern Distinctiveness: Tobacco and Society in Danville, Virginia, 1780–1865* (Chapel Hill, 1987).

10. Herbert Aptheker, *American Negro Slave Revolts* (New York, 1943); C. L. R. James, *The Black Jacobins: Toussaint L'Ouverture and the San Domingo Revolution*, 2d rev. ed. (New York, 1963); Michael Craton, *Testing the Chains: Resistance to Slavery in the British West Indies* (Ithaca, N.Y., 1982); Robin Blackburn, *The Overthrow of Colonial Slavery, 1776–1848* (Verso: London, 1988).

11. Eugene D. Genovese, *From Rebellion to Revolution: Afro-American Slave Revolts in the Making of the New World* (Baton Rouge, La., 1979). Genovese also compared the various political contexts within which New World slaveholding classes emerged, in "The Slave Systems and Their European Antecedents," *The World the Slaveholders Made* (New York, 1969), 21–102. See also "The Political Crisis of Social History: Class Struggle as Subject and Object," in Eugene D. Genovese and Elizabeth Fox-Genovese, *Fruits of Merchant Capital: Slavery and Bourgeois Property in the Rise and Expansion of Capitalism* (New York, 1983), 179–212.

CHAPTER 1. *Outsiders*

1. Willie Lee Rose, ed., *A Documentary History of Slavery in North America* (New York, 1976), 176.

2. M. I. Finley, *Ancient Slavery and Modern Ideology* (London, 1980), 74–77; Orlando Patterson, *Slavery and Social Death: A Comparative Study* (Cambridge, Mass., 1982), 35–76 and passim.

3. Paul Finkelman, *The Law of Freedom and Bondage: A Casebook* (New York, 1986), 218.

4. Frederick Law Olmsted, *The Journey through the Seaboard Slave States* (New York, 1856), 618.

5. Roman eunuchs, see Keith Hopkins, *Conquerors and Slaves: Sociological Studies in Roman History*, I (Cambridge, 1978), 172–196.

6. The anarchy of slavery and the unpredictability of the masters, though a strong theme in slave narratives, has received little attention from historians. Two works that stress this aspect of slavery are Lawrence W. Levine, *Black Culture and Black Consciousness* (New York, 1977); Leon Litwack, *Been in the Storm So Long: The Aftermath of Slavery* (New York, 1979).

7. Eugene D. Genovese, *Roll, Jordan, Roll: The World the Slaves Made* (New York, 1974), effectively evokes this aspect of the master-slave relationship.

8. Peter Kolchin, *Unfree Labor: American Slavery and Russian Serfdom* (Cambridge, Mass., 1987), emphasizes the fundamental similarity of slavery and Russian serfdom. See esp. pp. 42–43.

9. Richard Hellie, *Slavery in Russia, 1450–1725* (Chicago, 1982), argues that the rise of serfdom in Russia depended on the decline of Russian slavery. This interpretation posits a fundamental dissimilarity between slavery and serfdom.

10. Ibid., passim; Jerome Blum, *Lord and Peasant in Russia, From the Ninth to the Nineteenth Century* (Princeton, 1961).

11. Robert Edgar Conrad, comp., *Children of God's Fire: A Documentary History of Black Slavery in Brazil* (Princeton, 1983), 242.

12. David Brion Davis, *The Problem of Slavery in Western Culture* (Ithaca, N.Y., 1966), 104–106.

13. Kolchin, *Unfree Labor*, 114–120. In addition to the statistical evidence cited by Kolchin, see Herbert Gutman and Richard Sutch, "The Slave Family," in Paul A. David et al., *Reckoning with Slavery: A Critical Study in the Quantitative History of American Negro Slavery* (New York, 1975), 94–133. Gutman and Sutch speculate that two million slave marriages took place from 1820 to 1860, and they estimate that 29 percent of the marriages were broken—producing a figure of just under 600,000 broken families.

14. Blum, *Lord and Peasant*, 469.

15. A. N. Radishchev, *A Journey from St. Petersburg to Moscow*, trans. Leo Wiener (Cambridge, Mass., 1958), 158–159.

16. S. T. Aksakov, *The Family Chronicle*, trans. M. C. Beverley (New York, 1961), 55–57.

17. Radishchev, *Journey*, 159; Aksakov, *Family Chronicle*, 55, 71.

18. Conrad, comp., *Children of God's Fire*, 244.

19. For a general discussion of honor, with a few tantalizing observations about dishonor, see Julian Pitt-Rivers, "Honor," in David L. Sills, ed., *International Encyclopedia of the Social Sciences* (New York, 1968), 6:503–511.

20. Patterson, *Slavery and Social Death*, 77–101, shows honor and dishonor are exaggerated in all slave societies. The classic study for the Old South is John Hope Franklin, *The Militant South* (Cambridge, Mass., 1956), which ties the southern concern for honor closely to slavery and social inequality. Ber-

tram Wyatt-Brown, *Southern Honor: Ethics and Behavior in the Old South* (New York, 1982), questions slavery's role in generating a distinctly southern cult of honor. More recently, Wyatt-Brown, "The Mask of Obedience: Male Slave Psychology in the Old South," *American Historical Review*, 93 (1988), 1228–1252, explores the powerful impact of honor and dishonor within the slave community. See also Steven Stowe, *Intimacy and Power in the Old South: Ritual in the Lives of the Planters* (Baltimore, 1987); Edward L. Ayres, *Vengeance and Justice: Crime and Punishment in the 19th-Century American South* (New York, 1984).

21. Philip D. Curtin, ed., *Africa Remembered: Narratives by West Africans from the Era of the Slave Trade* (Madison, Wis., 1967), 133. The definitive study of the slave trade is now Joseph C. Miller, *Way of Death: Mercantilism and the Angolan Slave Trade, 1730–1830* (Madison, Wis., 1988), which, among its many virtues, unravels the historical process that has until now been obscured by the "confusion and anarchy" the trade seemed to generate.

22. Ibid., 299–304.

23. Far less frequently parents abandoned or sold their children into slavery, or individuals were enslaved by public authorities to pay off debts or taxes. For concise summaries of the origins of enslavement, see M. I. Finley, "Slavery," *International Encyclopedia of the Social Sciences*, 14:307–313; Patterson, *Slavery and Social Death*, 105–171.

24. Adrienne Koch and William Peden, eds., *Selected Writings of Thomas Jefferson* (New York, 1944), 278.

25. Solomon Northup, *Twelve Years a Slave*, ed. Sue Eakin and Joseph Logsdon (Auburn, N.Y., 1853; Baton Rouge, La., 1968), 196, 201.

26. John W. Blassingame, ed., *Slave Testimony: Two Centuries of Letters, Speeches, Interviews, and Autobiographies* (Baton Rouge, La., 1977), 132–133.

27. Charles H. Nichols, ed., *Black Men in Chains: Narratives by Escaped Slaves* (New York, 1972), 97, 98.

28. Gilbert Osofsky, comp., *Puttin' On Ole Massa: The Slave Narratives of Henry Bibb, William Wells Brown, and Solomon Northup* (New York, 1969), 180.

29. Ibid., 80–81.

30. Quoted in James Oakes, *The Ruling Race* (New York, 1982), 159.

31. Theodore Rosengarten, ed., *Tombee: Portrait of a Cotton Planter* (New York, 1986), 347–348.

32. Nichols, ed., *Black Men in Chains*, 104–105.

33. Blassingame, ed., *Slave Testimony*, 161. See also pp. 171–172.

34. Rose, ed., *Documentary History of Slavery*, 148.

35. Thomas Wiedemann, ed., *Greek and Roman Slavery* (Baltimore, 1981), 24.

36. Davis, *Problem of Slavery in Western Culture*, 108–109.

37. Wiedemann, ed., *Greek and Roman Slavery*, 15.

38. Aristotle, *The Politics*, 1253b23, 1254b16.

39. Joseph Vogt, *Ancient Slavery and the Ideal of Man*, trans. Thomas Wiedemann (Cambridge, Mass., 1975), 9; Aristotle, *The Politics*, 1254b16.

40. *Republic*, V:469 (A. D. Lindsay, trans., Dutton paper ed., 1957).

41. Wiedemann, ed., *Greek and Roman Slavery*, 62–63, 30, 72.

42. Davis, *Problem of Slavery in Western Culture*, 91–121. See also the brief but eloquent observations of Robin Lane Fox, *Pagans and Christians* (New York, 1987), 295–299.

43. Winthrop D. Jordan, *White Over Black* (Chapel Hill, N.C., 1968), 20–24; Albert Raboteau, *Slave Religion: The "Invisible Institution" in the Antebellum South* (New York, 1978), 96–128.

44. Paul E. Lovejoy, *Transformations in Slavery: A History of Slavery in Africa* (Cambridge, 1983), 29, 30.

45. Captain Theophilus Conneau, *A Slaver's Log Book, or Twenty Years' Residence in Africa*, intro. by Mabel M. Smythe (Englewood Cliffs, N.J., 1976), entry for December 10, 1826, p. 69. See also, Frederick Cooper, *Plantation Slavery on the East Coast of Africa* (New Haven, Conn., 1977), 23–27, 242 ff.

46. Conrad, comp., *Children of God's Fire*, 205, 244, 429–430.

47. On Brazilian racism, see Carl Degler, *Neither Black nor White: Slavery and Race Relations in Brazil and the United States* (New York, 1971).

48. Koch and Peden, eds., *Selected Writings of Thomas Jefferson*, 256–262.

49. The distinctively racist character of New World, and especially southern, slavery, is examined in Davis, *Problem of Slavery in Western Culture*, 47–54; Alan Watson, *Roman Slave Law* (Baltimore, 1987).

50. Alfred Taylor Bledsoe, *Liberty and Slavery: or, Slavery in the Light of Moral and Political Philosophy*, printed in E. N. Elliott, ed., *Cotton Is King, and Pro-Slavery Arguments* (Augusta, Ga., 1860), 295, 300.

51. Thomas R. R. Cobb, *An Inquiry into the Law of Negro Slavery in the United States of America* (1858; New York, 1968), 17, 18, 51.

52. Paul E. Lovejoy, ed., *The Ideology of Slavery in Africa* (Beverly Hills, 1981).

53. Richard Hellie, *Slavery in Russia, 1450–1725* (Chicago, 1982).

54. Suzanne Miers and Igor Kopytoff, eds., *Slavery in Africa: Historical and Anthropological Perspectives* (Madison, Wis., 1977), 26–40.

55. Hopkins, *Conquerors and Slaves*, 115–132.

56. Frederick P. Bowser, *The African Slave in Colonial Peru 1524–1650* (Stanford, 1974), 272–301.

57. Degler, *Neither Black Nor White*, 39–47; Stuart B. Schwartz, *Sugar Plantations in the Formation of Brazilian Society: Bahia, 1550–1835* (Cambridge, 1985), 330–332.

58. The best examination of this topic is Davis, *Problem of Slavery in Western Culture*, 54–58.

59. Finkelman, ed., *Law of Freedom and Bondage*, 99.

60. Patterson, *Slavery and Social Death*, 285–293; Finley, *Ancient Slavery and Modern Ideology*, 109–110; Hellie, *Slavery in Russia*, 696–699.

61. Philip D. Curtin, *The Atlantic Slave Trade: A Census* (Madison, Wis., 1969), 89–93; Allan Kulikoff, *Tobacco and Slaves: The Development of Southern Cultures in the Chesapeake, 1680–1800* (Chapel Hill, N.C., 1986).

62. Kolchin, *Unfree Labor*, 114–120.

63. Kenneth M. Stampp, *The Peculiar Institution: Slavery in the Antebellum South* (New York, 1956), 34.

64. Bowser, *The African Slave in Colonial Peru*, 88–109; Cooper, *Plantation Slavery on the East Coast of Africa*, 79.

65. Finley, *Ancient Slavery and Modern Ideology*, 9. Finley's concept of a "genuine" slave society is now widely accepted, even among those who would add other societies to Finley's own list.

66. M. I. Finley, "Technical Innovation and Economic Progress in the Ancient World," *Economy and Society in Ancient Greece*, ed. and intro. Brent D. Shaw and Richard P. Saller (London, 1981), 176–195; Perry Anderson, *Passages from Antiquity to Feudalism* (London, 1974), 18–28; Douglass North, *The Economic Growth of the United States, 1790–1860* (Englewood Cliffs, N.J., 1961; New York, 1966), 122–134; Eugene Genovese, *Political Economy of Slavery: Studies in the Economy and Society of the Slavery South* (New York, 1965), 43–179; Gavin Wright, *Political Economy of the Cotton South: Households, Markets and Wealth in the Nineteenth Century* (New York, 1978); Wright, *Old South, New South: Revolutions in the Southern Economy Since the Civil War* (New York, 1986), 17–34. The most comprehensive counter-argument is Robert William Fogel and Stanley L. Engerman, *Time on the Cross*, 2 vol. (Boston, 1974).

67. Finley, *Ancient Slavery and Modern Ideology*, 77–92.

68. Drew Gilpin Faust, ed., *The Ideology of Slavery: Proslavery Thought in the Antebellum South, 1830–1860* (Baton Rouge, La., 1981), 30.

69. Robert A. Padgug, "Problems in the Theory of Slavery and Slave Society," *Science & Society*, 40 (1976), 3–27. Elizabeth Fox-Genovese, *Within the Plantation Household: Black and White Women in the Old South* (Chapel Hill, N.C., 1988), 55, argues that the "South had a slave system within a capitalist mode of production."

CHAPTER 2. *Slavery and Liberal Capitalism*

1. Steven M. Stowe, *Intimacy and Power in the Old South: Ritual in the Lives of the Planters* (Baltimore, 1987), 52.

2. Clement Eaton, *The Growth of Southern Civilization, 1790–1860* (New York, 1961), 114.

3. John Harley Warner, "The Idea of Southern Medical Distinctiveness:

Medical Knowledge and Practice in the Old South," in Ronald L. Numbers and Judith Walzer Leavitt, eds., *Sickness and Health in America: Readings in the History of Medicine and Public Health* (Madison, Wis., 1985), 53–70.

4. Michael O'Brien, *A Character of Hugh Legaré* (Knoxville, Tenn., 1985); O'Brien and David Moltke-Hanses, eds., *Intellectual Life in Antebellum Charleston* (Knoxville, Tenn., 1986).

5. David P. Handlin, *American Architecture* (London, 1985).

6. Rhys Isaac, *The Transformation of Virginia, 1740–1790* (Chapel Hill, N.C., 1982); Albert J. Raboteau, *Slave Religion: The "Invisible Institution" in the Antebellum South* (New York, 1978), 128–210; Donald G. Matthews, *Religion in the Old South* (Chicago, 1977).

7. Eric Hobsbawm, "The Crisis of the Seventeenth Century," in Trevor Aston, ed., *Crisis in Europe, 1560–1660: Essays from Past and Present* (London, 1965), 5–58; Jan DeVries, *The Economy of Europe in an Age of Crisis, 1600–1750* (Cambridge, 1976).

Among the countless works on the general economic background, I have relied especially on T. H. Aston and C. H. E. Philpin, eds., *The Brenner Debate: Agrarian Class Structure and Economic Development in Pre-Industrial Europe* (Cambridge, 1985); Carlo M. Cipolla, *Before the Industrial Revolution: European Society and Economy, 1000–1700*, 2d ed. (New York, 1980); Ralph Davis, *The Rise of the Atlantic Economies* (London, 1973); Maurice Dobb, *Studies in the Development of Capitalism* (London, 1946); Paul Sweezy et al., *The Transition from Feudalism to Capitalism*, intro. by Rodney Hilton (London, 1976).

8. Simon Schama, *The Embarrassment of Riches: An Interpretation of Dutch Culture in the Golden Age* (New York, 1987).

9. Jan DeVries, *The Dutch Rural Economy in the Golden Age, 1500–1700* (New Haven, Conn., 1974).

10. Perry Anderson, *Lineages of the Absolutist State* (London, 1975).

11. DeVries, *Economy of Europe in an Age of Crisis*, 30–83.

12. Harold Perkin, *Origins of Modern English Society* (London, 1969), 73–79 and passim, is particularly sensitive to the importance of absolute property.

13. Ibid., 128–146, 176–209.

14. Neil McKendrick, John Brewer, J. H. Plumb, *The Birth of a Consumer Society: The Commercialization of Eighteenth-Century England* (Bloomington, Ind., 1982).

15. Charles Verlinden, *L'Esclavage dans L'Europe Médiévale*, 2 v. (Brugge, DeTempel, 1955, 1977); Verlinden, *The Beginnings of Modern Colonization*, trans. Yvonne Freccero (Ithaca, N.Y., 1970); William D. Phillips, Jr., *Slavery from Roman Times to the Early Transatlantic Trade* (Minneapolis, 1985).

16. Sidney W. Mintz, *Sweetness and Power: The Place of Sugar in Modern History* (New York, 1985). See also Richard Sheridan, *Sugar and Slavery: An Economic History of the British West Indies, 1623–1775* (Baltimore, 1974).

17. Mintz, *Sweetness and Power.*

18. Philip D. Curtin, *The Atlantic Slave Trade: A Census* (Madison, Wis., 1969), 116, 119, 217, 235.

19. C. R. Boxer, *The Golden Age of Brazil, 1695–1750* (Berkeley, 1962), 24–25; Stuart B. Schwartz, *Sugar Plantations in the Formation of Brazilian Society: Bahia, 1550–1835* (Cambridge, 1985), 66, 161, 163.

20. Richard S. Dunn, *Sugar and Slaves: The Rise of the Planter Class in the English West Indies, 1624–1713* (Chapel Hill, N.C., 1972), 46–83, quotation on p. 67.

21. Ibid., 117–187; Franklin W. Knight, *Slave Society in Cuba During the Nineteenth Century* (Madison, Wis., 1970), 25–46. For case studies of sugar plantations, see Jerome S. Handler and Frederick W. Lange, *Plantation Slavery in Barbados: An Archaeological and Historical Investigation* (Cambridge, Mass., 1978), and Michael Craton, *Searching for the Invisible Man: Slaves and Plantation Life in Jamaica* (Cambridge, Mass., 1978).

22. Curtin, *Atlantic Slave Trade*, 95–126, 205–230; Paul E. Lovejoy, *Transformations in Slavery: A History of Slavery in Africa* (Cambridge, 1983), 19, 46.

23. Joseph C. Miller, *Way of Death: Mercantilism and the Angolan Slave Trade, 1730–1830* (Madison, Wis., 1988).

24. Lovejoy, *Transformations in Slavery*, 66–87.

25. T. H. Breen, "The Baubles of Britain," *Past & Present*, 119 (May, 1988), 73–104; Carole Shammas, "How Self-Sufficient Was Early America?" *Journal of Interdisciplinary History* xiii:2 (Autumn, 1982), 247–272.

26. Breen, "Baubles of Britain."

27. On the rise of consumer demand in the southern colonies, see Gloria L. Main, *Tobacco Colony: Life in Early Maryland, 1650–1720* (Princeton, N.J., 1982).

28. Edmund S. Morgan, *American Slavery, American Freedom: The Ordeal of Colonial Virginia* (New York, 1975).

29. On the preconditions for the emergence of slave society, see M. I. Finley, *Ancient Slavery and Modern Ideology* (London, 1980), 86.

30. Paul G. E. Clemens, *The Atlantic Economy and Colonial Maryland's Eastern Shore: From Tobacco to Grain* (Ithaca, N.Y., 1980); Allan Kulikoff, *Tobacco and Slaves: The Development of Southern Cultures in the Chesapeake, 1680–1800* (Chapel Hill, N.C., 1986), 23–44.

31. M. I. Finley, *Economy and Society in Ancient Greece*, ed. and intro. Brent D. Shaw and Richard P. Saller (Middlesex, 1981), 190; Perry Anderson, *Passages from Antiquity to Feudalism* (London, 1974), 18–28.

32. Charles G. Sellers, Jr., "Who Were the Southern Whigs?" *American Historical Review*, LIX (1954), 335–345; Thomas Brown, "The Southern Whigs and Economic Development," *Southern Studies*, 20 (1981), 20–38; J. Mills Thornton III, *Politics and Power in a Slave Society: Alabama, 1800–1860*

(Baton Rouge, La., 1978); Harry L. Watson, *Jacksonian Politics and Community Conflict: The Emergence of the Second American Party System in Cumberland County, North Carolina* (Baton Rouge, La., 1981).

33. Max Weber, *Economy and Society: An Outline of Interpretive Sociology*, eds. Guenther Roth and Claus Wittich (Berkeley, 1978), I, 399–634; Max Weber, *The Protestant Ethic and the Spirit of Capitalism*, trans. Talcott Parsons (New York, 1958).

34. This position is most forcefully represented by Immanuel Wallerstein, *The Modern World System: Capitalist Agriculture and the Origins of the European World-Economy in the Sixteenth Century* (New York, 1974).

35. The most thorough exploration of this theme is Eugene Genovese and Elizabeth Fox-Genovese, *Fruits of Merchant Capital: Slavery and Bourgeois Property in the Rise and Expansion of Capitalism* (New York, 1983).

36. For a critique of Wallerstein's and related positions, see Robert Brenner, "The Origins of Capitalist Development: A Critique of Neo-Smithian Marxism," *New Left Review*, 104 (1977), 25–92. Brenner, however, offers no alternative hypothesis to explain capitalism's influence.

37. Karl Marx, *Capital*, trans. Ben Fowkes (New York, 1977), v. I, 345.

38. Breen, "Baubles of Britain"; Mintz, *Sweetness and Power*, 42.

39. Eric Hobsbawm, *The Age of Revolution, 1789–1848* (New York, 1962); and for England, the cultural transformation is discussed in Perkin, *Origins of Modern English Society*, 218–339.

40. John of Salisbury, *Policraticus*, V:II.

41. David Brion Davis, *The Problem of Slavery in Western Culture* (Ithaca, N.Y., 1966), 111–112.

42. Robert Filmer, *Patriarcha, or The Natural Power of Kings*, I:3–4, I:10.

43. Ibid., I:4, III:1.

44. Ibid., III:14.

45. Robert Filmer, *Observations upon Aristotle's Politiques* (1652), preface, in David Wootton, ed., *Divine Right and Democracy: An Anthology of Political Writing in Stuart England* (Harmondsworth, 1986), 110.

46. See especially the essay on "Atomism" in Charles Taylor, *Philosophy and the Human Sciences*, in *Philosophical Papers*, 2 (Cambridge, 1985), 188, and in general, 187–210.

47. Knight, *Slave Society in Cuba*, 110 ff.

48. C. L. R. James, *The Black Jacobins: Toussaint L'Ouverture and the San Domingo Revolution*, 2d rev. ed. (New York, 1963), 58–61. James notes the irony of planter representatives in Paris siding enthusiastically with the republican forces in the French Revolution: They "had tied the fortunes of San Domingo to the assembly of a people in revolution and thenceforth the history of liberty in France and of slave emancipation in San Domingo is one and indivisible." As we shall see, southern slaveholders put themselves in the same position.

49. On Brazilian liberalism, see Thomas Flory, *Judge and Jury in Imperial Brazil* (Austin, Texas, 1981); Emilia Viotti Da Costa, *The Brazilian Empire: Myths and Histories* (Chicago, 1985); Gilberto Freyre, *The Masters and the Slaves: A Study in the Development of Brazilian Civilization*, trans. Samuel Putnam, 2d ed., rev., intro. David H. P. Maybury-Lewis (Berkeley, 1986), lxxix.

50. John Locke, *Second Treatise of Government*, I:4.

51. Charles S. Hyneman and Donald S. Lutz, eds., *American Political Writing during the Founding Era, 1760–1805* (Indianapolis, 1983), I, 72, 75, 612–613.

52. Ibid., I, 83.

53. Ibid., I, 574.

54. Adrienne Koch and William Peden, eds., *The Life and Selected Writings of Thomas Jefferson* (New York, 1944), 437.

55. Francis Newton Thorpe, comp., *The Federal and State Constitutions, Colonial Charters, and Other Organic Laws . . .* (Washington, D.C., 1909), v. 3, 1277, 1381.

56. Hyneman and Lutz, eds., *American Political Writing*, I, 92–96, 567. On the "materialism" of southern republicans (versus the moralism of their northern counterparts), see Forrest McDonald, *Novus Ordo Saeculorum* (Kansas, 1985).

57. Ibid., I, 92–96; II, 712.

58. Ibid., I, 334–335.

59. Marvin Meyers, ed., *The Mind of the Founder: Sources of the Political Thought of James Madison*, rev. ed. (Hanover, N.H., 1981), 64. See, in general, Gordon Wood, *The Creation of the American Republic, 1776–1787* (Chapel Hill, 1969).

60. Thorpe, comp., *Federal and State Constitutions*, v. 2, 664; v. 3, 1274, 1686; v. 7, 3813.

61. The influence of liberal ideals on planter families may be traced in three excellent studies: Daniel Blake Smith, *Inside the Great House: Planter Family Life in Eighteenth-Century Chesapeake Society* (Ithaca, N.Y., 1980); Isaac, *Transformation of Virginia*, esp. 302–305; Jan Lewis, *The Pursuit of Happiness: Family and Values in Jefferson's Virginia* (Cambridge, 1983).

62. Hyneman and Lutz, eds., *American Political Writing*, II, 905.

63. Shearer Davis Bowman, "Planters and Junkers: A Comparative Study of Two Nineteenth-Century Landed Elites and their Regional Societies" (Ph.D. diss., Berkeley, 1986), sees this "Burkean" conservatism as the characteristic ideology of southern planters. Daniel T. Rodgers, *Contested Truths: Keywords in American Politics Since Independence* (New York, 1987), provides evidence of sectional distinctiveness but in general sees the emergence of a conservative obsession with "order" as a pervasive reaction to democratization in nineteenth-century America.

64. John Codman Hurd, *The Law of Freedom and Bondage in the United States* (Boston, 1858; New York, 1968), I, 248, 299.

65. Willie Lee Rose, ed., *A Documentary History of Slavery in North America* (New York, 1976), 176–178.

66. Ibid., 179–196.

67. Thomas R. R. Cobb, *An Inquiry into the Law of Negro Slavery in the United States* (1858; New York, 1968), 83, 3.

68. Hyneman and Lutz, eds., *American Political Writing*, I, 613; Locke, *Second Treatise of Government*, IV:25.

69. Locke, *Second Treatise*, IV:24, VII:85; Jean-Jacques Rousseau, *The Social Contract*, I:IV.

70. A. Leon Higginbotham, Jr., *In the Matter of Color: Race and the American Legal Process; The Colonial Period* (New York, 1978), 78.

71. Hurd, *Law of Freedom and Bondage*, II, 18.

72. Rose, ed., *Documentary History of Slavery*, 187.

73. Fredrika Teute Schmidt and Barbara Ripel Wilhelm, eds., "Early Proslavery Petitions in Virginia," *William and Mary Quarterly*, 3rd ser., XXX (1973), 139.

74. Quoted in James Oakes, *The Ruling Race* (New York, 1982), 134, 147.

75. Ibid., 134.

76. Alfred Taylor Bledsoe, *Liberty and Slavery: or, Slavery in the Light of Moral and Political Philosophy*, printed in E. N. Elliott, ed., *Cotton Is King, and Pro-Slavery Arguments* (Augusta, Ga., 1860), 275–276.

77. Benedict Anderson, *Imagined Communities: Reflections on the Origins and Spread of Nationalism* (London, 1983), 135.

78. M. L. Bush, *Noble Privilege*, v. 1 of *The European Nobility* (London, 1983); M. L. Bush, *The English Aristocracy: A Comparative Synthesis* (Manchester, 1984); Lawrence Stone and Jeanne C. Fawtier Stone, *An Open Elite? England 1540–1880* (Oxford, 1984); Arno J. Mayer, *The Persistence of the Old Regime: Europe to the Great War* (New York, 1981); David Spring, ed., *European Landed Elites in the Nineteenth Century* (Baltimore, 1977).

79. Hyneman and Lutz, eds., *American Political Writing*, I, 83, 611.

80. Thorpe, comp., *Federal and State Constitutions*, v. 3, 1274.

81. *Selections from the Letters and Speeches of the Hon. James H. Hammond of South Carolina*, intro. Clyde N. Wilson (New York, 1866; Spartanburg, S.C., 1978), 111.

CHAPTER 3. *Slaveholders and Nonslaveholders*

1. Gustavus W. Dyer and John Trotwood Moore, comps., *The Tennessee Civil War Veterans Questionnaires* (Easley, S.C., 1985), v. 3, 1285, and passim.

2. Ibid., 1285, 1009, 972, 926, 880. Geographical variations in the re-

sponses are examined in Fred A. Bailey, "Tennessee's Antebellum Society from the Bottom Up," *Southern Studies*, XXII (1983), 260–273.

3. Keith Hopkins, *Conquerors and Slaves* (Cambridge, 1978), 1–98.

4. Richard Dunn, *Sugar and Slaves: The Rise of the Planter Class in the English West Indies, 1624–1713* (Chapel Hill, N.C., 1972), 67, 95, 110–112.

5. Ibid., 131, 148, 150–151, 164–165.

6. Stuart Schwartz, *Sugar Plantations in the Formation of Brazilian Society: Bahia, 1550–1835* (Cambridge, 1985), 435.

7. Stanley J. Stein, *Vassouras: A Brazilian Coffee County, 1850–1890* (Cambridge, Mass., 1957), 47–48.

8. Frederick Cooper, *Plantation Slavery on the East Coast of Africa* (New Haven, Conn., 1977), 57–59, 100.

9. Franklin Knight, *Slave Society in Cuba During the Nineteenth Century* (Madison, Wis., 1970), 41–43.

10. Ira Berlin and Herbert Gutman, "Natives and Immigrants, Free Men and Slaves: Urban Workingmen in the Antebellum South," *American Historical Review* 88 (1983), 1175–1200; James Roark and Michael P. Johnson, *Black Masters: A Free Family of Color in the Old South* (New York, 1984); Robert S. Starobin, *Industrial Slavery in the Old South* (New York, 1970).

11. Daniel R. Hundley, *Social Relations in Our Southern States*, ed. William J. Cooper, Jr. (New York, 1860; Baton Rouge, La., 1979), 30.

12. John Taylor, *Arator*, ed. M. E. Bradford (Petersburg, Va., 1818; Indianapolis, 1977), 123.

13. Adrienne Koch and William Peden, eds., *The Life and Selected Writings of Thomas Jefferson* (New York, 1944), 368.

14. Frances Anne Kemble, *Journal of a Residence on a Georgian Plantation in 1838–1839*, ed. John A. Scott (New York, 1961), 93.

15. Ibid., 60.

16. Sally McMillen, "Mothers' Sacred Duty: Breast-feeding Patterns among Middle- and Upper-class Women in the Antebellum South," *Journal of Southern History* 51 (1985), 333–356; Lawrence Stone, *The Family, Sex and Marriage in England 1500–1800* (London, 1977), 428–432.

When poor health or inadequate lactation prevented them from nursing, mistresses turned most often to bottle-feeding or to relatives, friends, and neighbors. Slaves were sometimes used, but in planter families that option was often viewed as a last resort. "Child sucked well this morning," one South Carolina planter wrote shortly after the birth of his child in 1845. "Hope to God it will not have to suck a bottle & what is *ten times worse, a Negro*." Theodore Rosengarten, ed., *Tombee: Portrait of a Cotton Planter* (New York, 1986), entry for Sept. 27, 1845, p. 370.

17. Daniel Blake Smith, *Inside the Great House* (Ithaca, N.Y., 1980); Rhys Isaac, *The Transformation of Virginia* (Chapel Hill, N.C., 1982); Jan Lewis, *The Pursuit of Happiness* (Cambridge, 1983). Allan Kulikoff argues that al-

though Chesapeake planters "rejected the connection between male supremacy in the family and royal absolutism in government that lay at the heart of European patriarchal theory, they sought to retain patriarchal control over their families." Thus the same changes that other scholars see as the rise of a "modern" family Kulikoff sees as evidence for an emerging "domestic patriarchy"—the development of "separate spheres" for men and women, the "separation of public and private roles," and family relations grounded in affection. See Allan Kulikoff, *Tobacco and Slaves* (Chapel Hill, N.C., 1986), 166, and in general 165–204.

18. Suzanne Lebsock, *The Free Women of Petersburg: Status and Culture in a Southern Town, 1784–1860* (New York, 1984); Marylynn Salmon, *Women and the Law of Property in Early America* (Chapel Hill, N.C., 1986), 81–119.

19. Thomas R. R. Cobb, *A Digest of the Laws of the State of Georgia* (Athens, Ga., 1851), ch. 148; Salmon, *Women and the Law of Property*, 58–80.

20. Kulikoff, *Tobacco and Slaves*, 165–204; Catherine Clinton, *The Plantation Mistress: Woman's World in the Old South* (New York, 1982).

21. Bruce Collins, *White Society in the Antebellum South* (London, 1985), 19–20, 166.

22. Jane Turner Censer, *North Carolina Planters and Their Children: 1800–1860* (Baton Rouge, La., 1984), 125–127.

23. James Oakes, *The Ruling Race* (New York, 1982), 71, 72, 128–129.

24. Ibid., 37–68; Donald Schaeffer, "Yeomen Farmers and Economic Democracy: A Study of Wealth and Economic Mobility in the Western Tobacco Region, from 1850–1860," *Explorations in Economic History*, XV (October, 1978), 421–437.

25. Frederick F. Siegel, *The Roots of Southern Distinctiveness: Tobacco and Society in Danville, Virginia, 1780–1865* (Chapel Hill, N.C., 1987), 144.

26. Richard Sutch, "The Breeding of Slaves for Sale and the Westward Expansion of Slavery, 1850–1860," in Stanley L. Engerman and Eugene D. Genovese, eds., *Race and Slavery in the Western Hemisphere: Quantitative Studies* (Princeton, N.J., 1975), 191.

27. Dyer and Moore, comps., *Tennessee Veterans Questionnaires*, v. 4, 1711, and v. 2, 494.

28. Fred A. Bailey, "Class and Tennessee's Confederate Generation," *Journal of Southern History*, 51 (1985), 38; Bailey, "Tennessee's Antebellum Society"; Albert Fishlow, "The American Common School Revival: Fact or Fancy?," in Henry Rosovsky, ed., *Industrialization in Two Systems* (New York, 1966), 47; Fishlow, "Levels of Nineteenth-Century American Investment in Education," *Journal of Economic History* 26 (1966), 418–436.

29. Bailey, "Class and Tennessee's Confederate Generation."

30. Dyer and Moore, comps., *Tennessee Veterans Questionnaires*, v. 4, 1734. See also Clinton, *Plantation Mistress*.

31. J. D. B. DeBow, *The Interest in Slavery of the Southern Non-slaveholder* (Charleston, 1860).

32. Jan Lewis and Kenneth A. Lockridge, " 'Sally Has Been Sick': Pregnancy and Family Limitation Among Virginia Gentry Women, 1780–1830," *Journal of Social History*, 22 (1989), 5–19; John Thomas Scholtterbeck, "Plantation and Farm: Social and Economic Change in Orange and Greene Counties, Virginia, 1716–1860" (Ph.D. diss., Johns Hopkins University, 1980), 83–102; Colin Forster and G. S. L. Tucker, *Economic Opportunity and White American Fertility Ratios, 1800–1860* (New Haven, 1972), 43–45.

33. Dyer and Moore, comps., *Tennessee Veterans Questionnaires*, v. 3, 923.

34. Gavin Wright, *The Political Economy of the Cotton South: Households, Markets, and Wealth in the Nineteenth Century* (New York, 1978), 73–74. See also Dale Evans Swan, *The Structure and Profitability of the Antebellum Rice Industry, 1859* (New York, 1975), and Mark Schmitz, *Economic Analysis of Antebellum Sugar Plantations in Louisiana* (New York, 1977), both of which confirm Wright's finding that the larger the plantation the greater the proportion of land devoted to staple crops.

35. Roger Ransom and Richard Sutch, *One Kind of Freedom: The Economic Consequences of Emancipation* (Cambridge, 1977), 2–7, 15–19; Jacqueline Jones, *Labor of Love, Labor of Sorrow: Black Women, Work and the Family, from Slavery to the Present* (New York, 1985), 11–43.

36. D. Clayton James, *Antebellum Natchez* (Baton Rouge, La., 1968), 145–146.

37. Oakes, *Ruling Race*, 69–95.

38. Thomas R. R. Cobb, *An Inquiry into the Law of Negro Slavery in the United States of America* (1858; New York, 1968), ccxv. See also Gavin Wright, *Old South, New South: Revolutions in the Southern Economy since the Civil War* (New York, 1986), 24–26.

39. David Brion Davis, *Slavery and Human Progress* (New York, 1984).

40. Richard Graham, "Slavery and Economic Development: Brazil and the United States South in the Nineteenth Century," *Comparative Studies in Society and History* 23 (1981), 620–655. See also Robert William Fogel and Stanley L. Engerman, *Time on the Cross: The Economics of American Negro Slavery* (Boston, 1974), 247–257.

41. Harold Woodman, "Economic History and Economic Theory: The New Economic History in America," *Journal of Interdisciplinary History*, 3 (1972), 337–340; Woodman, "New Perspectives on Southern Economic Development: A Comment," *Agricultural History*, XLIX (1975), 362–373. Where Woodman stresses the "irrationality" of the slave economy, Ralph V. Anderson and Robert E. Gallman, "Slaves as Fixed Capital: Slave Labor and Southern Economic Development," *Journal of American History*, LXIV (1977), 24–46, hold that the limits slavery placed on economic development

were the consequence of "rational" economic behavior on the part of individual masters.

42. Alva Fitzpatrick to Phillips Fitzpatrick, August 20, 1849, Benjamin Fitzpatrick Papers, Southern Historical Collection, UNC Chapel Hill, quoted in Oakes, *Ruling Race*, 74.

43. Kulikoff, *Tobacco and Slaves*, 64–77.

44. Randolph B. Campbell, "Intermittent Slave Ownership: Texas as a Test Case," *Journal of Southern History*, LI (1985), 21; Donald F. Schaefer, "Yeoman Farmers and Economic Democracy: A Study of Wealth and Economic Mobility in the Western Tobacco Region, 1850–1860," *Explorations in Economic History*, XV (1978), 427–428, found that 15 percent of the yeomen farmers became slaveholders; Schaefer, "Agricultural Displacement at the Southern Frontier: A Test of the Phillips Hypothesis" (unpublished paper, 1987), 16–17, used the Parker-Gallman sample of the cotton South and found that 26 percent of the yeomen became slaveholders. Schaefer's studies also reveal significant numbers of small slaveholders losing their slaves altogether in the same years, suggesting a steady pattern of both upward and downward mobility.

45. Randolph B. Campbell, "Slave Hiring in Texas," *American Historical Review*, 93 (1988), 107–114; Sarah S. Hughes, "Slaves for Hire: The Allocation of Black Labor in Elizabeth City County, Virginia, 1782–1810," *William and Mary Quarterly*, 3d ser., XXXV (1978), 260–286.

46. Schaefer, "Agricultural Displacement," 12, finds that cotton-belt yeomen were more likely to move than were slaveholders.

47. James D. Foust, *The Yeoman Farmer and the Westward Expansion of U.S. Cotton Production* (New York, 1975), 128; Steven Hahn, *The Roots of Southern Populism: Yeoman Farmers and the Transformation of the Georgia Upcountry, 1850–1890* (New York, 1983), 26; Lacy K. Ford, Jr., "Social Origins of a New South Carolina: The Upcountry in the Nineteenth Century" (Ph.D. diss., Univ. of South Carolina, 1983), 40.

48. Ford, "Social Origins of a New South Carolina," 91.

49. Forrest McDonald and Grady McWhiney, "The Antebellum Herdsmen," *Journal of Southern History*, XLI (1975), 147–166. In addition to the specific sources cited, my interpretation of the southern yeoman is based on the following: Paul Escott, *Many Excellent People: Power and Privilege in North Carolina, 1850–1900* (Chapel Hill, N.C., 1985); J. William Harris, *Plain Folk and Gentry in a Slave Society: White Liberty and Black Slavery in Augusta's Hinterlands* (Middletown, Conn., 1985).

50. Dyer and Moore, comps., *Tennessee Veterans Questionnaires*, v. 3, 963.

51. Ibid., v. 4, 1356.

52. Quoted in Stuart Bruchey, *Roots of American Economic Growth, 1607–1861* (New York, 1968), 18.

53. Hundley, *Social Relations in Our Southern States*, 216.

54. Dyer and Moore, comps., *Tennessee Veterans Questionnaires*, v. 3, 963.

55. David Weiman, "Petty Production in the Cotton South: A Study of Upcountry Georgia, 1840–1880" (Ph.D. diss., Stanford Univ., 1983), 80 ff.; Hahn, *Roots of Southern Populism*, 52–77.

56. Weiman, "Petty Production in the Cotton South," 91–103.

57. Hahn, *Roots of Southern Populism*, 45–49.

58. David Weiman, "Farmers and the Market in Pre-industrial America: A View from the Georgia Upcountry," *Journal of Economic History* (forthcoming).

59. Hundley, *Social Relations in Our Southern States*, 258–267.

60. Hinton Rowan Helper, *The Impending Crisis of the South: How to Meet It*, ed. George M. Fredrickson (New York, 1857; Cambridge, Mass., 1968), 44–45, 18, 22.

61. Among those who detect a "modernization" crisis in the 1850's, see the essays by William Barney, Stephen Hahn, and John T. Scholtterbeck, in Orville Vernon Burton and Robert C. McMath, Jr., eds., *Class, Conflict, and Consensus: Antebellum Southern Community Studies* (Westport, Conn., 1982); Ford, "Social Origins of a New South Carolina," 269–368.

62. *Virginia Gazette* (Purdie & Dixon), March 30, 1789, quoted in T. H. Breen, *Tobacco Culture: The Mentality of the Great Tidewater Planters on the Eve of the Revolution* (Princeton, N.J., 1985), 160.

63. Taylor, *Arator*, 93–94.

64. John Ashworth, *"Agrarians" and "Aristocrats": Party and Political Ideology in the United States, 1837–1846* (London, Royal Historical Society, N.J. Humanities Press, 1983; Cambridge, 1986), 11.

65. Ibid., 14.

66. Quoted in Alison Goodyear Freehling, *Drift Toward Dissolution: The Virginia Slavery Debate of 1831–1832* (Baton Rouge, La., 1982), 53–54.

67. Ibid., 60.

68. Richmond *Enquirer*, Convention Supplement 27, April 1851.

69. Ashworth, *"Agrarians" and "Aristocrats,"* 12.

70. Chilton Williamson, *American Suffrage: From Property to Democracy, 1760–1860* (Princeton, N.J., 1960), 266; Carl N. Degler, *Place over Time* (Baton Rouge, La., 1977), 90–91.

71. Dyer and Moore, comps., *Tennessee Veterans Questionnaires*, v. 3, 1025.

72. Robert Dawidoff, *The Education of John Randolph* (New York, 1979), 57–59. This theme is fully elaborated in William Freehling, *Prelude to Civil War: The Nullification Controversy in South Carolina, 1816–1836* (New York, 1966).

73. Quoted in Siegel, *Roots of Southern Distinctiveness*, 56–57.

74. Benedict Anderson, *Imagined Communities: Reflections on the Origin and Spread of Nationalism* (London, 1983), 135–136.

75. For general observations, see Arno J. Mayer, "The Lower Middle

Class as Historical Problem," *Journal of Modern History*, 47 (1975). Case studies include Philip Nord, *Paris Shopkeepers and the Politics of Resentment* (Princeton, N.J., 1986); Sean Wilentz, *Chants Democratic: New York City and the Rise of the American Working Class* (New York, 1984); Shulamit Volkov, *The Rise of Popular Antimodernism in Germany: The Urban Master Artisans, 1873–1896* (Princeton, N.J., 1978); Robert Gellately, *The Politics of Economic Despair: Shopkeepers and German Politics, 1890–1914* (London, 1974); Eugene H. Berwanger, *The Frontier Against Slavery: Western Anti-Negro Prejudice and the Slavery Extension Controversy* (Urbana, Ill., 1967); V. Jacque Voegeli, *Free But Not Equal: The Midwest and the Negro During the Civil War* (Chicago, 1967).

76. This is most effectively argued in George M. Fredrickson, *The Black Image in the White Mind* (New York, 1971).

77. Cobb, *Inquiry into the Law of Negro Slavery*, ccxiii.

78. Ira Berlin, *Slaves Without Masters* (New York, 1974); Michael P. Johnson and James L. Roark, *Black Masters: A Free Family of Color in the Old South* (New York, 1985), includes an excellent analysis of the interplay of class conflict and slavery in Charleston.

79. Henry Steele Commager, ed., *Documents of American History*, 8th ed. (New York, 1968), I, 340.

CHAPTER 4. *Slaves and Masters*

1. *State v. Mann*, 13 N.C. (2 Dev.) 263 (1824).

2. *State v. Will*, 18 N.C. (1 Dev. & Bat.) 121 (1834).

3. The literature on slave resistance is immense, but among the most important studies are Raymond A. Bauer and Alice H. Bauer, "Day to Day Resistance to Slavery," *Journal of Negro History*, 27 (1942), 388–419; Herbert Aptheker, *American Negro Slave Revolts* (New York, 1943); Kenneth M. Stampp, *The Peculiar Institution: Slavery in the Antebellum South* (New York, 1956); Gerald W. Mullin, *Flight and Rebellion: Slave Resistance in Eighteenth Century Virginia* (New York, 1972); Peter Wood, *Black Majority: Negroes in Colonial South Carolina from 1670 Through the Stono Rebellion* (New York, 1974).

4. *Southern Cultivator*, V (April, 1847), 62; *American Cotton Planter*, II (Dec., 1854), 356.

5. *Cotton Planter and Soil of the South*, I (Dec., 1857), 374.

6. *American Farmer*, III (July 27, 1821), 141.

7. *American Farmer*, XII (Nov., 1856), 131.

8. *DeBow's Review*, XIII (Aug., 1852), 194.

9. Stampp, *Peculiar Institution*, 34–140.

10. [Natchez] *Southern Planter*, I (1842), 21.

11. *Southern Agriculturist*, XI (Feb., 1838), 80.

12. *Southern Cultivator*, IV (March, 1846), 43.

13. *Southern Agriculturist*, XI (Oct., 1838), 512.

14. *Farmers' Register*, VII (June, 1839), 372.

15. *Southern Planter*, XVI (Feb., 1856), 51.

16. *Southern Cultivator*, IV (Aug., 1846), 113.

17. *Southern Cultivator*, XIV (Jan., 1856), 17.

18. [Natchez] *Southern Planter*, I (1842), 19.

19. *Southern Cultivator*, IV (Aug., 1846), 127.

20. *Southern Agriculturist*, IX (Nov., 1836), 584.

21. *Cotton Planter and Soil of the South*, I (Dec., 1857), 375.

22. *Southern Agriculturist*, XI (Feb., 1838), 77.

23. Elizabeth Fox-Genovese, *Within the Plantation Household* (Chapel Hill, N.C., 1988).

24. *Farmers' Register*, VIII (April, 1840), 230; *Farmers' Register*, III (June, 1836), 115.

25. Eugene D. Genovese, *Roll, Jordan, Roll: The World the Slaves Made* (New York, 1974).

26. Jacqueline Jones, *Labor of Love, Labor of Sorrow: Black Women, Work, and the Family from Slavery to the Present* (New York, 1986), 11–43.

27. Deborah Gray White, *Arn't I a Woman: Female Slaves in the Plantation South* (New York, 1985).

28. On fictive kinship and the slave family, see Herbert Gutman, *The Black Family in Slavery and Freedom, 1750–1925* (New York, 1976).

On slave culture generally, I defer to some of the extraordinary studies upon which my brief observations rely: Sterling Stuckey, "Through the Prism of Folklore," *Massachusetts Review*, 9 (1968); John Blassingame, *The Slave Community: Plantation Life in the Antebellum South* (New York, 1972); George P. Rawick, *From Sundown to Sunup: The Making of the Black Community* (Westport, Conn., 1972); Genovese, *Roll, Jordan, Roll*; Leslie Howard Owens, *This Species of Property: Slave Life and Culture in the Old South* (New York, 1976); Lawrence W. Levine, *Black Culture and Black Consciousness: Afro-American Folk Thought from Slavery to Freedom* (New York, 1977); Albert J. Raboteau, *Slave Religion: The "Invisible Institution" in the Antebellum South* (New York, 1978); Paul D. Escott, *Slavery Remembered: A Record of Twentieth Century Slave Narratives* (Chapel Hill, N.C., 1979); Charles Joyner, *Down by the Riverside: A South Carolina Slave Community* (Urbana, Ill., 1984); Sterling Stuckey, *Slave Culture: Nationalist Theory and the Foundations of Black America* (New York, 1987).

29. Stuckey, *Slave Culture*, chap. II and passim.

30. Genovese, *Roll, Jordan, Roll*.

31. J.-C. Dumont, "Le signification de la révolte," *Revue des études latine*, 45 (1967), 97, quoted in M. I. Finley, "Revolution in Antiquity," in Roy Porter and Miculas Teich, eds., *Revolution in History* (Cambridge, 1987), 54.

32. For a different interpretation see Genovese, *Roll, Jordan, Roll*, 597–

598, in which the author argues that " 'day-to-day resistance to slavery' generally implied accommodation" and that it was "at best prepolitical and at worst apolitical." Genovese's interpretation is profoundly significant, for it properly shifts the focus away from the questions of whether resistance existed and how much there was to the neglected issue of its political significance.

33. John Codman Hurd, *The Law of Freedom and Bondage in the United States* (Boston, 1858); I:42. On the legal regulation of masters in general, see David Brion Davis, *The Problem of Slavery in Western Culture* (Ithaca, N.Y., 1966).

34. Thomas R. R. Cobb, *An Inquiry into the Law of Negro Slavery in the United States of America* (T. & J. W. Johnson & Co., 1858), 66–67.

35. S. A. Cartwright, M.D., "Slavery in the Light of Ethnology," in E. N. Elliott, ed., *Cotton Is King, and Pro-slavery Arguments* (Augusta, Ga., 1860; New York, 1968), 689–728; Josiah C. Nott, *Two Lectures on the Natural History of the Caucasian and Negro Races*, in Drew Gilpin Faust, ed., *The Ideology of Slavery: Proslavery Thought in the Antebellum South, 1830–1860* (Baton Rouge, La., 1981), 208–238. For the context in which such ideas developed, see William Stanton, *The Leopard's Spots: Scientific Attitudes Toward Race in America, 1815–1859* (Chicago, 1960); George M. Fredrickson, *The Black Image in the White Mind: The Debate on Afro-American Character and Destiny, 1817–1914* (New York, 1971).

36. Barbara J. Fields, "Ideology and Race in American History," in James M. McPherson and J. Morgan Kousser, eds., *Region, Race and Reconstruction* (New York, 1982), 149.

37. Hurd, *Law of Freedom and Bondage*, II:19.

38. Willie Lee Rose, ed., *A Documentary History of Slavery in North America* (New York, 1976), 177.

39. Ibid., 187; Hurd, *Law of Freedom and Bondage*, II:17.

40. Hurd, *Law of Freedom and Bondage*, I:42.

41. *State* v. *Mann*, 13 (2 Dev.) 263 (1829).

42. *State* v. *Will*, 18 N.C. (1 Dev. & Bat.) 121 (1834).

43. Ibid.

44. Ibid.

45. Cobb, *Inquiry into the Law of Slavery*, 83–84.

46. See, for example, Louis Masur, *Rites of Execution: Capital Punishment and the Transformation of American Culture, 1776–1865* (New York, 1989).

47. *State* v. *Hoover*, 20 N.C. (4 Dev. & Bat.) 365 (1839).

48. *State* v. *Caesar*, 31 N.C. (9 Ired.) 391 (1849).

49. Paul Finkelman, *The Law of Freedom and Bondage: A Casebook* (New York, 1986), 191–273.

50. Cobb, *Inquiry into the Law of Slavery*, 93–94n.

51. William W. Freehling, *Prelude to Civil War: The Nullification Controversy in South Carolina, 1816–1836* (New York, 1966).

52. Kenneth M. Stampp, *The Imperiled Union: Essays on the Background of the Civil War* (New York, 1980), 3–36.

53. John C. Calhoun, *A Disquisition on Government*, ed. C. Gordon Post (Indianapolis, 1953), xxii.

54. Thomas D. Morris, *Free Men All: The Personal Liberty Laws of the North, 1780–1861* (Baltimore, 1974).

55. Stanley W. Campbell, *The Slave Catchers: Enforcement of the Fugitive Slave Law, 1850–1860* (Chapel Hill, 1970), 49–95.

56. William M. Wiecek, *The Sources of Antislavery Constitutionalism in America, 1760–1848* (Ithaca, N.Y., 1977), 20–39; Paul Finkelman, *An Imperfect Union: Slavery, Federalism, and Comity* (Chapel Hill, N.C., 1981); Don E. Fehrenbacher, *The Dred Scott Case: Its Significance in American Law and Politics* (New York, 1978).

57. Paul Finkelman, "*Prigg* v. *Pennsylvania* and Northern State Courts: Anti-Slavery Uses of a Pro-Slavery Decision," *Civil War History*, 25 (1979), 5–35; Paul Finkelman, *Slavery in the Courtroom: An Annotated Bibliography of American Cases* (Washington, D.C., 1985), 60–64.

58. [Theodore Dwight Weld], *American Slavery as It Is: Testimony of a Thousand Witnesses* (New York, 1839).

59. Harriet Beecher Stowe, *Uncle Tom's Cabin* (1852).

60. On the value of slave autobiographies, see Blassingame, *Slave Community*, revised and enlarged ed. (1979), 367–382.

61. Dwight Lowell Dumond, ed., *Southern Editorials on Secession* (New York, 1931), 217. For the conservative roots of proslavery intellectuals, see Larry E. Tise, *Proslavery: A History of the Defense of Slavery in America, 1701–1840* (Athens, Ga., 1988).

62. Drew Gilpin Faust, ed., *The Ideology of Slavery: Proslavery Thought in the American South, 1830–1860* (Baton Rouge, La., 1981), 64, 29, 28, 41.

63. Ibid., 29, 41.

64. Ibid., 78–135.

65. See Michael A. Bernstein, "Northern Labor Finds a Southern Champion: A Note on the Radical Democracy, 1833–1849," in W. Pencak and C. Wright, eds., *New York City and the Rise of American Capitalism* (Charlottesville, 1989), 147–167.

66. Quoted in Eric L. McKitrick, ed., *Slavery Defended: The Views of the Old South* (Englewood Cliffs, N.J., 1863), 80, 81.

67. George Fitzhugh, *Cannibals All! or, Slaves Without Masters*, ed. C. Vann Woodward (Cambridge, Mass., 1960), 228.

68. George Fitzhugh, *Sociology for the South* (1854) in Harvey Wish, ed., *Ante-Bellum* (New York, 1960), 57–58.

69. Dumond, ed., *Southern Editorials on Secession*, 360, 3.

70. Roy P. Basler, ed., *The Collected Works of Abraham Lincoln*, 8 vols. (New Brunswick, N.J., 1953–1955), IV, 263.

71. Benjamin Quarles, *The Negro in the Civil War* (Boston, 1953), 42–56; John Hope Franklin, *The Emancipation Proclamation* (New York, 1963); Leon F. Litwack, *Been in the Storm So Long: The Aftermath of Slavery* (New York, 1979), 3–63. Extensive documentation of this interpretation can be found in the monumental project by Ira Berlin et al., eds., *Freedom: A Documentary History of Emancipation, 1861–1867*, ser. 1, v. 1, *The Destruction of Slavery* (Cambridge, 1985).

72. Bell Irvin Wiley, *The Plain People of the Confederacy* (Baton Rouge, La., 1944), 70–104; James M. McPherson, *The Negro's Civil War* (New York, 1965), 19–36, 55–68; Quarles, *Negro in the Civil War*, 57–77; Litwack, *Been in the Storm So Long*, 104–166.

73. *New York Times*, June 2, 1861; Robert Engs, *Freedom's First Generation: Black Hampton, Virginia, 1861–1890* (Philadelphia, 1979), 18–22.

74. *U.S. Statutes*, XII, 319.

75. *Congressional Globe*, 37th Cong., 1st sess. (1861) 411–412.

76. *War of the Rebellion: A Compilation of the Official Records of the Union and Confederate Armies* (Washington, D.C., 1880–1901), ser. 1, vol. 2, p. 649; Frank Moore, ed., *The Rebellion Record*, II (New York, 1861), 437–438.

77. Moore, ed., *Rebellion Record*, II, 493; Basler, ed., *Collected Works*, IV, 506, and V, 222–224.

78. Barbara J. Fields, *Slavery and Freedom on the Middle Ground: Maryland during the Nineteenth Century* (New Haven, Conn., 1985), 108–112.

79. Edward McPherson, ed., *The Political History of the United States During the Great Rebellion* (New York, 1864), 196–197.

80. Ibid., 198.

81. Georgia Lee Tatum, *Disloyalty in the Confederacy* (Chapel Hill, N.C., 1934); Stephen Ambrose, "Yeomen Discontent in the Confederacy," *Civil War History*, 8 (1962), 259–268.

82. The classic critique of the Proclamation is Richard Hofstadter, *The American Political Tradition, and the Men Who Made It* (New York, 1948), 131–132. Details of the slaves' reaction to the British offer of emancipation during the American Revolution are presented in Benjamin Quarles, *The Negro in the American Revolution* (Chapel Hill, N.C., 1961), 19–32, 111–181.

83. Frederick Douglass, *Life and Times of Frederick Douglass* (rev. ed., 1892; reprinted, London, 1962), 358.

84. Franklin, *Emancipation Proclamation*, 100–103, 108–112.

85. Ibid., 120–123, 132–133; Quarles, *Negro in the Civil War*, 163–182; Bell Irvin Wiley, *Southern Negroes: 1861–1865* (New Haven, Conn., 1938), 83.

86. For a different view of the significance of northern racism, see Louis S. Gerteis, *From Contraband to Freedman: Federal Policy Toward Southern Blacks, 1861–1865* (Westport, Conn., 1973). On black troops, see Dudley Taylor Cornish, *The Sable Arm: Black Troops in the Union Army, 1861–1865* (New York, 1956); Litwack, *Been in the Storm So Long*, 65–103.

87. M. I. Finley, *Ancient Slavery and Modern Ideology* (London, 1980), 110; Finley, *Economy and Society in Ancient Greece* (London, 1981), 104–111.

88. Paul E. Lovejoy, *Transformations in Slavery: A History of Slavery in Africa* (Cambridge, 1983), 246–268.

EPILOGUE. *The Meaning of the Civil War*

1. Ulrich B. Phillips, *American Negro Slavery* (New York, 1918; Baton Rouge, La., 1966), 313.

2. Leon F. Litwack, *Been in the Storm So Long* (New York, 1979); Jay R. Mandle, *The Roots of Black Poverty: The Southern Plantation Economy after the Civil War* (Durham, N.C., 1978), 20.

3. Roger L. Ransom and Richard Sutch, *One Kind of Freedom: The Economic Consequences of Emancipation* (Cambridge, 1977), 86–87; Leon F. Litwack, "The Ordeal of Black Freedom," in Walter J. Fraser, Jr., and Winifred B. Moore, Jr., eds., *The Southern Enigma: Essays on Race, Class and Folk Culture* (Westport, Conn., 1983), 5–24; John W. Cell, *The Highest Stage of White Supremacy: The Origins of Segregation in South Africa and the American South* (Cambridge, 1982), 103–170.

4. Harold D. Woodman, "Post-Civil War Southern Agriculture and the Law," *Agricultural History*, 53 (1979), 319–338; Harold D. Woodman, "Postbellum Social Change and Its Effects on Marketing the South's Cotton Crop," *Agricultural History*, 56 (1982), 215–230; Jonathan Wiener, *Social Origins of the New South* (Baton Rouge, La., 1978); Ronald L. F. Davis, *Good and Faithful Labor: From Slavery to Sharecropping in the Natchez District, 1860–1890* (Westport, Conn., 1982); Michael Wayne, *The Reshaping of Plantation Society: The Natchez District, 1860–1900* (Baton Rouge, La., 1983).

5. Forrest McDonald and Grady McWhiney, "The South from Self-Sufficiency to Peonage: An Interpretation," *American Historical Review* 85 (1980), 1095–1118; Steven Hahn, *The Roots of Southern Populism* (New York, 1983). For somewhat different analyses, both of which emphasize the long-term rather than the immediate dislocations of the Civil War, see Lacy K. Ford, "Rednecks and Merchants: Economic Development and Social Tensions in the South Carolina Upcountry, 1865–1900," *Journal of American History* 71 (1984), 294–318; David Weiman, "The Economic Emancipation of the Non-Slaveholding Class: Upcountry Farmers in the Georgia Cotton Economy," *Journal of Economic History*, XLV (1985), 71–93.

6. The unprecedented significance of land in the postbellum economy is examined in Gavin Wright, *Old South, New South: Revolutions in the Southern Economy Since the Civil War* (New York, 1986), 17–33.

7. Eric Foner, *Nothing But Freedom: Emancipation and Its Legacy* (Baton Rouge, 1983), 39–73; Wayne K. Durrill, "Producing Poverty: Local Gov-

ernment and Economic Development in a New South County, 1874–1884," *Journal of American History* 71 (1985), 764–781. See also Charles L. Flynn, Jr., *White Land, Black Labor: Caste and Class in Late Nineteenth Century Georgia* (Baton Rouge, La., 1983).

8. J. Crawford King, Jr., "The Closing of the Southern Range: An Exploratory Study," *Journal of Southern History*, XLVIII (1982), 53–70, argues that "the planter class did not get what it had been seeking until after" the Civil War.

9. Eric Foner, *Reconstruction: America's Unfinished Revolution* (New York, 1988), provides a comprehensive survey of black politics in the Reconstruction South.

10. V. O. Key, Jr., *Southern Politics in State and Nation* (New York, 1949), 513–517, and passim. In the absence of a complete study of the origins of legislative malapportionment, the argument that follows must remain tentative.

11. On the disruptive influence racism had on class-based political insurgency in the postwar South, C. Vann Woodward, *Origins of the New South* (Baton Rouge, La., 1951), remains unsurpassed. See also the important essay by Armstead L. Robinson, "Beyond the Realm of Social Consensus: New Meanings of Reconstruction for American History," *Journal of American History* 68 (1981), 276–297.

12. Francis Newton Thorpe, comp., *The Federal and State Constitutions* (Washington, D.C., 1909), IV, 2049–2063, 2069–2089.

13. Ibid., IV, 2083–2084, lists the number of representatives per county. Adult male population is derived from Joseph C. G. Kennedy, comp., *Population of the United States in 1860* (Washington, D.C., 1864), 264–269. These statistics include twenty-one-year-olds who could not vote; but this should have no significant effect on the conclusions.

14. Lawrence Goodwyn, *Democratic Promise: The Populist Moment in America* (New York, 1976); Leon Fink, *Workingmen's Democracy: The Knights of Labor and American Politics* (Urbana, Ill., 1983), 149–177.

15. Alabama. *Official Proceedings of the Constitutional Convention of the State of Alabama, May 21st, 1901, to September 3rd, 1901* (Wetumpka, Ala., 1940), III, 2780.

16. J. Morgan Kousser, *The Shaping of Southern Politics: Suffrage Restriction and the Establishment of the One-Party South* (New Haven, Conn., 1974). For a useful explanation of the variations from state to state, see Joel Williamson, *The Crucible of Race: Black-White Relations in the American South Since Emancipation* (New York, 1984), 225–246.

17. Louisiana. *Official Journal of the Proceedings of the Constitutional Convention of the State of Louisiana held in New Orleans, Tuesday, February 8, 1898* (New Orleans, 1898), 31. Similar attacks on the Reconstruction constitutions as a pretext for disfranchisement can be found in: Alabama. *Address of Hon. Jno.*

B. *Knox on his Installation as President, May 22, 1901* (Montgomery, Ala., 1901), 1; J. N. Brenaman, *A History of Virginia Conventions* (Richmond, Va., 1902), 80–81 (Brenaman was Assistant Secretary to Virginia's 1901–1902 Constitutional Convention); South Carolina. See *Journal of the Constitutional Convention of the State of South Carolina* (Columbia, S.C., 1895), opening remarks by Robert Aldrich.

18. William Archibald Dunning, *Essays on the Civil War and Reconstruction and Related Topics* (New York, 1897), 249–252, 353–385. See also Dunning, *Reconstruction: Political and Economic, 1865–1877* (New York, 1907), 109–123.

19. Dunning, *Essays*, 383.

20. Ibid., 384.

21. Quoted in Dwight Billings, Jr., *Planters and the Making of the "New South": Class, Politics, and Development in North Carolina, 1865–1900* (Chapel Hill, N.C., 1979), 210.

22. Ulrich B. Phillips, *Life and Labor in the Old South* (Boston, 1929), 198–201.

Index

elves are slaves, but are they sold into slavery? or turn to it willingly?